ABNORMAL RETURNS

WINNING STRATEGIES FROM THE FRONTLINES OF THE INVESTMENT BLOGOSPHERE

TADAS VISKANTA

New York   Chicago   San Francisco   Lisbon   London   Madrid   Mexico City
Milan   New Delhi   San Juan   Seoul   Singapore   Sydney   Toronto

The *McGraw·Hill* Companies

1 2 3 4 5 6 7 8 9 10   DOC/DOC   1 8 7 6 5 4 3 2

ISBN   978-0-07-178710-9
MHID   0-07-178710-0

e-ISBN 978-0-07-178711-6
e-MHID   0-07-178711-9

This publication is designed to provide accurate and authoritative information in regard to the subject matter covered. It is sold with the understanding that neither the author nor the publisher is engaged in rendering legal, accounting, securities trading, or other professional services. If legal advice or other expert assistance is required, the services of a competent professional person should be sought.
—*From a Declaration of Principles Jointly Adopted by a Committee of the American Bar Association and a Committee of Publishers and Associations*

Library of Congress Cataloging-in-Publication Data

Viskanta, Tadas E.
    Abnormal returns : winning strategies from the frontlines of the investment blogosphere / by Tadas Viskanta.
        p.   cm.
    ISBN 978-0-07-178710-9 (alk. paper)—ISBN 0-07-178710-0 (alk. paper)
    1. Investments.   2. Portfolio management.   3. Investment analysis.
    4. Risk management.   I. Title.

    HG4521.V57 2012
    332.6—dc23   2011048927

McGraw-Hill books are available at special quantity discounts to use as premiums and sales promotions or for use in corporate training programs. To contact a representative, please e-mail us at bulksales@mcgraw-hill.com.

This book is printed on acid-free paper.

To my parents, who have always loved and supported me.
To their credit I am right where I am supposed to be.

Contents

Acknowledgments

IF IT WEREN'T FOR THE RECALCITRANCE OF THE PUBLISHING INDUS-
try some seven years ago, this book would likely have never come to
fruition. At that time, I was actively pitching another investment-
related book, *The Alpha Revolution: How Hedge Funds Have Changed
Investing and What It Means for Your Portfolio*. Unfortunately for the
wider reading public, and me, no publisher wanted to publish it.
Rather than go the then arduous route of self-publishing, I turned in
another direction.

At this time, blogs were coming into vogue, and the investment blogosphere was starting to get off the ground. After some
initial reluctance, I entered the investment blogosphere with a
blog *Abnormal Returns* that continues up to this day. So in a certain respect, I have to thank all those book editors from way back
who passed on my book, because without them there would be no
Abnormal Returns book or blog.

I want to thank the team at McGraw-Hill Professional who helped
bring this project to its conclusion. They include Stephanie Frerich, Gaya
Vinay, Janice Race, Ruth Mannino, Sarah Hendrickson, and Lydia
Rinaldi. As well, I want to thank Robert Meitus, who in a short period
of time helped turn my book proposal into a signed book contract.

The *Abnormal Returns* blog has been a solo effort from the outset,
but for the past two-plus years it has been published in collaboration
with the team at StockTwits. In particular, I would like to thank
Howard Lindzon, who has been a consistent champion of the blog,
and Phil Pearlman, who has been especially supportive and always
has my back. The best thing I can say about StockTwits is that if it
did not already exist, someone would have to invent it.

I want to thank fellow blogger Josh Brown, who has been traveling along the first-time author track at the same time. I also want to thank all those who kindly provided generous testimonials for the book jacket.

Claude Erb, my former boss and coauthor of mine, greatly influenced the way I think about investing to this day. My other investment influences are too many to list here, but they include the dozens, if not hundreds, of bloggers whom I follow and who provide the daily fodder for *Abnormal Returns*.

Books are by their nature solitary efforts. My life is anything but a solitary effort. I am lucky to have in my wife, Colleen, the best partner I could ever hope for. We count ourselves blessed each day for the good fortune we have been granted.

Introduction

Investing is hard.

—TADAS VISKANTA

THE ABOVE IS A SENTIMENT I HAVE REPEATED IN MY BLOG TOO MANY times to count. It never ceases to amaze me how even the most sophisticated investors can so often get caught with their proverbial pants down. For any number of reasons, sophisticated investors make fundamental mistakes, often out of overconfidence, that belie their high status. We see it all the time—investors get sucked into (in hindsight) obvious Ponzi schemes, or blow up their portfolios through the abuse of leverage, or invest in vehicles so complex that they did not understand them to begin with.

Investor overconfidence manifests itself in other ways as well. The media is rife with so-called market gurus or pundits that are quick to make bold forecasts with little or no thought of how investors will use, and likely abuse, their advice. Dan Gardner, in his book *Future Babble,* notes that the media craves these "confident and conclusive" forecasts because it makes for a better story.[1] The implicit assumption is to let the viewers themselves deal with the consequences of poor forecasts.

When the best investors—the ones that other investors talk about in hushed tones—make public market pronouncements, they are much more circumspect in their use of language than the "gurus." They talk about probabilities, possibilities, and alternative scenarios, not absolutes. They recognize that the financial markets, especially in the turbulent age in which we live, are not hospitable to definitive statements.

If there is one overriding theme in this book, it is that we all need to approach the markets and our investments with a sense of humility. The reasons are twofold. It is the height of hubris to think that we can say with a great deal of certainty how global markets function. Our knowledge of the markets is slender compared with their complexity.

Second and more important, our ability to understand and control our own actions is limited. Investors since time immemorial have been slapping themselves on the forehead after a bad trade, muttering, "stupid, stupid, stupid!" While the financial markets have become increasingly global and complex, human nature has remained stubbornly stuck in an age when stocks and bonds had not yet been invented.

If investing is hard even for professional investors, what chance do individual investors have? As adults in today's society, we are largely set adrift in the investment world with little in the way of guidance or objective advice. Whether you are saving for your retirement or a child's education or are simply looking to build a better life, you need to possess some basic investment skills. Some argue that traditional investing is in a certain sense dead.[2] Investing isn't dead, but the odds are currently stacked against us all. Whatever the odds, we still need to make an effort to save and invest for our futures.

What does that entail? The vast majority, let's say 99%, of Americans don't want to be active traders glued to their computer screens throughout the day. Not that there is anything necessarily wrong with trading. We just need to recognize that most people are focused on other things: building a career, maintaining their health insurance, or funding their 401(k) plans. They aren't traders. They are trying to earn a modest return on their hard-earned savings. When it comes to your investments, you certainly don't need to have all the answers. No one does, but you do need to be able to ask the right questions.

The good thing is that your needs are not likely unique. Therefore, some straightforward investment education should serve you well. A mutual fund insider writes: "The fact of the matter is that good, basic investment advice doesn't need to be customized to any large extent. Setting someone on the road to investment success requires, first and foremost, nothing more than implementing some very basic, general principles. Keep costs low. Diversify broadly. Find an asset allocation you'll be comfortable with over the long term, and for crying out loud leave it alone."[3] We will discuss those principles, but we should also recognize that the challenge often arises not with the plan, but with the planner.

From the discussion so far, you should have some sense that this book is not going to provide you with the "secret" to investing success. This is because *there is no secret*. Our goals are much more modest. For most investors, investment mediocrity is an eminently achievable and worthy goal. The great thing is that investment mediocrity is now easier and cheaper to accomplish than at any other time in history.

Some might say that investment mediocrity is an unworthy goal. And that may be true, because who wants to be mediocre? In today's winner-take-all society, this sort of attitude is an anathema. However, a quick review of what it takes to be an outstanding investor might persuade you that mediocrity is not shooting too low.

The skills involved in becoming an accomplished investor are not easily acquired in the classroom, although that is as good a place to start as any other. Great investors exhibit an interest in finance, accounting, history, and psychology, to name but a few topics, and to that you can add a heavy dose of self-awareness. To a large degree, these skills are acquired over time through hard work and good old-fashioned hard knocks. This description from Barry Ritholtz, is apt, "Great investors are savvy generalists."[4] Robert G. Hagstrom describes investing as "the last liberal art."[5] To get downright philosophical, Michael J. Mauboussin discusses the importance of consilience, or linking principles across disciplines, to help one become a better investor.[6]

If we take this a step further and try and put a figure on just how many investors possess the skills necessary to invest successfully, we get some bleak numbers. William J. Bernstein came up with a pessimistic estimate of the number of capable investors as 1 in 10,000.[7] Even if you fiddle with these estimates, you still are likely to arrive at only a small fraction of people who are truly proficient in the field of money management. In that light, becoming a merely competent investor seems like a worthy goal.

This does not mean that investors should throw up their hands and give up. While investing is a challenge, its mastery is also an opportunity. If you are reading this book, you recognize the importance of trying to gain a measure of investing skills. The opportunity lies not only in potential financial gains, but rather the confidence in knowing you have the ability to manage your own portfolio. That ability is a lifelong asset that can pay for itself many times over.

There is also another aspect that is quite enticing. There are few arenas in which an amateur can compete against professionals on an equal footing. In the financial markets, that is the reality with nearly every trade. Some would surely argue that the playing field isn't level; but in the end, for every buy there is a sell, and on the other side of a trade is likely a professional investor—although today the other side of the trade is just as likely to be a computerized trading algorithm.

The other prominent arena in which amateurs take on professionals directly is poker. Events like the World Series of Poker allow amateur players to go up against the pros, for a price of course. The entry fee into the WSOP Main Event is currently $10,000. For that buy-in, you can compete at the same table with the pros. Going up against the best poker players in the world has to be for amateurs both anxiety inducing and a tremendous thrill.

That being said, investing and trading *shouldn't be* too thrilling. Investing should in fact be boring. The clichéd view of investing is one of frenetic trading and wild market action. A look at the best traders and investors at work would likely show you a very different picture. You probably couldn't tell from their demeanor whether they were up big or down big on the day.

This idea of making investing boring is an important one, in part because it touches on the responsibilities of those who write about investing. The Latin phrase *primum non nocere* is translated as "First, do no harm."[8] This is a longstanding principle of medical ethics that directs doctors to do no harm to a patient in trying to heal them.

The same ethos should be applied to investing as well, leaving aside the issue of whether most strategies presented to investors actually work or even make sense. Most investment books present strategies and tactics to investors that, if misapplied, are likely to do an investor more harm than good. The challenges facing investors are already numerous enough. We don't need to add the potential misapplication of investment advice to the list. The counterargument being that people are responsible adults and should understand the risks inherent in any investment strategy.

That is a shortsighted argument in my opinion. The biggest challenges facing investors of all types are not necessarily the hard issues we commonly think of, like the global economy, the Fed's latest moves, or the trend in corporate earnings. Rather they are psychological and emotional. The point is that analysts, and the books they write, should focus on simplifying and clarifying ideas in an attempt to make life easier for investors, instead of tempting them into the latest hot strategy. Life is too short to add complexity to our lives when simplicity is a far more sustainable strategy.

For that reason, this book should be read more as an exploration of a series of investment topics as opposed to some sort of doctrinaire investment philosophy. As noted earlier, a humble approach to the markets is the only one that matches the reality of investing. Investment strategies perform best when they match the personality of the individual implementing them. We often can't say that one investment strategy is right or that another is wrong. Any strategy may be right or wrong for an individual given the person's outlook, experience, and goals.

Simplicity does not come easily for anyone who follows the markets on a regular basis. It is deceptively easy to get caught up in the day-to-day goings-on in the markets. The breathless tone of financial television and the bold headlines of the investment blogosphere all lead you to believe that the next piece of news or the next opinion is the most important thing you will hear all day. In the end, they aren't selling news or analysis but rather a sense that you are in on the action.

Many of the fears that market participants have turn out to be either unfounded, of temporary importance, or far less critical than originally thought. This building, and rebuilding, of the proverbial "wall of worry" is an ongoing feature of the financial markets. Still, of course, there are times when the market's fears turn out to be well founded. Anyone who lived through the financial crisis of 2007–2009 now recognizes that the global financial system came very close to running completely off the rails.

The market is therefore generating and rejecting hypotheses on a continuing basis. My job as a blogger is to try and sort through the noise and extract some semblance of a signal from the flow of news. This curation process parallels my motivation for writing this book. The ideas and concepts I discuss are ones that keep jumping out at me in the process of my daily blogging. When putting together the plan for this book, these ideas came to me quickly, probably because I have spent years immersed in them.

That is not to say that I view these ideas with any proprietary interest. Rather the concepts that follow are best thought of as "things I think I think." As with all investment boilerplate, I reserve the right to change my mind at a moment's notice given sufficient evidence to the contrary.

When I first started blogging some 6 years ago, what feels like 60 in blog years, I created for my blog, *Abnormal Returns*, the tagline "A wide-ranging, forecast-free blog." Over thousands of blog posts, that tagline has stuck. I haven't changed it partly because I didn't have the time to craft a smarter one, but also because it still reflects the ethos of the blog. In light of the tagline, the structure and content of this book should not be surprising.

We are going to range over the entire landscape of investing, with an emphasis on concepts that, it is hoped, stand up to some rigor but also have a half-life in excess of the current news cycle. We will start with a look at the building blocks of investing—risk and return. We will then explore the characteristics of the main asset classes— equities and fixed income. Next we will turn our attention to how investors put portfolios together and how investors might attempt to outperform the market.

We then examine three big decade-long trends that have permanently changed investing. First we note how the introduction of exchange-traded funds has dramatically changed the way we invest. Next we investigate the increasingly global nature of investing. Last we look at the rise of alternative asset classes that investors use in an attempt to create a better risk-return trade-off.

In the final section of the book, we look more at the ways in which we can become better investors. First we take a closer look at some ways we can try and combat the many behavioral biases we all possess. Second we focus on how we all can become smarter consumers of financial media. In conclusion we are able to draw some broader lessons from what has been a difficult decade, some say a lost decade, for investors.

Whether we want to admit or not, we are all already in the midst of an investing journey. It usually starts off with low stakes but builds quietly and quickly into an important adult responsibility. It's not a sprint. It's a marathon. The only way you can win, let alone finish, a marathon is to get off the couch and stay on course.

1

Risk

Risk is a four-letter word. Like other less polite four-letter words, it is hard to imagine living without it. An understanding of risk is crucial in any attempt at becoming a competent investor. While risk may be unavoidable, its definition is, at best, fluid. Risk can mean different things to different people at different times. When investors discuss investing, they say "risk and return." *Risk* first, *return* second. Likely they say it this way partly because risk rolls off the tongue better, but also because risk represents the fundamental building block of finance and investments.

If risk and return are a matched pair, why then is so much emphasis laid at the feet of risk and not returns? Returns are in a certain sense easy. Returns are visible. Whenever we turn on financial television or access the Internet, we are confronted with stock prices. Returns are not all that difficult to measure. In the vast majority of cases, to calculate returns we only need the change in price of a security along with any dividends or interest paid along the way. We also have pretty good return measures going back decades, if not centuries, across a range of countries and asset classes.

As transparent as returns are, risk is that much more opaque. If you ask most people what is risk in regard to investing, they would likely mimic the dictionary definition: "the chance that an investment (as a stock or commodity) will lose value."[1] There is no database where we can look up historical levels of risk for any security. We can't even state with any certainty the current risk of any particular security.

This lack of precision in the definition of risk left an opening for academia. Academic finance was forced to come up with its own definitions of risk. Depending on how you look at it, finance took a more mathematical route in defining risk. In the most established model of finance—the capital asset pricing model (CAPM)—risk isn't some measure of potential loss; rather it is measured by volatility, or the degree to which a security's price fluctuated in value.[2] Finance types will recognize this as a gross simplification of the CAPM, but the fact is that volatility takes into account all price fluctuations, not just those that are negative.[3]

In other models that followed the CAPM, there is also a linear relationship between risk and return. The higher the expected riskiness of an asset, the higher the expected return on the asset. Pretty simple. This is embodied in the phrase "nothing ventured, nothing gained." It is important to recognize that we are talking about averages here, the theory being that, on average, higher risk is compensated in the form of higher returns.

Much of academic finance in the past three decades has been dedicated to showing the many ways in which the CAPM fails. Academics have created newer models that add additional factors to explain security returns, based on the assumption that these factors proxy for various kinds of risk, which presumably are compensated for on average and over time. In that time, academic finance has begun focusing on measuring risk when asset returns, and the overall economy, are performing poorly.[4]

This academic conception of risk is very different from that of many investment practitioners. This difference is palpable in this quote by James Montier, who writes, "Risk is the permanent loss of capital, never a number."[5] Those investors who look at securities on a case-by-case basis—or in the parlance of the industry, from a bottom-up perspective—hew much more closely to our intuitive sense of the word *risk*.

These investors, often value investors, see not a linear relationship between risk and return but rather an inverse relationship. Those securities that are the least risky have the highest return potential. This is because these securities have been beaten down and the risk has been wrung out of them. In short, these assets have much less farther to fall and are therefore less risky.

Even in this world, the conception of risk is still opaque. No security comes attached with an estimate of its risk. Analysts are forced to make an estimate of a security's fair value. However, these fundamental investors feel that if they focus on securities that trade far below their fair value, they work within a margin of safety.[6]

If you are able to unearth enough securities trading with an adequate margin of safety, you can generate returns both in excess of the market and with less overall risk, the idea being that this buffer between what a security's true value is and where it is trading will make up for any errors the investor makes in judgment or analysis. The concept of a margin of safety puts the risk management process at the forefront of investing. Noted investor Howard Marks makes the point by saying, "Skillful risk control is the mark of a superior investor."[7]

We would all like to be superior investors. However, as discussed in the introduction, that goal may be a stretch for many of us. You can bet that successful investors, like Howard Marks, got to that stage in part by focusing on risk management. Getting from one period to the next with your portfolio largely intact should be the first goal of any investor. In investing, like in a marathon, you can't finish the race if you don't pass each checkpoint along the way.

What should be clear is that whether you conceive of risk in this fundamental framework or in the academic sense, risk is unavoidable. Some people never take that first crucial step to becoming investors because they are paralyzed by the fear of investing. They feel that if they don't step off the sidewalk, they cannot be at risk from oncoming traffic. Unfortunately for them, they have not taken into account the possibility of a car making its way onto the sidewalk.

This somewhat gruesome analogy is important because financial risk is everywhere. It is explicit in the investments we already own. It is implicit in the trade-offs we make by choosing to invest or not invest. It would be great to believe otherwise, but a lifetime of investing is also a lifetime of risk taking.

There Is No Such Thing as a Risk-Free Asset

Risk taking does not come naturally to most people. For every inveterate risk taker, there are a handful of individuals happy to stay as far away from risk as possible. For the rest of us, risk taking is much more of a learned response. In fact, there is evidence of a large genetic component in our willingness to take on financial risk.[8] This mismatch between our innate desire to take risk and our need to take risk to generate returns represents the lifeblood of the financial industry. Much of what the financial industry does is to create vehicles that mitigate risk. At its worst, the industry tries to fudge or hide the risk of certain investments altogether.

Sometimes society as a whole decides it is in our collective interest to mitigate risk. One of the most visible instances is FDIC insurance. Bank deposits for individuals are now guaranteed up to $250,000 per bank. The government does this so that individuals are not at risk to the failure of a bank, in addition to trying to prevent bank runs. The FDIC is proud to note, "Since the FDIC began operation in 1934, no depositor has ever lost a penny of FDIC-insured deposits."[9] That guarantee, however, is not absolute. In the midst of the financial crisis, the limit was increased to what it is now. There is nothing that prevents, however difficult politically, a future government from reducing the limit.

The point is that in the above case, government—and in other cases, the financial services industry—acts in a way to try and entice risk-averse investors to take on investment risk. A perfectly reasonable way of doing this is through collective vehicles such as mutual funds and, more recently, exchange-traded funds (ETFs). To a person, investors recognize that investing in a portfolio of stocks is less risky than investing in any individual or handful of stocks. By mitigating the risk of an individual stock, the hope is that a fund investor is able to enjoy a general rise in stock prices over time.

For most this is a welcome development because the stock market is a cruel place. The high-profile Dow Jones Industrial Average recently celebrated its 115th anniversary. It might surprise you that only one company, GE, has been in the index from the outset.[10] Clearly permanence is not a feature of the equity markets. We need not look out over an entire century to see equity risk; we need only look a year or two in advance.

In 2001 Enron Corporation went bankrupt.[11] It is not news that companies go bankrupt. Companies large and small go bankrupt all the time. What is news was that Enron had been one of the largest companies in market capitalization in the United States and had been named for six years running as "most innovative" among *Fortune*'s Most Admired Companies. This stunning turn of events is a lesson in the risks of any individual company, even one as widely held and admired as Enron.

Market participants recognize that equities, individually and as a whole, are risky. Academics can debate the precise types and amounts of risk, but suffice it to say that few today believe that equities are risk free in any sense of the term. The picture when it comes to fixed income is very different. Risk in the fixed-income market is a different beast altogether.

In the bond markets, investors are worried about two things: "When am I supposed to get paid back?" and "Am I going to get paid back in full, and if not, how much will I receive?" Everything else really stems from these two questions. The bond market, compared with the equity market, is therefore more up front in its approach to risk taking (and risk avoidance).

Despite its many flaws and its woeful performance in light of the financial crisis, the rating agency paradigm is still the way in which the bond markets stratify risk. At the very bottom of the risk scale are bonds issued by the U.S. Treasury. These securities are assumed by most market participants to be risk free, despite recent political turmoil that threatened the U.S. Treasury's ability to manage the debt. Every other bond is subsequently priced in reference to Treasuries.

If the fixed-income story ended there, it would be a straightforward one. On average, lower-rated bonds default more often than higher-rated bonds, and fixed-income investors on average price bonds accordingly. So when a company as big and as high profile as General Motors declares bankruptcy, it does not come as that great a shock to the markets.

Other times investors can be caught flat-footed. One could argue that the onset of the financial crisis was caused by the rapid decline in Lehman Brothers' liquidity position and its subsequent bankruptcy. Among the investors caught unaware were many money market mutual funds that were ill equipped to deal with securities that faced a permanent markdown in value. Funds that were supposed to be risk free were shown to be anything but.

This shock was a primary reason why the global financial system essentially locked up overnight. One could argue that the financial crisis was an ongoing series of miscalculations on the part of issuers and investors. Issuers created securities, nominally rated as risk free by the ratings agencies, that came along with higher coupons. Investors were more than happy to purchase these securities in the hope of garnering additional yield.

This highly stylized view of the financial crisis of 2007–2009 just happens to confirm the proposition made earlier that a primary role of the financial markets is to coax risk-averse investors into risky securities. Sometimes bankers and their clients fool themselves into thinking that financial alchemy is possible, that somehow we can turn risky securities into risk-free ones. While diversification can mitigate some risks, it cannot eliminate them. If we learn one lesson, it is that risk is inherent in the financial markets. We can try to identify and reduce those risks through careful portfolio construction, but those risks still remain.

Nor should we ever believe that any security is truly risk free.[12] Even Treasuries that are assumed to be risk free are not. Let's leave aside interest rate risk for the moment. While there is little risk that those securities will not be paid off in whole, there is a range of outcomes that make Treasuries risky. For foreign investors, a continued decline in the U.S. dollar would make U.S. government securities a money-losing proposition.

For domestic investors, currently much of the Treasury yield curve is trading below expected inflation. Investors are therefore likely to experience negative real, after inflation, returns. We are also leaving the issue of taxes aside at the moment. This is not an unusual situation for the past couple of years. In fact, talk of "financial repression" is rearing its head. This would be a policy of keeping interest rates low for a long time, which would make the available real return on Treasuries in any foreseeable scenario negative.

So if securities that are assumed by everyone to be risk free actually entail real risks, we should recognize that *every* investment entails risk. The great challenge for investors is to accurately identify these inherent risks before they come to pass. Unfortunately our minds ensure that we will get fooled from time to time. Extrapolating past returns into the future is a common mistake that investors make time and time again.

When the Walls Come Down

Investors chase market returns. Anyone who has looked at the data sees this phenomenon play out over time and across asset classes. As a market declines, investors pull their money out. As that market rises, investors put their money back in. On the whole, investors earn less than they would have had they simply stayed put. Carl Richards coins this phenomenon the "behavior gap."[13] By one estimate, investors lose up to 1% per annum by poorly timing their buys and sells.[14]

Research indicates that investors aren't necessarily trying to time the market; rather they are extrapolating returns several years into the future.[15] A likely explanation for this is that risk-averse investors need to see some confirmation that it is "safe" to invest in a particular asset. The only visible sign to most investors that a market is safe is that the price has gone up. The opposite case holds when prices decline.

This goes back to our differing explanations of risk. To the investor who is solely extrapolating returns, the market that has fallen in price seems more risky because all you see is further losses down the road. However, to fundamental investors, an asset that has fallen in price, absent any additional bad news, has become cheaper and is therefore less risky. It will take at least the absence of bad news to bring investors back into the market.

In that sense, it is often said that markets climb a "wall of worry." We can best think of a wall of worry as the market's list of real, potential, and imagined risks. A stock is always in the process of pricing in those risks. As time goes on and those risks are proved to be either unfounded or less impactful than previously thought, investors become more comfortable. More comfortable investors make for a higher stock price. The opposite is true as well: if risks not foreseen come to pass, a stock will decline as investors rate it as riskier than previously thought.

At any point, there is a cornucopia of potential risks. There are your run-of-the-mill economic concerns focused on growth and inflation. Any individual company or industry faces another whole set of specific risks focused on sales growth, disruptive technological innovation, and competition. Then there are your more existential risks like global warming or terrorism. It is not hard to come up with any number of risks with wildly varying probabilities of occurrence.

Indeed, some analysts make their living by focusing on a particular risk to the exclusion of all others. This risk might be hyperinflation, or it might be deflation; whatever it is, according to these analysts it is devastating, and it is often just around the corner. These analysts usually have some preferred asset that is assumed to be a shelter from the coming storm.

We find it ridiculous when the term *guru*, which has its origin in religion, is applied to investing. However, in the case of those analysts who are wedded to a single overarching worldview, the term is appropriately applied. The world of investing is too complicated a place to rely on so-called gurus whose advice withstands any factual refutation.

So most of the time and for most assets, there exists a wall of worry. It takes a lot to convince the general public to achieve a level of willful disbelief that the risk in any asset has been eliminated. For any market, or stock, to achieve this level of risk blindness, something else needs to occur. A market needs to eliminate the proverbial wall of worry before it can seem like it is bulletproof to investors. Ironically those markets that have performed the best, that have supplanted whatever worries existed and now seem invulnerable, are actually the riskiest. This perception of invulnerability sows the seeds of the market's eventual and inevitable decline.

One need only look back a few years to see how this played out in the great housing boom and bust of the early twenty-first century. A slow and steady rise in house prices eventually morphed into a full-on housing frenzy. It seemed to many that there was little or no risk that housing prices could ever fall on a sustained basis. In some cases, buyers were able to refinance in excess of the entire value of a home in the belief that price appreciation would make up the difference. One can trace the financial crisis that followed in part to the belief in ever-rising home prices.

The models that Wall Street used to price the many complicated securities that came out of this housing boom did not take into account the potential for a sustained, nationwide decline in home prices. However, here we sit with home prices at or near postpeak lows.[16] The effects of the housing boom (and bust) are still reverberating through the banking system and global economy.

This example shows the real-world consequences of pushing the concept of risk to the back burner. Housing booms and busts don't come around all that often, but when they do, they can have systemic effects on the economy and the financial system. Booms and busts are a fixture in market history. The challenge is not to allow risk blindness to cloud your judgment about future possible returns.

The question for investors today is whether these periods of excessive optimism are becoming more frequent. One could argue, like Barry Ritholtz does, that we are experiencing a "bubble in bubbles."[17] Whether these bubbles are real or imagined, it matters for investors who have to live in their wake.

Bubble Trouble

It seems that we are living in an age where bubbles are almost commonplace. The Internet bubble of the late 1990s and early 2000s and the housing bubble of the mid-2000s are recent examples of bubbles at work. Due in part to this rapid succession of bubbles, it seems now that everyone is on a hair trigger to be the first to declare every notable price rise (or fall) a bubble.

Bubbles, properly defined, are rare things. However, the past decade we seem to be caroming from one boom-bust cycle to the next. Some might lay the blame for this at the foot of the Federal Reserve for fostering risk taking, but for our purposes the underlying cause is irrelevant. This is because bubbles have been a feature of markets across time, culture, and geography.

The defining characteristic of a bubble is price. Bubbles are characterized by a rapid increase in price. Those prices rise above any reasonable indication of intrinsic value. The rise in price is accompanied by a marked increase in public participation in the market and is supported by claims of a fundamentally new pricing regime. The final piece of the bubble puzzle is the inevitable rapid decline in price that washes away whatever optimism existed prior.[18]

The great challenge of bubbles is that they can really only be identified in hindsight. A bubblelike market can remain aloft far longer than its detractors can believe. As long as the market's apogee is still unknown, there is always a ready source of market defenders. It takes the passage of time and a clear peak in price to convince the vast majority of market participants that a bubble did indeed take place.

Most discussions of bubbles focus on price, in part because a bubble is defined by the rapid rise and subsequent fall in price. It may seem strange that we have included a discussion of bubbles in a chapter devoted to risk. However, bubbles not only play havoc with expectations about asset prices but also have a large effect on investors' emotions and their changing tolerance for risk. Indeed, much of the recent research on bubbles emphasizes how discount rates, or investors' willingness to take on risk, change over time.[19]

If you assume that the intrinsic value of a stock (or market) is generally slow moving, then a rapid increase in price, by definition, increases the stock's risk. If the stock were to revert to fair value, a loss is therefore more likely. The problem is that our emotions give us very different messages. As a stock's price increases, it provides positive feedback to investors that their initial decision was correct. For those investors still on the sidelines, it gives them the emotional kick to move off the sidelines.

This cycle plays itself out in the markets over scales large and small and over time frames short and long. Where a bubble differs is that it subsequently induces individuals who don't normally participate in markets to join in. It also helps that journalists, albeit unconsciously, can get caught up in bubbles as well—especially how journalists converge on certain language surrounding market moves.[20] A bubble also induces people to act in clear violation of their own, more reasoned judgments.

As Meir Statman writes, "Investors everywhere run in herds, large or small, bullish or bearish."[21] These herds can play a disproportionate role in individual decision making. Statman notes that, at the height of the Internet bubble, a poll showed that investors knew stocks were overvalued but remained in the market in hope of capturing some further upside. This willful suspension of disbelief makes it nearly impossible for investors to recognize when the inevitable trend change occurs.

We could have included in the definition of a bubble that most investors, even those who got into a market relatively early, don't end up profiting from a bubble. To profit from a bubble, one needs to both buy and sell. Nearly all investors, large and small, focus on the purchase decision with little or no thought to their exit plan. To many the risk of not being in the market seems far more urgent than any future price decline. That is why investors who escape scot-free from a bubble are rare indeed.

Even in the case of a company such as Amazon.com, which successfully threaded its way through the bubble, it has taken a full decade for Amazon.com stock to retrace its losses from its peak in 1999. Remember, this company is maybe the best-known survivor of the bubble. Other companies and their investors are not so lucky. The point is that most investors in Amazon.com likely did not have the wherewithal to hold the stock for the decade that followed.

This shows the high stakes that are involved in market dislocations like those seen in the Internet bubble. As mentioned earlier, we are still living with the aftermath of the housing bubble with home price indexes still showing little sign of recovery and a backlog of houses waiting to change hands. A bubble is a rare event that increases the stakes of investing for both the individual and the economy as whole.

That is not to say that every aspect of a bubble is necessarily bad. Daniel Gross makes the case that in some instances the aftereffects of some bubbles actually provide a public good to the economy.[22] Gross explains how the construction of the railroads in nineteenth-century America provided generations of benefits to the country despite the poor financial performance of the original rail companies. One could also argue that were it not for the Internet bubble of the prior decade, we would not be experiencing the numerous benefits of what is best described as Web 2.0.

If bubbles represent a case study in risk, what can be done to combat them? One of the clear implications is that investors of all stripes need to have a plan. This is a theme we will return to time and again.

In this framework, a bubble is simply another event against which investors execute their plan. Of course, that is easier said than done.

Having some experience with bubbles is desirable, but that experience is not exactly something one can acquire easily. A substitute is having some understanding of the history of financial markets. A broader understanding of how markets experience these cycles time and again, under widely different circumstances, can help gird one for the challenges that follow.

Achieving this wider understanding is really a larger component of trying to put a bubble into context. Investors also need to put the effect of a bubble into context within the framework of an overall portfolio. Bubbles tend to have a spotlight effect by forcing all of an investor's attention onto the bubble to the detriment of the portfolio as a whole. When viewed in light of an entire portfolio, decisions regarding a bubblelike asset become clearer.

This idea of garnering some broader context may require outside intervention. Stephen P. Utkus notes the importance of seeking out third parties to help bring some additional information and judgment into a situation.[23] Bubbles are characterized in part by groupthink, and therefore consulting with someone who is not part and parcel of the group can bring some much-needed perspective.

Bubbles are insidious because they affect the way investors manage and process information. Nor should we be sanguine that identifying bubbles in real time is an easy task. Perhaps because it is so difficult to do, Benjamin Graham suggested investors never go below 25% equities over above 75% equities.[24] If bubbles represent an overshooting of price to the upside, then the flip side of a bubble is a panic. Panics, however, play out under different circumstances than bubbles do and toy with our emotions in a very different way.

Panic Rarely Pays

The unwinding of a bubble is a long, drawn-out, often torturous process. The drama is extensive because it takes time and evidence to convince all the classes of investors that the run-up in prices was not founded in reality. This unwinding is not over until the hard-core true believers capitulate. People never like to admit that they were wrong, and the deflation of a bubble is a most extreme example.

While there may be periods of panic in the bubble deflation process, panic is a very different beast. *Panic* is, by definition, a sudden, uncontrollable fear among a group of people that induces hasty or irrational actions.[25] Three important points arise from this definition. The first is that it is sudden. Panics are driven by events that seem to come out of left field. Second, panics generate fear, fear of the unknown. Third, they affect a large group of people, the proverbial herd, and anyone familiar with herd behavior will tell you that it is impossible to predict the actions of a herd.

There is never a good time for disaster to strike. Whether that disaster is natural, such as a 9.0 Richter scale earthquake in Japan, man-made like a terrorist attack, or some combination thereof like a plane crash, disasters always seem untimely. The sudden onset of a disaster makes it difficult for market participants to put the event into context. Because these events have their origin outside the financial system, it may take time for investors to get up to speed on the issues involved. This gap in time between an event and the recognition of the likely outcome provides risk-averse investors all the excuse they need to panic.

It should be noted that not every panic starts out with some sort of calamitous event. The financial crisis of 2007–2009 was a prolonged affair with many significant events along the way. The failure of investment banks Bear Stearns and Lehman Brothers are obvious signposts, but there were any number of other events that played a role in the near total collapse of the global financial system. The seeds of that crisis were sown years, if not decades, earlier.

In the financial crisis, the gap between what was known and unknown was especially acute and played out over a long period of time for the markets. Few outside of the halls of power really knew how bad things were, how bad they could have gotten, and what steps needed to be taken to shore up the system. We are only now learning, three years later, the full extent of support the Federal Reserve provided to banks during the acute phase of the crisis.[26] We humans fear the unknown. These information gaps force investors (and the media) to try and come up with explanations for the current goings-on even if they have to make things up. Our need for a sense of control forces us to grab at whatever plausible story presents itself.

A panic isn't recognized as such without mass participation. One person's panic attack isn't newsworthy; a society's collective panic attack is worth noting. The same could be said for an event's impact on the markets. To induce a significant market downturn, there has to be fear, fear of loss. In theory you could have a panic to the upside, but it would play on different psychological effects and biases.

Markets decline precipitously and suddenly because investors who would normally step up to buy an undervalued security recognize that when a market falls, there is no indication where it might eventually bottom out. Mebane Faber writes, "The difficulty with investing during drawdowns is that they can always get worse."[27] The ultimate fear of investors is that a security is going to go to zero. We have already mentioned the case of Enron, a once admired company that quickly went bankrupt. These cases of companies that eventually go to zero are highly salient to investors.

The other reason why investors are so wary of drawdowns—or more simply put, losses—is that they are difficult to make up. A 10% decline in a stock's price requires an 11% increase to return to break even. A 50% decline requires a 100% return to break even. The math of losses is unforgiving, especially for the large losses associated with periods of panic and disaster.

A recent paper that examined how markets react to aviation disasters helps show just how panicky a market can get. Kaplanski and Levy find that markets will price in losses an order of magnitude larger than the actual economic losses.[28] Investors who panic and sell will generate losses that are offset by the brave (or foolhardy) who are willing to take the other side of the trade. In the case of aviation disasters, markets eventually bounce back, but the earlier panics do leave a residue of higher risk estimates.

Ultimately this discussion of panics is one about risk, or more accurately the *mis*estimation of risk. These errors in risk estimation play out in three dimensions. The first is at the macro level. We all recognize that there is always a chance of natural and human-caused disasters. No matter what the cause, they are always shocking when they occur. This shock is because we have collectively misestimated the probability and/or the consequence of an event.

By extension, we misestimate the effect of these rare events on specific assets and our portfolio as a whole. In short, we have underestimated the risk, however temporary, of just such an event. Panic is induced because a stock falls farther and faster than we ever thought possible. An unmitigated fall in stock prices is often driven by sellers who must sell—in short they must sell at any price. Price-sensitive investors witnessing seemingly endless and relentless selling by the likes of margin clerks can easily get discouraged. This disconnect between expectation and reality makes hasty actions all the more likely.

Last, sudden events cause us to reexamine our own tolerance for risk. Many advisors use surveys to sort investors based on their tolerance toward risk. But no survey is able to accurately capture the emotional trauma of real-world events in real time. We don't make investing decisions using questionnaires; instead those decisions happen under pressure in real time.

Panic is an irrational act, and irrational acts rarely pay off. Panic, or at least hasty selling, is sometimes appropriate in the markets. Anything you can get for a stock that is headed for zero is a good sale. As well, if you have dramatically misestimated the risk of a stock, or your own tolerance for risk, then selling, however rushed, may make perfect sense. In other cases, selling into a panic is simply the result of our base instincts coming to the fore. A desire for control and safety takes over, and we take action, however ill advised, because in the moment it makes us feel better. Anyone interested in tranquillity should not be messing about in the financial markets in the first place.

Risk versus Uncertainty

Investing would be a whole lot easier if we could easily characterize how the return-generating process worked. We could invest knowing the possible range, however poor, of outcomes. However, the world doesn't work that way. Investing is not like a board game with all the pieces laid out and a set of rules to follow. It is more like playing a board game where occasionally, and seemingly out of the blue, a basketball lands on the board, distributing the pieces randomly and generally making a big mess.

During any period of time, you may be able to play the game undisturbed by some random event, but you never really can say.

This is the essence of the difference between uncertainty and risk. Risk is a characterization of all the known possible outcomes. Uncertainty represents "unknown unknowns," things we have not even thought could occur—maybe more accurately described as events with probabilities so small, but not zero, that we don't even consider them in the normal course of events.

In the non-board-game real world, these surprise events are almost always negative in nature. A little bit of imagination could conjure up some really positive events that could affect the world for the better. However, from an investor's standpoint, these positive shocks to the system should really just be thought of as found money; it's great if it happens, but not something you can really ever count on.

What investors need to do in the meantime is think about risk in two very distinct ways. The first way is trying to get a better handle on the risks in front of us. The second way is trying to determine the ways in which the world could surprise us.

Frank Knight was one of the first to make the distinction between uncertainty and risk, drawing the distinction in part because our means of forecasting the future are limited at best. We humans have a tendency to take history as it happens and extrapolate into the future. About Frank Knight, Peter Bernstein wrote, "In the end, he considered reliance on the frequency of past occurrences extremely hazardous."[29]

This tendency to view the future as being much like the past gets us humans into trouble in many ways, not just financially. As Howard Marks writes, "Projections tend to cluster around historic norms and call for only small changes... The point is, people usually expect the future to be like the past and underestimate the potential for change."[30] A couple of things are at play here.

The first is that we humans are an overconfident lot. Study after study shows that we humans have a tendency to overestimate our abilities. This includes our ability to forecast the future. This over-confidence leads us to take on risks that we do not even know we are taking on.[31] In future chapters we will see that the stock (and bond) markets can generate negative returns lower and for longer than most people think.

A related issue is hindsight bias, or our tendency to see past events as being inevitable—we knew that would happen all along. If we view the past as something that had to happen in a certain way, it will make it difficult for us to peer into the future looking for disruptive changes. It may be hard to believe, but Argentina at the beginning of the twentieth century was counted among the world's developed markets.[32] The intervening century was not kind to the Argentinean economy as it badly lagged its wealthy and not-so-wealthy competitors. In hindsight Argentina looks like an awful bet, but a hundred years earlier the case for Argentina as an investment was much more compelling.

Financial markets don't go much for this type of alternative reality. The best that finance does is to use historical returns to estimate future risks. This itself has its own problems because it is culling data from a very specific history. Much of the modern financial risk management infrastructure is built on top of these data. If the data are in some way biased, they will not provide the right answers to their users.

One could argue that the financial crisis occurred in part by Wall Street's reliance on a particular model that was used to price and manage the risk of mortgage securities. Everyone was pricing securities based on recent data that showed a very low likelihood of a generalized decline in national home prices. We all know what happened next. As Felix Salmon writes: "In the world of finance, too many quants see only the numbers before them and forget about the concrete reality the figures are supposed to represent. They think they can model just a few years' worth of data and come up with probabilities for things that may happen only once every 10,000 years. Then people invest on the basis of those probabilities, without stopping to wonder whether the numbers make any sense at all."[33]

For whatever reason, we live in a world where 10,000-year events seem to happen on a regular basis. Traditional risk modeling can capture some of the risks involved in investing but, by definition, miss the most important risks. This gets to the difference between risk and uncertainty. Risk, while not modeled all that well, is generally captured by the markets. That is why most earnings or economic releases come along with a collective shrug of the shoulder from the markets. The news was already well anticipated.

A healthy respect for uncertainty changes your fundamental outlook for investing. It makes you think about building redundancies into your portfolio. While it is unpleasant to think about worst-case scenarios, it does help clarify your thinking. Thinking about how to construct an "all-weather portfolio" that you can live with through good times and bad is a useful exercise. The worst investment strategy is one that cannot be followed because we feel compelled to jump ship at the most inopportune times.

Any investor interested in having a long-lasting and fulfilling investing career needs to avoid too many losses of too large a magnitude. This is why we started our discussion of investing with risk and not returns. As Benjamin Graham wrote, "The essence of investment management is the management of risks, not the management of returns."[34]

Key Takeaways

+ There is no such thing as a risk-free investment. Investors can mitigate risk but should recognize that *every* investment entails risk.
+ Markets are always in the process of incorporating new fears, beliefs, and information; hence, there is the constant presence of a "wall of worry."
+ Bubbles represent an extreme expression of investor behavior. Investors should not be sanguine that spotting a bubble in real time is easy.
+ The flipside of a bubble is a panic. However only in rare occasions does panic selling pay off.
+ Risk and uncertainty are not the same thing. Financial markets generally do a decent job of pricing risk but are unable to capture the uncertainty inherent in an uncertain world.

2

Return

Nobody gets involved in investing because of a burning desire to manage risk. As important as understanding and managing risk is, it often gets left out of discussions of investing. The concept of risk is opaque and works against our intuition. On the other hand, returns are transparent and highly publicized. There are few industries where a manager's performance is quoted on a daily basis as happens in the investment industry.

Because performance is quoted on shorter-term time frames like days, months, and quarters, we often neglect to discuss a feature of returns that is relevant across time and asset classes: inflation. Inflation is the general rise in prices that occurs over time. Whether we like it or not, we live in a nominal world, meaning that the wages we earn, the investments we make, and the goods we end up buying are all affected by inflation.

Economists often talk about economic statistics on what they call a real basis. In short, they strip out the effects of inflation to allow for comparisons across economic series, time, and even countries. For example, a period of 5% economic growth is far more impressive when inflation is 1% than when it is 4%. However, this focus on real measures clouds the issue for investors, because investors live in a nominal world.

Rampant inflation has not been a problem in the United States for decades. So for many, the issue of inflation has faded from our collective memories. In one sense, this is a good thing. Inflation can greatly distort the way people collectively make decisions in an economy. Not having to contend with these effects can make for a more efficient economy.

However, for investors, inflation has never really gone away. It is always there lurking in the background. An analogy can help bring the point home. In this increasingly eco-conscious age, people now worry about the "waste" electricity we use from so-called phantom devices. These devices—such as your TV—draw power even when they are turned off. Inflation is a lot like that. Even when we are not paying attention to it, inflation is still there, reducing the purchasing power of your hard-earned savings and investments.

Some might say that we can safely ignore 2% inflation, such as we have seen of late. However, a quick lesson in the power of compounding should dissuade you of this view. In a world of 2% inflation, an investor needs to earn 2% just to stay even with inflation. (We are ignoring the effect of taxes at this point.) After 10 years, that initial dollar invested would have to grow to $1.22 just to stay even with inflation. If you substitute 5% for 2%, you would have to grow a dollar into $1.63 just to break even. This quick example shows you the power of not only inflation but also compounding.

Like many things in life, inflation is something individuals and the economy can get accustomed to. Individuals internalize the effect of higher future prices, workers demand pay hikes, and businesses build into their contracts higher prices to counteract the effects of inflation. In this example, some of the effects of expected inflation can be managed, but the larger costs to society still remain. And what is a bigger danger to investors is unexpected inflation.

When inflation really gets rolling, it can take some time for investors to come to terms with higher inflation. In the meantime, all manner of financial assets, for instance, bonds, get repriced, i.e., get priced lower. From this perspective, the worst-case scenario is a steadily increasing rate of inflation. These recurring negative surprises wreak havoc on asset prices as investors repeatedly try to ratchet up their expectations.

On the other hand, the best-case scenario is one in which inflation is high but steadily declines.[1] This reduction in the rate of inflation, or disinflation, represents what happened through much of the 1980s and 1990s in the United States. The wringing out of inflation from the system represented a healthy tailwind to both the bond and equity markets during this time period.

There are some securities these days that take into account the effects of inflation. In the United States these are called TIPS, or Treasury inflation-protected securities. TIPS provide investors with a coupon, or interest rate, over and above consumer price inflation. Other sovereign nations, and a handful of corporations, also issue these types of securities, but they represent a small part of the overall bond market. These securities represent a unique way for individuals to hedge, in part, the risk of higher inflation.[2]

In the midst of the inflationary decade of the 1970s, Warren Buffett wrote an article for *Fortune* magazine describing the negative effects of inflation on companies and their shareholders. He makes the point that inflation serves as a tax on investment. Buffett writes: "The arithmetic makes it plain that inflation is a far more devastating tax than anything that has been enacted by our legislatures. The inflation tax has a fantastic ability to simply consume capital. It makes no difference to a widow with her savings in a 5% passbook account whether she pays 100% income tax on her interest income during a period of zero inflation, or pays *no* income taxes during years of 5% inflation. Either way, she is 'taxed' in a manner that leaves her no real income whatsoever."[3]

Investors need to recognize that taxes play the same role that inflation does for the tax-paying individual. In the investment world, taxes are rarely taken into account when discussing returns. Taxes fall by the wayside in large part because investing entities like pensions, endowments, and even mutual funds don't pay taxes. They either are tax exempt or simply pass along their tax obligations to their investors. The other complicating factor is that every individual faces a unique tax situation, making it difficult to generalize. Just because the financial media frequently avoids the issue of taxes does not mean you should. Taxes play as important a role as inflation in generating returns over time.

It has often been said that there is nothing certain in this life besides death and taxes. From an investor's perspective, you can add inflation to that list. Even small amounts of inflation add up over time to degrade returns. What matters for investors is generating real, after-tax returns. Once you recognize the important role that real and after-tax returns play, we can move on to the challenge of understanding how those returns are generated in the first place.

The Equity Risk Premium

In the desire to generate real, after-tax returns, it would be great if we could count on the financial markets to generate steady, real returns in exchange for taking on financial risk. Academics call the return premium for equities versus bonds the *equity risk premium* (ERP). However, it is difficult to pin down what the ERP is. At best, we can say that the premium for investing in equities is much lower than it has been. At worst, the ERP is a myth.

Investors need to believe in an ERP. They need to believe that the efforts required to create and manage an equity portfolio should earn them some sort of additional return over time. Otherwise what is the point? Given the importance that the ERP plays for investors and companies alike, you would think that we would have a good handle on it. Unfortunately you would be mistaken.

Aswath Damodaran, who writes extensively on the topic, notes: "Equity risk premiums are a central component of every risk and return model in finance and are a key input into estimating costs of equity and capital in both corporate finance and valuation. Given their importance, it is surprising how haphazard the estimation of equity risk premiums remains in practice."[4] Just how haphazard are these estimates?

Practitioners, companies, and academics are in the same ballpark when it comes to estimating the ERP. Surveys by Fernandez, Aguirreamalloa, and Avendaño show an estimated 5–6% ERP in the United States.[5] Given the way finance is taught in the United States, we shouldn't be that surprised that all the parties in the surveys came in with roughly the same estimates.

What is surprising is just how big a spread there is in the estimates. Estimates of the ERP run anywhere from below 2% on the low side all the way up to 10–15% on the high side.[6] You could argue that this diversity in opinion is what makes markets. However, this wide a spread calls into question whether we are in fact talking about the same thing altogether.

What is clear is that estimates of the ERP have been coming down over time. In part that has to do with the poor performance of the equity markets ever since the year 2000. And in part it has to do with a growing recognition that the ERP simply can't be as high as earlier thought.

For a long period of time, the case for equities above all other asset classes was based on the high ERP seen historically. The ERP was so high that it was classified by academics as the "ERP puzzle." However, over time academics have been lowering their estimates of the ERP. A survey of academic textbooks by Fernandez shows a 3% decline in the estimated ERP over the past two decades.[7] It is safe to assume this estimate will come down even further.

The past decade or so has been a lost decade for U.S. stocks. The poor performance has dragged down all sorts of historical measures of the ERP. In the case of the United States, from 1986 to 2010 the ERP versus bonds has only been 0.9%.[8] So for a 25-year period, equity investors earned not even 1% more than long-term Treasury bonds. If you look at this number on a global basis, the number since 1986 is actually negative![9]

To get numbers like those seen in the survey data, you have to use data going all the way back to the beginning of the twentieth century. In the case of the United States, Dimson, Marsh, and Staunton find a 4.4% ERP for the United States and a 3.8% ERP for a globally diversified index. Other researchers go back to the beginning of the nineteenth century to generate even longer-term estimates.

There are two issues with going back this far to generate long-term estimates of the ERP. The first is that there are real methodological problems with trying to extract data from back then. There are no computer files one can consult to generate these data time series. Jason Zweig at the *Wall Street Journal* looked at many of the problems with the old data and found any data before 1870 to be suspect.[10] In short, we have data that are a lot less reliable than commonly thought.

Second and more important, what relevance do equity returns from these early periods really have to us today? The process of equity investing was very different back then. It took a much more intrepid investor to invest in equities in those earlier times. Information was scarcer, and the costs were much higher. Equities must have seemed like a much more speculative proposition back then than they do today. Today we have nearly unlimited data, nearly free commissions, and the ability to trade stocks with a mouse click. Today's equity investor is no longer facing the hurdles an investor a century ago would have faced. We should therefore take these long-run estimates of the ERP with a big grain of salt.

Not mentioned in all this discussion is another issue. All these estimates are based on theoretical returns to some sort of market basket of stocks. While today market baskets, or index funds, are commonplace and transparent, all these estimates of market returns are not necessarily based on investable indexes—again another reason to be skeptical of these estimates.

Given these limitations, the ERP is likely lower than previously thought and lower than most people's estimates. What if the ERP is even lower than these low-end estimates? As mentioned, the ERP does not take into account certain real-world effects, all of which lead to lower estimates of the ERP.

Eric Falkenstein, author of the book *Finding Alpha,* has been a critic of the literature on the ERP.[11] Falkenstein believes that after you take into account a number of adjustments, the ERP is actually zero![12] For example, index returns don't take into account the variable dollar flows into equities.[13] Therefore, buy-and-hold results overestimate the returns investors actually earned. Another factor not taken into account is taxes, an issue we have already touched on. Falkenstein notes that all these estimates are based on pretax returns and should therefore be lowered for taxable investors. He also mentions a number of other factors, some technical, that serve to reduce the ERP. He notes that any of these factors puts a big dent in the ERP, and when taken as a whole, they make prior estimates of the ERP seem far off base.

This discussion is admittedly abstract and filled with somewhat conflicting statistics. The question of the ERP is important for a couple of reasons. The first is simple. Equities are the linchpin of most people's long-term portfolios. If the estimates used to justify this status are flawed, we need to understand this. Second, we need to understand the limitations of the ERP. If we can't trust the estimates many people use to justify a role for equities, then we need to rethink our entire approach to investing.

Then again, you don't have to buy the case that the equity premium is strictly zero to rethink your approach to investing. If the ERP is more modest than previously thought, it makes the idea of a 100% equity portfolio seem decidedly risky. Blogger and investment advisor David Merkel writes: "One can gain moderately over the very long haul in stocks versus bonds, but with significant volatility. Don't risk what you can't afford to lose in the stock market, and other risky investment vehicles."[14] This seems like good advice whether the ERP is 0% or 5%.

The Drawdown Dilemma

There is a big disconnect between the research that academic finance and investment professionals conduct and the real world. The prior discussion of the ERP is a perfect example. Researchers talk about average returns, which, on the face of it, makes sense. How else can we summarize decades of market returns? Unfortunately we don't live in an average world. We live in a world where we go to work, save, invest, and (the hope is) retire.

Many financial planners move beyond the use of simple average returns with more sophisticated models. To the degree to which these models show investors that they need to spend less and save more, they are useful. However, if they are used to more precisely predict the future outcomes of the market, then they are simply dressing up uncertainty with a false sense of precision.

Everybody's experience in the markets is unique. Nobody earns the average return of the market. We all are going to experience different market conditions at different points in our financial lives. Therefore, talking about average returns really hides the much more complicated investing equation we all face over time. Nobody lives a perfectly average life. Therefore, nobody lives a perfectly average investing life either.

Peter Bernstein is quoted as saying, "The market's not a very accommodating machine; it won't provide high returns just because you need them."[15] In that sense, you can think of the market as a slot machine. Just because you put a quarter in, you are not entitled to a payoff. So in the abstract, we can talk about average market returns, but everyone's experience with the market is going to be different.

Timing plays a big role in our investing experiences, which is another way of saying that luck matters. A brief review of the history of the markets shows decade-long periods of high and low returns, with few average decades in between. Therefore, investors who are in their prime savings and investing years in the midst of a rip-roaring bull market are going to have a much better experience than they might have over the past lost decade for stocks.

A concept to keep in mind when thinking about investing over the long run is the idea of drawdowns. A drawdown is the reduction in the value of an asset (or market) as the asset falls in price. Once an asset reaches a new high price, the drawdown is complete. Drawdowns are the bane of investors large and small. Drawdowns are best thought of as the manifestation of downside risk. Risk management is in a very real sense an attempt to minimize drawdowns.

Drawdowns are unavoidable. Markets cannot continually reach new highs. The challenge for investors is not the transient drawdown but the ones that last decades and wreak havoc with a portfolio. These drawdowns can greatly harm those who are coming up on significant milestones like retirement. In the past decade for stocks, there has been no shortage of examples of people who delayed their retirement because of the drawdown in the stock market.

The stock market in the United States has experienced a handful of significant drawdowns in the past 100 years. The most notable drawdown was in the wake of the market crash of 1929 and the ensuing Great Depression. The stock market did not recover until 1945. Most recently we have seen two big drawdowns. The first was in the wake of the Internet bubble, the second occurring in the wake of the financial crisis of 2008. Both of these pushed the market down some 50% from its highs.

Equity market drawdowns highlight the importance of valuations. In the case of 1929 and 1999, the equity market was undergoing a bubble. By any measure, the market before starting its descent was richly priced. These high valuations turned out to be an indication that risk was high as well. The subsequent market fall served to normalize the market's valuation. In the case of 1929, the state of the economy played an important role in the long climb back for the stock market. The economy also plays a crucial role in the performance of bonds.

It should not be altogether surprising that the stock market can undergo long periods of underperformance. What may be more surprising is that the bond market can undergo protracted drawdowns as well. While valuation also plays a role in the bond market, what matters most is unexpected inflation. The entire decade of the 1970s was characterized by high inflation and a decline in the real value of bonds. The ensuing multidecade-long bull market in bonds was a function of three decades of disinflation.

Dimson et al. highlight the role that simple diversification can play in reducing the magnitude of drawdowns in either equities or bonds. They present the performance of a 50:50 portfolio of equities and bonds and state: "Individually, equities and bonds have on several occasions lost more than 70% in real terms. But since 1900, this 50:50 blend has never (USA) or virtually never (UK) suffered a decline of over 50%. Furthermore, the duration of drawdowns is briefer for the blend portfolio than for the supposedly low-risk fixed income asset."[16]

They go on to note that this portfolio is a naïve one and that investors would be well served by a portfolio more diversified than a simple 50:50 split. Diversification into international markets could help diversify the risks of any single country. Another surprising diversifier comes to mind as well—cash. James Montier, in a discussion of hedging tail risks, highlights the attractions of cash. As he states: "When constructing portfolios ex-ante, the aim should be robustness, not optimality. Cash is a more robust asset than bonds, inasmuch as it responds better under a wider range of outcomes."[17]

We will talk more about cash in a future chapter, but this discussion of cash highlights the importance of what Montier calls a robust solution. The goal of every investor is to survive drawdowns and reach the finish line with portfolio intact. Drawdowns are important not only because of the financial havoc they can wreak but also because of the psychological damage they can inflict. Drawdowns bring out the worst behavior in investors, such as panic. The best portfolio solutions recognize the dangers that drawdowns pose to our portfolios and our behaviors.

In a more philosophical light, we need to recognize that luck plays a big role in investing. Some investors are going to experience muted drawdowns and robust market returns; others just the opposite. The market owes us nothing. The most recent lost decade for stocks shows that the best laid plans of investors can be upended by all manner of calamities.

This discussion of long-term returns glosses over an important point. For investors the long term is really made up of a series of short terms. We can't get to 10-year or 20-year returns without passing a number of milestones along the way. Therefore, looking at how returns evolve over the intermediate term will give us a better sense of how returns are generated.

Momentum

Momentum equals mass times velocity. In the context of the financial markets, momentum simply means that stocks and asset classes that performed well (poorly) in the recent past on average continue to outperform (underperform) in the future. Momentum in that sense is about as simple as simple gets when it comes to the financial markets. All you need are historical prices to do the calculations.

There are many ways to calculate momentum. At its most basic level, it involves measuring past performance, usually over a 3- to 12-month time frame, and comparing the performance of a set of assets. The assets with the best past performance are expected to continue that performance in the future. Likewise those assets with the worst performance are expected to continue to underperform in the future. Portfolios are formed accordingly and updated as new returns come in. In this formulation, momentum is an intermediate-term phenomenon. Momentum eventually fizzles out, and mean reversion eventually kicks in.

In our earlier discussion of bubbles and their aftermath, we saw how momentum works at its most extreme. What we are talking about here is garden-variety booms and busts, not bubbles and panics. Markets everywhere undergo these types of cycles. On the face of it, momentum, or relative strength, should not exist. However research by James P. O'Shaughnessey shows it working decade after decade in U.S. equities.[18] The patterns we are discussing are very simple, and as trading strategies go, momentum strategies are relatively easy to implement.

Maybe the most intriguing aspect of momentum is that it is such a persistent feature in financial markets. Momentum shows up in all sorts of places, including within and across asset classes. As Antti Ilmanen states, "Momentum strategies perform well in virtually all asset classes we study."[19] If momentum strategies showed profits only in select time periods or geographies, we could dismiss momentum as a phenomenon, but the evidence is too strong that momentum exists.

In a much-cited paper, Asness, Moskowitz, and Pedersen study the existence of value and momentum factors together across a range of asset classes. In agreement with Ilmanen's statement above, the authors find momentum effects in a range of asset classes.[20] Intriguingly, they also find that the returns to momentum strategies in different markets seem to be correlated. As well, they find that momentum strategies perform best in periods of declining liquidity like that seen during financial crises. This jibes with the performance of managed futures during the tumultuous year of 2008.

One thing Asness et al. don't do is say definitively why momentum exists. Then again, no one really has any single explanation for why momentum effects persist. Most attempts rely on behavioral factors to explain the stylized facts of momentum and the eventual reversal in returns. These include some combination of an underreaction to news and an overreaction to past returns. If behavioral factors are the reason driving momentum, then it is a pretty good bet that it will persist over time.

Momentum strategies have become ever-more popular over time. In part this has to do with education. In their book *The Ivy Portfolio,* Mebane Faber and Eric W. Richardson discuss how investors can implement strategies based on trailing 10-month returns within and across asset classes.[21] On the managed futures side, a book like *Trend Following* by Michael W. Covel has played a large role in getting the message out about these types of strategies.[22] There is more to it than mere publicity.

A structural shift in the financial markets has made the implementation of momentum strategies cheaper and easier than ever before. The emergence of ETFs for nearly every asset class, industry sector, country, currency, and commodity has brought momentum strategies to the masses. Prior to this, momentum strategies were more expensive and difficult to implement. We will see later just how much ETFs have changed the financial markets, but for investors and traders the existence of so many asset classes has been a boon.

One of the more prominent areas where momentum investing takes place is in the commodity futures markets. The managed futures industry is made up mostly of investors who follow momentum strategies in various markets, including commodities, currencies, and equities.[23] We will discuss managed futures later in the book, but the success of trend followers has garnered a great deal of attention and capital. The challenge for trend followers has never been in formulating a strategy. Trend-following strategies are pretty straightforward. The challenge has always been one of discipline.

The discipline required to follow a momentum-type strategy is largely overlooked in these discussions. Momentum works because it calls on investors to do things that do not come naturally. Momentum strategies require investors to buy things that have already increased in value and are trading near their highs, not their lows. Successful momentum strategies also have strict and well-defined selling, or switching, strategies. Both these pieces of the momentum puzzle are difficult for investors to master.

There is another piece to the momentum puzzle, and it relates to our earlier discussion of drawdowns. Just as markets and asset classes can have sizable drawdowns, so can strategies. Momentum strategies are notorious for having sizable drawdowns. As noted, not only do large drawdowns have an effect on returns; they have a large psychological cost as well. Momentum strategy followers are plagued by the desire to bail out on the strategy when returns are the worst. In short, the returns to momentum come with a high psychological price tag.

The publicized returns to investments made using mechanical momentum strategies are therefore not necessarily reflective of what we mere humans are able to do on our own. When it comes to implementation, a computer is more disciplined than any human can be. There is some hope though. In the areas of equities and managed futures, new exchange-traded products (ETPs) have arisen that follow momentum strategies. These ETPs take the guesswork and psychological difficulties out of the implementation of momentum strategies for individual investors.

The question for investors is whether these prepackaged momentum solutions will eventually erode the returns obtained with these types of strategies.[24] If momentum investing becomes so simple that anyone can do it, the returns gained using the strategy may disappear over time. This possibility is not altogether farfetched. A number of so-called market anomalies have largely disappeared after being studied and popularized.

So if momentum seems to rule markets in the intermediate term, what happens in the longer term? We have already hinted at this earlier, but over the long run, value effects win out as markets come back to reality, or mean-revert. Let's take a look at the number of ways that valuation eventually comes into play.

Value Will Out

If we go back to our discussion of bubbles, we see how markets can move through periods of euphoria when momentum rules. When this momentum reverses, it oftentimes takes prices not only toward fair value but past fair value into undervalued territory. Every market move is obviously not a bubble bursting, but this stylized view of market behavior gives us a clue to the other part of our return puzzle: value.

Just like momentum, value effects are a well-established fact of the financial markets. There are a number of types of value investors, including those that like to call themselves contrarians. One manifestation of value is the reversal effect. Reversals occur over many time frames, but most typically they occur outside the window of momentum—that is, just outside of a year. Longstanding research indicates that those stocks that performed worst over the past three to five years undergo a "reversal effect" and begin outperforming.[25] We see just the opposite effect for those stocks that have performed best, with their stocks beginning to underperform.

If reversals didn't occur, returns would in theory just continue on indefinitely. Expensive assets would get more expensive, and cheap assets would keep on getting cheaper. We know that is not how the world works. Public investors are only one side of the equation. On the other side of the equation are issuers and private investors. These players get paid to recognize when things get expensive and, conversely, cheap.

Think back to the Internet bubble. When things were getting frothy, every company, new or old, that had any business tangentially related to the Internet moved to go public. Those companies took advantage of high valuations to issue overpriced stock. This cycle of initial public offerings (IPOs) has been going on for a long time. That is in part why IPOs in general underperform the market.[26] Companies initially issue stock when valuations are high, and the stocks subsequently underperform. If these issuers in a certain sense "sell high," who buys low?

In some cases, other corporations. If a company's price gets too low relative to that of its competitors, one of those competitors could make a bid, at a premium, to acquire or merge. Other types of bidders can get involved as well. Over the past few decades, private equity has become an important player in the market for corporate control. If private equity investors see a public company trading at a level at which they believe they can purchase, finance, and operate the company profitably, they will attempt to do so. This sort of real-world activity helps bridge what we see going on in the stock market and the actual market for corporate control.

This is not an equity market phenomenon only. Companies that issue bonds take advantage of favorable market conditions as well. Throughout 2011, corporations issued record amounts of debt, taking advantage of rock-bottom interest rates. With Treasury yields at historically low levels and low credit spreads, some companies with AAA ratings were able to issue bonds at rates not much higher than that of the U.S. government.[27] Could rates have gone lower? Sure, but these companies recognized a favorable environment to issue debt and took advantage of it.

From an investing perspective, there are a couple of ways of looking at and implementing value investing strategies. The first takes a more quantitative, or academic, approach; it looks at statistical measures of value to build portfolios. Value-based approaches have been shown for some time to outperform the market. These value stocks outperform in part because their valuations eventually converge with the rest of the stock market.[28] The question is whether these statistical approaches can continue to work in an era where knowledge and network effects, which are difficult to value, play an increasingly larger role in companies than plant and equipment do.

David Swensen, head of the Yale University endowment fund, describes these approaches as "naïve contrarianism."[29] In his view, value investing is a more thoughtful process of looking for value in whatever corner of the markets that provides it. This is a more challenging task than simply buying stocks that are statistically cheap. Swensen writes, "In many instances, value investing proves fundamentally uncomfortable, as the most attractive opportunities frequently lurk in unattractive or even frightening areas."[30]

Value, or contrary, investing is therefore like momentum investing in that it is psychologically difficult to stick with over time. In the case of value investing, it requires consistently going against the crowd. As noted investor Howard Marks writes: "To boil it all down to just one sentence, I'd say the necessary condition for the existence of bargains is that perception has to be considerably worse than reality. That means the best opportunities are usually found among things most others won't do."[31] The most successful value investors are able to do things that most investors are unable or unwilling to do and are therefore able to generate returns not available to index investors.

The fact that momentum and value can coexist shows that the investment world is, to say the least, a complicated beast. Some investors do very well plying their trade in either the world of momentum or value. To some degree, this has to do with their investment disposition, as one or the other of these approaches feels right to a certain group of investors. This is an important point, because as we discussed, both these approaches work in part because they are psychologically difficult to follow. Those investors that are best suited to the psychological rigors of either momentum or investing are most likely to succeed with that approach.

For the rest of the world, there is a middle approach, and that involves combining value and momentum in a portfolio. We can look at this in a couple of different ways. Combining value and momentum on a microscale or within an asset class makes these returns less vulnerable to the returns for any single return factor. On a broader scale, it makes sense to combine value and momentum across asset classes in part because the returns for value and momentum are negatively correlated with each other.[32]

Research indicates that portfolios focused on these strategies can outperform those simply focused on broad asset classes.[33] An investor who combines the two approaches has a chance to create a portfolio that provides less volatile returns in an attempt to generate abnormal returns. This is the crux of the matter for investors. Our discussion of risk and return has focused on trying to create portfolios that keep investors on track and in the game. Finding a middle path between momentum and value within and across asset classes gives investors a better chance of creating a portfolio that they can stick with over time.

Key Takeaways

- Investors should never forget that their goal is to generate real, after-tax returns and that inflation and taxes play key roles in our returns.
- Estimates of the equity risk premium have been coming down for some time. There are good arguments why we should contemplate and plan for a lower, even zero, equity risk premium.
- The market owes us nothing. Investors need to contemplate dealing with significant drawdowns in the equity and fixed-income markets during their lifetime.
- Over the short and intermediate term, momentum rules markets. However, following a momentum strategy comes with significant psychological costs.
- Eventually momentum fizzles out and value wins out. The links between the financial markets and corporate finance ensure some balance between prices and reality.
- Investors have a better chance of earning balanced returns by combining strategies, like value and momentum, in their portfolios.

3

Equities

WHEN PEOPLE ASK WHAT THE MARKET DID TODAY, THEY USUALLY mean the stock market. This is because, for better or worse, the stock market remains the investment choice for those investors looking to save for long-term goals like retirement—this despite the fact that by one measure equities only make up 25% of the value of the global capital markets.[1]

Investors these days are in a desperate search for returns. That is in part why asset classes and themes seem to go in and out of fashion so rapidly nowadays. For investors unable to access other more exclusive and esoteric asset classes, equities remain the one opportunity to generate real returns over time.

In a certain sense, governments at present are not giving investors much of a choice. The compression in interest rates has made the potential returns on all manner of government bonds decidedly negative after taking into account inflation and taxes. Equities at least offer the prospect for future growth in earnings and dividends that investors hope can offset the costs of increasing longevity. Growth is certainly important, but investors should recognize that growth is a more nuanced story than it seems on the surface.

The Stock Market Is Not the Economy

It is common wisdom that the stock market and the economy are inextricably linked. When the economy does well, the stock market does well, and vice versa. As Bradford Cornell writes: "The long-run performance of equity investments is fundamentally linked to growth in earnings. Earnings growth, in turn, depends on growth in real GDP."[2] This relationship makes intuitive sense. If the economy is doing well, people are working, sales are strong, and presumably profits are up. Higher profits imply higher stock prices.

Our understanding of economic history bolsters this simple story. The worst time for the U.S. stock market was during the Great Depression. On the flip side, the decades of the 1980s and 1990s were filled with falling inflation, consistent economic growth, and rising stock prices. The challenge is that the links between the stock market, corporate earnings, and the economy play out over time horizons that are longer than most investors' time horizons. This simple story also leaves out two important pieces of the puzzle. The first is that the companies that make up the stock market are only a part, albeit an important part, of the overall economy. Second, research shows that only current economic growth and the stock market are related. That means that economic growth today tells us nothing about future stock market returns.

The U.S. economy today is a poster child for the disengagement of the corporate sector from the economy. While the U.S. economy continues to operate with generally tepid economic growth, headline unemployment rates well in excess of 9%, and a budget deficit well in excess of a trillion dollars, the stock market has not (yet) collapsed. There is increasing frustration among many Americans who see corporate America profiting while so many workers continue to struggle. Why then is there such a disconnect between Wall Street and Main Street?

First, corporate profit margins are at record highs. Companies have optimized their workforces for lean economic times. Unfortunately these high profit margins are coming at the expense of workers. Second, a large part of corporate America today is made up of multi-national companies that generate significant portions of their profits from overseas sales. These sales (and profits) have little bearing on what is going on in the U.S. economy today. There is little doubt that the U.S. economy at present represents a historical outlier.

The long arc of economic history shows that the recent example of corporate earnings growing faster than GDP is an anomaly. Why is that? Over the long run, measures of earnings growth have to trail GDP growth. Bernstein and Arnott make the point that much of what constitutes economic growth comes not from the already existing (and publicly traded) sector, but rather from new companies.[3] While the economy as a whole benefits from innovation, advances in technology, and the formation of new companies, much of this occurs outside the existing universe of publicly traded companies. Ritter says it another way: "The point is that economic growth does result in a higher standard of living for consumers, but it does not necessarily translate into a higher present value of dividends per share for the owners of the existing capital stock. Thus, whether future economic growth is high or low in a given country has little to do with future equity returns in that country."[4]

This phenomenon is not unique to the United States. Bernstein and Arnott show that in a broad cross section of countries over a century a measure of corporate profits, i.e., dividend growth, trails a measure of economic growth, GDP. So while over shorter periods of time the stock market can disengage from the economy, over the longer term this dilutive effect eventually weighs on the stock market.

While this result is interesting, it does not tell us whether investing in high-growth countries leads to higher stock market returns. This is what we would expect. Faster growth should lead to a higher stock market. But that is not what history tells us. In a study that covers over a century of stock market returns, Ritter explains that there is in fact a negative relationship between equity returns and per capita GDP growth.[5] Paradoxically, slower-growing countries had better returns.

On the face of it, this makes no sense. Why should slower-growing countries experience better returns? What this analysis leaves out is valuation. Countries that grew the fastest tended to have higher starting valuations. So the faster economic growth was weighed down as those valuations normalized. In that sense, growth countries are not all that different from growth stocks. The past decade in the U.S. stock market can be viewed in this light, in which many large, well-known U.S. companies have spent the past decade working off excessive valuations from the turn of the century.[6]

These results are still widely ignored in the investment community. It is a common refrain that investing in emerging markets makes sense because that is where the growth resides. The rise of the emerging markets, particularly China, India, and Brazil, has reinforced in people's minds the link between economic growth and stock market returns. However, this story is now well known. What really mattered is that these countries started with relatively modest equity market valuations *and* surprised everyone with increasingly rapid growth.

These recent high-profile examples should overrule research that shows a more tenuous relationship. A more recent study by Dimson, Marsh, and Staunton that takes into account the experience of the emerging markets over the past 20 years again shows a negative relationship between economic growth and equity market returns.[7] The authors note that in this regard countries are a lot like companies: value countries tend to outperform growth countries.

A great deal of effort is expended trying to forecast growth rates in the United States and around the world. Wall Street is awash in economists who are more than happy to provide detailed economic forecasts for the entire globe. There is little reason to believe that economists have the ability to accurately forecast economic growth, and even if they did, these forecasts leave out a big part of the equation. What this means is that chasing growth in the emerging markets, or any other market, is a recipe for disappointment. Simply think of the emerging markets as another pond in which to fish for bargains.

Rapid economic growth can serve a country's interests in many ways, but for investors the importance of valuation should not be ignored. The stock market is not the economy, and so when a commentator comes on the air discussing economic forecasts, don't think, "How fast?" Think more along the lines of "How much?"

Lower Risk = Higher Returns

We previously discussed how the ERP is an example of how modern finance is still dealing with really basic questions. If market participants can't come to terms with the ERP, maybe it shouldn't be all that surprising that the relationship between risk and return within the equity markets themselves is jumbled as well.

A strand of research has been consistently showing that, however measured, lower-risk stocks tend to outperform higher-risk stocks. To anyone steeped in the idea of risk and return being positively related, this is a real puzzle. In academic finance, this finding is called the *low-risk anomaly*. One could call this the *high-beta anomaly* as well. Baker, Bradley, and Wurgler show that over a 41-year time period low-risk stocks trounced high-risk stocks. No matter how you slice the data, this relationship held up.[8]

The biggest effect was the particularly poor performance of the riskiest stocks. For whatever reason, the stocks with the highest risk stood out for their market-lagging performance. Two other points are worth making. First, Baker et al. found that the return path for the lowest-risk stocks was much smoother, or as they write, "genuinely lower risk." Second, unlike with other anomalies, this inverse risk-return relationship is holding steady, if not getting a bit stronger, over time.

A skeptic may wonder if this is simply an isolated example of U.S. equities behaving in some unique fashion. A good test is to see if these sorts of results show up in other markets as well. Even though the U.S. capital markets are the biggest and deepest, it is useful to see if these kinds of findings also hold in other equity markets.

Luckily for us, Frazzini and Pedersen have conducted similar research on a global basis.[9] They found that the high-beta and low-risk anomalies were present in the global equity markets too. Whether they looked at global equities pooled, that is, all together, or looked within 19 individual markets themselves, these results held up. Lower-risk stocks outperformed higher-risk stocks.

The big question in all of this is why. One would think that this sort of phenomenon would have been eliminated or at least reduced over time. Baker et al. put forth two explanations for the persistence of this phenomenon. The first is that individuals have an unexpected preference for high-risk stocks. The so-called lottery effect shows why it is that investors would be interested in taking on these risky stocks. In addition, the existence of overconfidence helps explain why overoptimistic investors help set the price of the riskiest stocks.

The second explanation Baker et al. put forth is that there are real institutional impediments to managers trying to exploit this effect. Most institutional managers, and the vast amounts of money they manage, are judged by their performance against a benchmark like the S&P 500. The risk they are concerned with is not the high-beta anomaly but rather career risk, that is, the risk that they underperform their benchmark for an extended period of time.

Ideally, to take advantage of the low-risk anomaly, a manager would systematically short high-risk stocks. Absent that, a manager would have to avoid certain stocks and load up on low-risk stocks. This portfolio will perform in a fashion substantially different from that of the benchmark. Although a "low-risk" portfolio should outperform on a risk-adjusted basis, a portfolio manager could very well experience periods of underperformance against the benchmark, thereby making this strategy in an ironic fashion risky.

Frazzini and Pedersen note that the low-risk anomaly is consistent with investors preferring risky, unleveraged assets—for example, high-beta stocks—compared with leveraged low-risk assets. Institutions and individuals are often loath to take on leverage, or borrowing, to buy any financial asset, even those that are generally believed to be safe. Leverage, both explicit and implicit, is abundant in the financial markets, but so long as large swaths of the investment industry are constrained, these low-risk anomalies could continue for some time to come.

How can investors take practical advantage of this anomalous situation? For investors who have the capacity, creating portfolios that systematically short risky assets and go long less risky assets is the preferred route. This allows investors to target how much exposure they want to any particular market. In contrast, Eric Falkenstein proposes two relatively straightforward strategies to exploit the low-volatility and high-beta anomalies.[10]

The first is described simply as a low-volatility portfolio. This portfolio owns a basket of stocks with the lowest volatilities. This portfolio from 1962 generates both a higher return and a lower risk, as measured by volatility, than the S&P 500 does. In fact, ETF providers have already launched funds that follow this very approach.

The second strategy is what Falkenstein describes as a beta 1.0 portfolio. This portfolio is constructed with stocks that have betas approximately equal to 1.0. Since 1962, this portfolio has generated substantially higher returns, roughly 2.0% per annum, than the S&P 500 with a little bit more risk. For an investor looking for an approach to the high-risk anomaly, with market risk, this is an interesting solution.

Whatever the explanation, markets are generating returns that fly in the face of standard finance. Given the returns involved, we are not talking about money machines here. We are talking about subtle market effects that provide some additional return with limited additional risk. These strategies are not risk free. They are risky in the sense that they generate returns that are different from standard benchmarks. Could these trends dissipate in the future? Sure, but it would involve a concerted effort on the part of institutional investors to reverse this inverse risk-return relationship. The introduction of low volatility ETFs may be the first step in this process.

Dividends Matter

Dividends matter. Historically dividends have generated a substantial part of the return of owning stocks. Dividends matter in how a company is managed. Companies that pay dividends to their shareholders are forced to think more carefully about their cash flows and the projects they choose to fund. The last thing a company wants to do is cut its dividend.

Some of the most recognizable companies in the United States show up on the list of companies that have maintained or increased their dividends over the years. However, somewhere along the way it became trendy for companies to not pay dividends. Maybe we can blame the market's infatuation with all things Warren Buffett, whose company, Berkshire Hathaway, has never paid a dividend. The prevailing market belief is that companies should use their cash to buy back shares instead of being forced to pay out regular cash dividends. We can trace this attitude to the rise of the widespread issuance of executive stock options.

Unfortunately there is little evidence that these share buybacks do much for shareholder value. There is evidence that those companies that use the largest percentage of their cash flow on share buybacks tend to have the lowest shareholder returns.[11] Share buybacks these days are used in large part to sop up the shares created on the exercise of executive stock options. It is therefore in the interest of company management to play up the role of share buybacks relative to dividends as a way of "enhancing shareholder value." Companies that actually reduce the number of shares outstanding via buybacks are a rarity.

Investors focused more on their own bottom line, instead of management's, should see through this facade since the evidence points toward the importance of dividends to investors. Investors who ignore dividends, due in part to the market's relatively low (sub 2%) dividend, are ignoring stock market history. From 1900 to 2010, the U.S. stock market with dividends reinvested returned 9.4% per annum; without dividends reinvested it returned 5.0%.[12] Over this time period, the dividend yield averaged around 4%. So dividends have made up a substantial part of investor returns. To simply ignore dividends is to ignore the history of the stock market.

Not only have dividends mattered over the long run for investors; they have also played a role in the relative performance of stocks within the stock market. The superior performance of the highest-yielding stocks generates what researchers call the *yield premium*. The yield premium is evident in U.S. stock market history but also seems to be a universal phenomenon. Dimson et al. find convincing evidence of the yield premium in 20 of 21 markets studied.[13] Not only does the yield premium exist, but high-yield portfolios also accomplish this with less risk than the stocks with no yield.

The yield-premium phenomenon is likely related to the low-volatility anomaly we discussed earlier. Both these findings show a portfolio of lower-risk stocks outperforming in both absolute and relative terms. This gives us some comfort that we are onto something real and enduring here. Another likely explanation for the yield premium is that it is another manifestation of the value effect. High dividend yields proxy for other measures of fundamental value—yet another indication that the value effect is something we should pay attention to.

Why might dividend-related strategies work? There may be a really simple explanation. Dividends are pretty sticky. Companies try to maintain or increase their dividends on an annual basis. Therefore, the volatility of dividend returns is rather low. Capital gains that make up the other part of an investor's total return are much more volatile. Imagine a case where you could choose to earn the same annual return, in one case a mix of dividends and capital gains and in the other case only capital gains. The first set of returns is, by definition, going to have a lower volatility than the capital gains–only case. Therefore, the risk-adjusted returns are going to be higher. The antidividend investor would have to generate higher annual returns to offset this volatility drag.

The argument against dividends would make more sense if there were evidence that when dividend payouts were low and retained earnings were high, corporations subsequently grew faster. This would give some ammunition to those who argue that companies should retain cash flow for their own use. Unfortunately the evidence shows just the opposite. In a paper they coauthored, Arnott and Asness show that for the aggregate U.S. stock market when dividend payout ratios are high, future earnings growth is fastest, and vice versa.[14] When dividend payout ratios are low, future earnings growth is at its slowest.

This result is surprising, but was replicated by ap Gwilym, Seaton, Suddason, and Thomas in research covering 11 international markets. They found once again that when aggregate dividend payout ratios were high, earnings growth was subsequently faster than when payout ratios were low.[15] Unfortunately for investors, this provided little benefit when it came to trying to forecast future returns.

These findings all used broad market indexes. For stock investors, an important question is whether the findings on payout ratios also hold for individual stocks. Zhou and Ruland looked at individual U.S. companies over a 50-year time period and found the relationship between high payout ratios and subsequent earnings growth held.[16] They argue these findings are likely related to a company's tendency to overinvest when management has ample free cash flow.

There is no theory of the valuation of corporate equities that does not rely on a company's ability to generate cash flow distributable to shareholders. Whether a company actually distributes that cash to shareholders, and in what form, is another question entirely. Historically the way in which companies distributed cash was in the form of dividends. And dividends remain an important indicator for individual stocks and for the market as a whole both in the United States and internationally. Don't be surprised if dividends recapture investor imaginations. When more Americans are reaching retirement age in search of investment income, dividends are once again likely to rise in importance in investors' eyes.

Asymmetric Returns

There is an important aspect of equity returns that we oftentimes overlook. The return to equities is asymmetric. Returns are asymmetric because equity returns characteristically have a downside floor of −100%. An unleveraged investor in a stock can lose his or her entire investment, but no more. On the other hand, there is no cap on the potential returns over time.

This fact has very important implications not only for how individual stocks perform but also for how the broader stock market averages perform. This property is also becoming more important as the very nature of what it means to be a company in the Internet age is changing. As companies become more virtual and rely less on brick-and-mortar infrastructure, it is possible to generate returns on capital that were unheard of in the industrial age.

We have so far only talked about the return on equities in relation to broad market averages. Within those broad market averages, thousands of stocks are generating returns therein. The returns to stocks over time do not follow a neat, normal bell-shaped curve. Stocks actually generate a set of returns that are far from normal. It is what Wilcox and Crittenden call the "Capitalism Distribution, a nonnormal distribution with very fat tails that reflects the observed realities of long-term individual common stock returns."[17]

What they found is that on one end of the return spectrum, a significant percentage, roughly 20%, of stocks are significant losers. And on the other end of the return spectrum, a significant percentage, again approximately 20%, of stocks are significant winners. Over the time period 1983–2006, some 39% of stocks in the Russell 3000 actually had negative total returns, and 64% of stocks underperformed the index. Some 25% of stocks were responsible for all the market's gains.[18]

This is a remarkable finding when you think about it. If you threw a dart at a list of stocks, on average the stock the dart hit would have underperformed the market. In fact, there is a pretty good chance the stock significantly underperformed the market. On the flip side, if you miss out on those stocks that are the big winners and drivers of overall market returns, you are in for disappointing returns. We can now see why Wilcox and Crittenden call the spectrum of returns the *capitalism distribution*. These results demonstrate the competitive forces at work in the economy that make it difficult for most companies to succeed. In a certain respect, the spoils are accruing to a small subset of companies and their investors.

Just in case you thought this was a U.S.-only phenomenon, in further research Wilcox and Crittenden found similar results with U.K. and Canadian stocks. That is, the bulk of each market's return was driven by just a handful of stocks.[19] The fact that this observation is consistent across markets gives us some comfort that this phenomenon is genuine and worth relying upon when investigating investment strategies.

These findings have two very important investment implications. The first is that these results provide a logical foundation for momentum, or trend-following, strategies. The companies that make up the bulk of the market's returns in a certain respect have to undergo periods of momentum. A stock cannot get to new 52-week highs without having already reached 52-week highs. Strategies that focus on stocks that are experiencing momentum are likely to find those stocks that go on to have extended periods of outperformance. That is not to say that this is some sort of money machine. We have seen that momentum strategies are costly to follow in terms of turnover and can undergo periods of notable underperformance.

Ironically these results that show an asymmetric return pattern to stocks also support an index-centric investment approach. If the returns to the stock market are driven by a small percentage of stocks, it is risky to undertake a strategy that potentially misses out on those stocks. Ideally, a profitable strategy would filter out these underperformers, but that is by no means guaranteed. A capitalization-weighted index will capture the returns to these multiyear high fliers along with the majority of stocks that underperform. This approach assures the investors that they will capture these returns with minimal turnover and, if done correctly, minimal costs.

What if this pattern of returns not only holds in the future but also becomes even more pronounced? There is evidence that in the

Internet age companies that are able to generate high returns for extended periods of time are becoming more prevalent. Michael Mauboussin writes: "In addition, the data show that the distribution of economic return on investment is wider in corporate America today than it was in the past. The spoils awaiting the wealth creators, given their outsized returns, are greater than ever before. As in the St. Petersburg game, the majority of the payoffs from future deals are likely to be modest, but some will be huge."[20]

The point is that building a web business, like a Facebook, with hundreds of millions if not billions of users, is a very different animal from building a traditional industrial business, like an automobile manufacturer. A company that can scale indefinitely has potentially a very different return pattern from that of a more traditional, capital-intensive company. The challenge for investors in the public market is when, or if, they will ever get a crack at investing in these types of companies. If a company does not need much in the way of capital, it may also have little need to come to the public markets. Therefore, the people who profit from the company's growth are the founders, employees, and venture capital firms as opposed to the general public.

Equity investors should be aware of this return pattern for stocks. These findings do not necessarily imply every investor should focus on momentum. Rather they should highlight the fact that the tails of the distribution matter a great deal. An equity strategy that plays in the mediocre middle of the return distribution is prone to have below-average returns. If you believe that the future is going to see more companies with the potential for extended periods of high growth, then it becomes all the more important to have a strategy that takes this into account.

If momentum is helpful in identifying market winners, then the flip side should also hold. Those stocks that are underperforming should lead to profitable short-selling strategies. Unfortunately in practice it has not worked out that way for short sellers.

Short Is Hard, Really Hard

If investing is hard, then short selling is really hard. Selling short a stock is not simply the opposite of buying a stock. It is something altogether different and markedly more complicated. That is why when you scan the list of the Forbes 500, you find plenty of investors who made their fortunes going long stocks, but very few, if any, who made their money on the short side.

The best analogy to describe short selling is to liken it to vomiting. As everyone knows, the digestive system is built to reliably move food one way. When that food chooses to reverse course, it is a violent and unpleasant act. The financial markets were built to facilitate transactions among investors seeking to profit on the rise in equity prices, not their decline. This is why blogger Joshua Brown writes, "For anyone looking to get into the game of outright short-selling, my advice is to go in with eyes wide open, it's a real bloodsport."[21]

Short sellers are perennial villains on Wall Street and around the world. Whenever markets decline, short sellers are targeted as being a prime mover behind the declines. When markets become really unhinged, authorities have historically banned short selling outright or made it so difficult that it was impossible. It does not matter to the general public that short sellers are often the first to identify companies with major issues like Enron or Lehman Brothers. As blogger Eddy Elfenbein writes: "Short-selling is crucial to an orderly market. It's difficult to overstate how important this is ... I find it interesting that regulators continue to blame short-sellers. The fact is that regulators overwhelmingly failed in finding problem spots in the economy and that's exactly what the shorts did."[22]

One reason why short selling is so difficult is because the mechanics of doing it are more complicated than purchasing stocks. To sell short a stock, it first has to be borrowed. Your broker must identify and borrow the stock in question. Once the short sale is in place, it is also more difficult to keep in place because at any time the lender can call in the stock. That is in part why short squeezes occur, where short sellers are required to repurchase the stock to satisfy these demands. Even when short sellers are correct in their assessment, as has been the case with a number of Chinese reverse-merger stocks. Short sellers can still lose, as has been the case when trading in these stocks has been halted for an extended period of time.[23] There simply is no short equivalent of buying a stock and forgetting about it.

It is often said that a short position can only earn a profit of 100% when a stock goes to zero, whereas a successful long position can go up indefinitely. Therefore, the dynamics of short selling are more difficult, despite the fact that the same techniques can be used to identify undervalued and overvalued stocks. David Swensen notes one way in which short selling is very different from going long.[24] When a targeted stock goes up, i.e., against a short seller, the value of the position actually increases. Errors therefore become magnified. The opposite is true on the long side, where when a stock goes down, its importance to the portfolio declines. For this reason, Swensen notes that short sellers need to maintain well-diversified portfolios and often experience high turnover.

There is another reason why few investors attempt the short side and fewer succeed. Many investors simply don't like the idea of betting against a stock and, ultimately, that company. It feels wrong to try and profit from the decline in value of a company. There are certainly exceptions, and these may include companies that are out-and-out frauds. But even in the case of frauds, these companies still have employees who are going to suffer from the company's demise. The vast majority of investors would rather participate in a company's success than profit from its demise. Despite this disparity, short sellers serve a very important role in identifying and publicizing companies that are at worst outright frauds and at best grossly overvalued.

There is ample evidence that short sellers do a good job of identifying those companies that are most overvalued. Whenever you see a company CEO complain about short sellers, you can be pretty sure that the short sellers are onto something. The market's perception is most often measured by the short-interest ratio. The short-interest ratio measures the number of shares sold short relative to average daily trading volume. A study by Boehmer, Huszar, and Jordan highlights the ability of shorts to identify overvalued stocks. They write, "Overall, we find evidence that short sellers are able to identify overvalued stocks to sell and also seem adept at avoiding undervalued stocks."[25] Their most interesting finding is that large, liquid stocks with little or no short interest have a tendency to outperform. Therefore, long-only investors can still benefit from the short-selling community's ability to identify not only overvalued stocks, but undervalued ones as well.

Despite this evidence, it is not clear that short selling will ever become a popular strategy. The stock market has been in the midst of what many call a "lost decade for stocks," and dedicated short-only funds are few and far between. There are well in excess of a thousand ETFs and only one ETF dedicated to short selling individual companies. Even after what has been an awful time for the stock market, there really is little demand for dedicated short-selling exposure. However, what there is ample demand for is vehicles that allow investors to hedge the value of their broader portfolio.

Shorting can take on this role as portfolio hedge. The whole idea behind hedge funds was to run portfolios balanced between long and short positions to hedge out overall market risk. Hedge funds have moved far beyond this original intention, but the idea of offsetting market risk with short positions is still a common one today. Hedging admittedly does not require shorting individual companies. In fact, most investors who hedge use instruments like futures, options, and ETFs that track broad market indexes. There are even ETFs, called inverse ETFs, designed to provide investors with returns opposite to that of the overall market. Hedging techniques that use these vehicles are easier to implement than shorting stocks and can reduce portfolio risk.

Despite the fact that most stocks end up underperforming the broad market indexes, it is difficult to profit by shorting stocks. This shouldn't be all that surprising or discouraging. More so than in other areas of the market, the shorts have the deck stacked against them. It is said that the market takes an escalator up and an elevator down. It is difficult for even the most patient, and stubborn, investors to wait for the payoff from their short bets. Fortunately we have seen how long investors can still benefit from the work of the shorts.

Most investors will never short a single stock in their lifetime and probably won't use various hedging techniques along the way. Most investors will, however, use good, old-fashioned bonds as ballast for their portfolios—a strategy that in light of recent performance looks like a good way to generate more balanced returns over time.

Key Takeaways

◆ The stock market is not the economy. The two can diverge for extended periods of time. In short, Wall Street is not Main Street.

+ In contrast with established theory, low-risk stocks have out-performed riskier stocks. Investors can now easily access these strategies but risk underperforming during bull markets.
+ Dividends matter. The long history of the U.S. and foreign stock markets show the importance of dividends. The increasing desire for yield may make dividends even more important in the future.
+ Research indicates that the distribution of individual stock returns is not normal. A small fraction of stocks generate out-size returns. This phenomenon may become more pronounced over time.
+ Short selling individual stocks is a hard way to generate returns. A number of obstacles prevent most investors from reliably prof-iting on the short side.

4

Fixed Income

SOME 10 YEARS AGO, THE HEAD OF THE YALE UNIVERSITY endowment fund, David Swensen, wrote, "In spite of promising lower returns than most other investment classes, bonds earn inclusion in portfolios by providing protection against the extraordinary circumstances of a financial crisis or economic deflation."[1] Little did Swensen know that the ensuing decade would so fully validate his advice.

If we look to the latter half of the past decade, we see both the effects of a major global financial crisis and the subsequent fears of economic deflation. During this time period, bonds—namely, Treasury bonds—served as ballast against the fears of a global financial meltdown brought on by the unwinding of the U.S. housing bubble and slow economic growth in the developed world. In short, bonds acted as advertised during this time period. In fact, over a recent 30-year period, long-term government bonds had higher returns than the S&P 500. It was the first time this happened since the Civil War.[2]

Despite this performance, some more adventuresome investors like to avoid bonds altogether, believing they are able to generate higher returns through riskier asset classes like equities or through their active investing. Two points stand out. One is that by doing so they are implicitly betting a large part, by one measure approximately 75%, of the global capital markets.[3] Second, this ignores entirely the insurancelike aspects of risk-free bonds like Treasuries.

Given the less than stellar fiscal situation in the United States, there has been a great deal of uncertainty about the risk of holding Treasury securities. It is a gross understatement to say that the United States could be doing a better job in managing its fiscal situation. That being said, there is not a ready list of candidates stepping up as risk-free substitutes. So while the United States has its problems, there are no obvious, large, liquid bond markets waiting in the wings to be the world's risk-free asset of choice.

The enemy of bonds is inflation, especially unexpected inflation. As mentioned earlier, investors now do have some options to combat against inflation in the form of TIPS, but these bonds still represent a fraction of the bond market and come with their own complexities. Economists are now using TIPS to extract market expectations about expected inflation.

So our interest in the bond markets is more than the role of bonds in a broadly diversified portfolio. The bond markets also present investors, in a more direct fashion, with important signals about what the Fed is intending to do and what investors are thinking about the state of the economy. So while many may view bonds merely as ballast against bad times, thoughtful investors can use the bond markets as a useful barometer about the world around them.

Yield-Curve Dynamics

The bond markets do more than just provide us with information about interest rates. More so than the equity markets, the bond markets are the lens through which investors compare the potential returns on all manner of investments. Every investor in the bond market compares the returns available on various bonds (corporate, mortgage, municipal) with the returns on the relevant Treasury bonds. Equity investors compare the dividend yield available on stocks versus bonds. CFOs compare where they can issue bonds or commercial paper against a relevant benchmark.

It seems logical then that the level of these yields should have some effect on the underlying real economy. Specifically we are talking about the slope of the yield curve, or the difference in interest rates between long-term bonds, typically the 10-year bond, and short-term interest rates, typically the 3-month Treasury bill. The yield curve is typically positive, indicating an upward-sloping yield curve. More rare is a negative term spread, or an inverted yield curve. The slope of the yield curve provides important signals to all kinds of economic actors; therefore, it logically plays a role as an economic indicator.

The modern financial markets are awash in economic indicators. Governments, central banks, investment banks, and various organizations are all generating an increasing number of economic indicators. All the sponsors of these indicators make some claim about the power of their indicators to forecast future economic activity. We can argue about whether having a more accurate forecast of economic growth will actually make you more money in the long run, but the quest for ever-more accurate economic forecasts is a fixture.

The best economic indicators don't rely on what people say they are going to do; rather they measure what people are actually doing with their dollars and cents. A great example of this is the slope of the yield curve. This indicator has been shown time and again to be a good indicator of future economic activity in the United States. The yield curve has inverted prior to each of the last seven economic recessions.[4] The slope of the yield curve is not a perfect indicator, especially in light of increasing Federal Reserve intervention throughout the yield curve. Since the slope of the yield curve is visible, easy to calculate, and real because it is based on trillions of dollars of bonds, we think it will once again be an unbiased economic indicator.

Just how does the yield curve work as an indicator? The idea behind how it works is pretty straightforward. When short-term interest rates exceed long-term interest rates, it indicates that credit is getting drained from the economy, usually with the help of a tight Fed policy. Blogger Cullen Roche states the idea succinctly: "Recessions, though not 100% accurate based on the yield curve, remain very high probability events when confronted with an inverted curve. And this makes a great deal of sense. An inverted curve is generally a sign that a credit binge is coming to an end and banks and investors are beginning to rein in their risk while also generally being accompanied by tighter government policy. An inverted curve is the equivalent of reaching the point where you're slamming the breaks on the car trying to stop her. And it generally works!"[5]

The yield curve works much better than the forecasts of professional economists. In a research paper, Rudebusch and Williams show that economists historically do not put not enough weight on the slope of the yield curve when it comes to forecasting recessions.[6] They find that a simple model based on the slope of the yield curve does a better job at forecasting recessions than do economists. The most recent recession was a prime example of this phenomenon. Prior to this most recent recession, there was a widespread disbelief about the usefulness of the yield curve as an indicator. It took a little longer this time than usual for the signal to work: the yield curve inverted in August 2006, and signs of stress were evident in 2007 before the full-blown recession hit in 2008. Those forecasters that doubted the yield curve were proved wrong in the worst possible way.

Still, as noted above, the slope of the yield curve, like every other indicator, is not perfect. There is some evidence that it is not as powerful an indicator in other countries as it is in the United States and that its predictive ability is fading over time.[7] Another important consideration at the moment is that current short-term interest rates are essentially zero. This situation is historically unprecedented and calls into question whether the slope of the yield curve can provide valid signals as long as this is the case. As important an indicator as the yield curve has been in the past, it likely has to be discounted for now until the Fed abandons its zero-interest rate policy and allows short-term interest rates to find their own level.

To be clear, the slope of the U.S. Treasury yield curve is not the only indicator worth paying attention to for signs about the state of the economy, just the most prominent. Another indicator of financial market conditions is the credit spread, or the spread in yields between riskless and riskier bonds. Credit spreads are most often measured by the AAA-Baa yield. Credit spreads are also important indicators to bond investors because they indicate the willingness of investors to take on risk. And credit spreads tell us something about the economy as well.

Credit spreads of all kinds were tracked closely during the financial crisis for signs of strain in the credit markets.[8] This is because, like the yield curve, credit spreads measure the real-time decisions of investors. As credit tightens and credit spreads widen, businesses of all sizes find it more difficult to borrow. Tight credit often leads to economic weakness. Because of their usefulness as economic indicators, the slope of the yield curve and credit spreads, as well as other means, have been used for some time now to forecast equity returns.

Researchers have looked at the forecasting ability of the slope of the yield curve on the equity market and not surprisingly found positive results.[9] Long before any of this research, equity investors have been keeping an eye on what the Federal Reserve has been doing. The Fed plays an all-important role in setting short-term interest rates, which are a necessary part of the slope of the yield curve.

Don't Fight the Fed

"Don't fight the Fed" is a well-worn cliché on Wall Street. Even before the extraordinary effort the Fed has taken during the financial crisis and its aftermath, much of Wall Street spent a great deal of time trying to read the proverbial tea leaves of the Federal Reserve. This is one area where Wall Street may not be wasting its money. Given our discussion about the importance of the shape of the yield curve, maybe it makes pretty good sense.

The idea that the Fed can have influential effects on the financial markets is not new. Norman Fosback, in his well-known book *Stock Market Logic,* helped popularize two rules based on Fed policy to guide stock market investors.[10] The "three steps and a stumble" rule and the "two tumbles and a jump" rule were designed to get investors in and out of the stock market based on Fed policy. In the first rule, if the Federal Reserve was raising rates, caution was warranted; in the second rule, if the Federal Reserve was cutting rates, optimism was warranted. The point is that the Fed has a notable influence on the economy and, by extension, the stock market.

There are complicated explanations about how the Fed affects interest rates, credit markets, and thus the economy. However, there is a much simpler explanation. The Federal Reserve has the power to set short-term interest rates. In terms of market rates, this is the one thing the Fed can unambiguously do. Other interest rates are more fully set by the normal ebb and flow of the markets.

These very short-term interest rates provide an important price signal to the financial markets. If the rates are set well below that of the rest of the yield curve, the market interprets this as an all-clear signal from the Fed. When the Fed hikes short-term interest rates above that of other market-derived interest rates, investors read this as a red light from the Fed. On the face of it, this seems like a gross oversimplification, but history bears out this interpretation.

A couple of notes of caution before proceeding any further. Due to the financial crisis and its aftermath, the Federal Reserve has conducted monetary policy in a number of unconventional ways. First, these new policies make reading the tea leaves of the Fed more difficult. Second, this discussion does not touch on any policy questions about how the Fed *should* be going about its business.

The Federal Reserve has come under a great deal of criticism for its lack of supervision of the nation's largest banks into the run-up to the financial crisis. That issue aside, the Fed was hiking interest rates leading up to what would be the end of the housing bubble and the economic and financial crisis that ensued. For our purposes, we do not have to agree on how the Fed should go about its business. All we need to agree on is that the Fed is a powerful force in the financial markets.

The Federal Reserve is admittedly a political institution. Any institution that has its leadership appointed by the president and confirmed by the Senate is, by definition, conscious of the political landscape. So both elected representatives and the Fed are acutely aware of the economic and political landscape they face. However, only the Fed seems to be able to affect the stock market all that much.

It is therefore ironic that so much time and effort is expended focusing on political elections and how they might affect the stock market. Historically, financial market returns are much more influenced by what the Fed is doing versus what political party is in power. Beyer, Jensen, and Johnson show that when the Fed is accommodative, equities outperform bonds that outperform cash. When the Fed is restrictive, equities still outperform but by a much narrower margin, and cash beats bonds.[11] The takeaway is that political conditions matter far less than monetary conditions.

The bigger question is how might monetary policy affect the stock market. According to research by current Federal Reserve chairman Ben Bernanke and Kenneth Kuttner, the stock market reacts to Fed changes not through changed expectations about real interest rates but rather through the ERP.[12] An easy Fed induces investors to lower their required risk premium. A tight Fed gets investors to do the opposite. From a speech on the topic, Bernanke stated: "However, easier monetary policy not only raises stock prices; as we have seen, it also lowers risk premiums, presumably reflecting both a reduction in economic and financial volatility and an increase in the capacity of financial investors to bear risk. Thus, our results suggest that easier monetary policy not only allows consumers to enjoy a capital gain in their stock portfolios today, but it also reduces the effective amount of economic and financial risk they must face."[13]

If true, this tells us why investors might change their behavior and maintain that change for an extended period of time. Fed policy typically stays in place over extended periods of time. Unlike other market-derived indicators that shift on a daily basis, the Fed's current policy stance is usually quite clear. The past shift in policy rates, whatever it was, indicates whether the Fed is easy or restrictive. In that regard, it makes sense for investors with longer-term time horizons to keep track of what the Fed is doing.

Ideally we would be able to anticipate what the Fed is going to do in the future. While the Fed has become increasingly more open to the public over time, it is still going to surprise the markets with decisions from time to time. Neither is the Fed infallible. Caveats aside, the signals the Fed provides to the markets are visible and powerful and affect the way investors approach risk. This combination makes it worthwhile to keep an eye on the Fed, and if at all possible, not fight it at every turn.

The Question of Cash

Cash is an asset, but not an investment. On the face of it, this seems like a false distinction. In this formulation, an asset is anything of value. An investment, on the other hand, is something that is expected to produce real, after-tax returns over time. In this light, cash is something we should value, but we should not expect it to provide us with real returns over time, as should equities or bonds.

Given our discussion of the yield curve, it makes sense to put into context how investors deal with the very shortest end of the yield curve: cash and cash equivalents. When discussing cash, we are not literally discussing currency. We are talking about short-term investments in income-producing securities, the most common of which are money market mutual funds, but also include Treasury bills, commercial paper, and short-term certificates of deposit. So when we are discussing cash, we are really talking about short-term investments that are easily accessible and highly liquid.

To be clear, we are not talking about the ready cash that makes up your emergency fund. Nearly every personal finance expert stresses the need for all individuals and families to have an emergency fund. An emergency fund is exactly that, a source of ready cash that can be accessed in case of unexpected and unplanned-for expenses. This ready source of cash helps buffer an investor's long-term portfolio from the vicissitudes of everyday life.

What we are talking about is the investment merits of cash for the long-term investor. It would be great if we could put our portfolios into short-term Treasury bills, and the like, and earn a return that would provide for our future needs. That is unfortunately not the case. Cash barely holds its own against inflation over the long run. Over a 110-year period, Treasury bills earned a 1% premium over inflation in the United States.[14] Coincidentally you find a similar return in the United Kingdom as well over this time period. Once you take into account taxes, the real, after-tax returns on cash for most investors are negative.

Under the best of circumstances, cash will hold its own against inflation and taxes. Unfortunately there are periods, like now, when cash is a notable loser. At present, with the Federal Reserve keeping interest rates essentially at zero, there is no return to cash; and after you take into account inflation and taxes, the real returns are decidedly negative. Things are so bad that firms are shuttering money market mutual funds because they have become unprofitable to manage.[15]

Even if you write off the current interest rate situation as an outlier, cash is not really an appropriate, strategic investment. A long-term investment should at least have the likelihood of increasing its value over time. For any number of reasons, cash is an inappropriate investment for anyone trying to accumulate wealth over time.

Why does cash provide such tepid returns? In a traditional risk-return framework, cash is a nearly riskless asset, and so we should not expect it to provide much in the way of returns. In that sense, there is likely an excessive amount of demand for cash. In addition to individual investors, institutions and corporations also have a need for ready access to cash. This demand for cash puts pressure on yields at the shortest end of the yield curve.

There is a supply component to the cash question as well. The U.S. Treasury can affect the relative price of its securities by choosing how much debt to auction at various maturities. These decisions don't change on a dime, but, for example, of late the U.S. Treasury has been lengthening the maturity of its debt, thereby reducing the relative amount of short-term T-bills outstanding.

Investors with some flexibility and a willingness to take on some additional risk can profit from excessive demand for money-market instruments. One way investors can find some additional return is by moving up the yield curve from the very shortest maturities to longer maturities, for example one year.[16] Because there is some institutional inflexibility, investors who venture out a little bit can pick up some additional yield without taking on much more risk. According to Eric Falkenstein, this is one of the few areas in finance where there is a consistent return to risk. We are still talking about risk-free Treasury securities in this regard. This observation is not a ticket to take on all sorts of incremental credit risk. It is simply an observation that there is a persistent institutional rigidity that allows investors to profit over time.

Cash is, above all, an asset that represents a haven from risk. Since the financial crisis, investors have been focusing on so-called tail risks. Tail risks are rare, unforeseen risks that can have devastating effects on financial markets and investor portfolios. Given that cash is a haven from risk, it should not be surprising that cash can serve as protection against tail risks. James Montier writes: "This is perhaps the oldest, easiest, and most underrated source of tail risk protection. If one is worried about systemic illiquidity events or drawdown risks, then what better way to help than keeping some dry powder in the form of cash—the most liquid of all assets."[17]

The description of cash as "dry powder" is apt. Cash is really a residual asset that comes into play after all other investment opportunities have been considered. In that way cash is at best a temporary holding when all other risky assets seem unattractive. Sometimes the opportunity cost of holding cash is negligible. Other times, like the last few years, the cost of holding cash has meant negative real returns.

In an ideal world, we could meet our future financial needs by investing in safe, liquid, short-term assets. Unfortunately we don't live in that world. To generate real returns, an investor needs to take on some risk. Treating cash as a long-term investment has been historically a money-losing proposition. We can offset some of those costs by pushing out the yield curve a little bit, but this only pushes the needle so far. Cash is at best a place for nimble investors to park assets, and avoid risk, while waiting for more attractive opportunities to present themselves.

Bond Funds Are Not Bonds

Bond funds (and ETFs) are not bonds. That seems like an obvious thing to state. But in the context of individual investors, bond funds are typically thought of as being synonymous with individual bonds. However, bond funds and bonds are very different things. Understanding the difference between the two is important because it means we understand what bonds are and how a collective vehicle like an open-end mutual fund or ETF can fundamentally change the nature of an asset like bonds.

We don't usually worry about the distinction between equities and equity funds. A company has an indefinite life. However, the bonds it issues most certainly do have a maturity date. That is why nobody thinks much about the nature of equity funds. Stocks keep trading until the companies go bankrupt, merge, or get acquired. An equity fund is just a more diversified vehicle than an individual stock. That is why substituting an equity fund for an individual equity is not all that interesting.

That is not the case when it comes to bonds. Bonds have maturity dates on which investors (the hope is) get back their principal. Once a bunch of bonds are bundled up into a fund, there no longer is any single maturity date. A bond fund is therefore characterized by its average maturity. There is no single day on which the typical fund returns an investor's principal. Any principal the fund receives is used to purchase additional bonds.

Bond fund managers, like all other fund managers, are very much focused on performing in line with their chosen benchmark. Those benchmarks don't shift much over time. If a fund's benchmark is three- to five-year Treasury bonds, you can bet that the manager is going to closely adhere to bonds that fit that criterion, whereas an individual investor with a five-year time horizon will after a year have a four-year horizon. Eventually the fund's and the investor's benchmark will diverge.

As discussed earlier, investors buy bonds to serve as an anchor to their portfolio and not necessarily to generate outsized gains. It has long been known that we use mental accounts. We segregate our investments into different buckets with different risk and return expectations. Presumably we put bonds into a "safe bucket." Therefore, when those bond investments go down in price, we feel greater amounts of regret. This regret makes us reluctant to realize the loss because recognizing that loss cements the mistake.

From an investment perspective, what would be perfect would be an investment that we can consider a "no-mental-loss investment." Meir Statman describes how individual zero-coupon Treasury bonds possess the feature of a no-mental-loss investment.[18] Even if the value of the zero-coupon bond declines, there is always the future promise of a payoff at par in the future. This feature makes it easier for investors to hold these bonds through thick and thin. Statman states: "Holders of individual bonds have greater no-mental-loss benefits than holders of bond mutual funds since they have the option to wait till the maturity date of each of their individual bonds and receive what they have been promised. In contrast, holders of bond mutual funds have no such option since mutual funds have no maturity dates. The prices of mutual funds are set at the market price at the end of each day, moving up or down. Holders of bond mutual funds are never assured that they will not incur a loss when they sell, no matter how long they wait."[19]

This sort of exercise is really only possible when talking about Treasury bonds. Therefore, bond funds exist for a very good reason. They allow smaller investors to diversify their holdings in a cost-efficient manner. The market for individual bonds remains pretty hostile to the individual investor. Outside of Treasury bonds, transacting in the municipal or corporate bond markets is for all intents and purposes cost prohibitive.[20] So from an investor's perspective, a bond fund that provided diversification, lower transaction costs, *and* a fixed maturity date would represent the best of both worlds.

Thankfully this innovation is slowly working itself through the mutual fund world. There are now ETFs that provide target-date exposure to municipal bonds and high-yield bonds. The big-fund firms, like Fidelity and Pimco, now offer target-date open-end bond exposure to muni bonds, TIPS, and zero-coupon Treasury bonds.[21] The fund industry doesn't often come up with truly novel solutions to investor problems, but target-date bond funds are a useful counterexample.

The idea of building a portfolio using a bond ladder is well established. Purchasing bonds of various maturities and using the proceeds from maturing bonds to purchase longer-dated bonds is a common practice. Now investors can use bond funds in the place of individual bonds. Judd, Kubler, and Schmedders coincidentally find that bond ladders represent a rational and cost-effective approach to investing.[22]

This discussion is bypassing the fact that the global bond markets are made up of many more types of bonds than just Treasuries or municipal bonds. A truly diversified bond portfolio includes mortgage-backed bonds, other asset-backed bonds, corporate bonds, and the whole wide world of international bonds. As you can see, the issue of diversification can greatly increase the complexity of managing a bond portfolio.

For anything other than Treasury bonds, it is difficult for individual investors, except for the very wealthiest, to assemble a portfolio of individual bonds. Bond funds therefore remain the vehicle of choice for most investors. The benefit of target-date bond funds is that they make it easier for some investors to stick with their goals by holding them to maturity. Any feature that makes it easier to stick to an investing plan should not be underrated. There is nothing worse than generating losses on bonds that were supposed to serve as ballast to a broader portfolio.

Bond math is pretty unforgiving because there are few ways to conjure up additional yield without taking on additional risk. The only surefire way to increase net returns is to focus on reducing costs. In bonds as in the rest of life, a penny saved is a penny earned. Historically investors have done well by taking on certain risks—and have been well advised to avoid other risks.

Risk and Some Return

Earlier we touched upon the role of bonds, specifically long-term Treasury bonds, to serve as insurance against extraordinary economic events like financial crises or deflation. There are also times during which this insurance is quite costly, such as now when 10-year Treasury bonds yield approximately 2%. As noted previously, during periods of unexpected inflation bonds can serve less as insurance and more like a deadweight cost. In that light, is it worth the time and effort of investors to try and improve upon the returns of plain vanilla Treasuries?

For investors with limited time, interest, and resources, the case for Treasuries is compelling. Again we are relying heavily on the full faith and credit of the U.S. government. Then again, if the U.S. government isn't able to pay its obligations in a timely fashion, then the United States (and the broader world) has a much bigger problem. The only decision an investor needs to make is what maturity bonds to buy. An investor can even purchase Treasury securities directly from the Treasury itself.[23]

Maturities do matter. We saw earlier in our discussion of the role of cash that we can boost returns, albeit modestly, simply by moving up the maturity ladder and away from where cash managers sit. Unfortunately investors in the past have been burned by fund managers who were not content with simply extending maturities but also ventured into riskier securities that came back to bite them when the financial crisis hit.[24] The question for investors is whether it is worth it to extend maturities.

Not really. Returning to the research of Frazzini and Pedersen, there is a clear relationship between risk-adjusted returns and Treasury maturities. Their research finds that the longer the maturity, the worse the bond performs on a risk-adjusted basis.[25] Extending maturities in this framework does little for investors. To take full advantage of the relationship, investors would have to be willing to leverage up their shorter-term bond positions.

If we take a look at the longer-term premium again, we find little advantage in investing in longer-term Treasury bonds versus intermediate-term Treasury bonds. From 1900 to 2010, the real return on an index of long-term Treasuries was nearly identical to that of an intermediate-term index—1.8% versus 1.7% per annum.[26] Given the additional volatility that comes along with the long-term bonds, it is not clear that they provide much benefit to the average investor.

What guidance do these numbers provide us in an extended and unprecedented period of low interest rates? At present an investor would have to go all the way out to a four-year Treasury note just to garner a 1.0% yield to maturity. This is a yield, we might add, that after inflation and taxes is decidedly negative. In this environment, the insurancelike aspects of a Treasury bond portfolio are coming at a very high cost in terms of returns.

One area where investors do seem to earn some return for taking on additional risk is in regard to credit. The results from Frazzini and Pedersen and from Falkenstein both show incremental returns to credit risk in the realm of investment-grade bonds.[27] Taking on some additional credit risk seems to pay off over time. What does not pay off over time is stretching into high-yield or junk bonds. It seems that the additional risk of these bonds never does add up to additional returns.

We should note a couple of caveats here. The first is that much of this additional return to credit accrued during the bond bull market that kicked off in the early 1980s.[28] Therefore, investors should be careful projecting these returns going forward absent the same underlying conditions.

The other caveat is that adding credit risk obviates some of the insurancelike characteristics of Treasury bonds. During the financial crisis of 2007–2009, the spreads on investment-grade bonds increased dramatically, thereby pushing returns down on these bonds. Also we have to be careful about what we mean by investment-grade bonds. One of the great lessons of the financial crisis was that even bonds rated AAA could carry a great deal of risk. Many a fund manager woke up to this realization in 2008.

Neither Frazzini and Pedersen's nor Falkenstein's study addresses municipal bonds, which would be interesting for this discussion. Individual investors often use municipal bonds as a substitute for Treasuries, the assumption being that there is a yield pickup due both to some additional credit risk and to the benefits of having a tax-free status. The municipal bond market is much more like a bazaar than the Treasury market, with thousands of issuers both large and small. In addition, the threat, real or imagined, of municipal bankruptcy has more fully entered the consciousness of municipal bond investors.

To some degree, we need to put all these results on ice as long as we are in an ultralow interest rate environment. As Samuel Lee writes: "An implication of Frazzini and Pedersen's model is that investors reaching for yield in a low-interest environment may be setting themselves up for disappointment. When investors decide that current yields aren't good enough, they start adding riskier assets to their portfolios. Their collective shift reduces the expected return of high-beta securities; the old calculus of high risk, high reward becomes one of higher risk, low reward."[29]

An understanding of historical returns is important in that it allows us to put the current state of affairs into perspective. As we alluded to earlier, following a conservative, low-beta strategy in a low-interest-rate environment leads to negative real returns. The temptation is therefore strong for investors to deviate from this original game plan to try and pick up additional yield wherever they may find it. There are times when this may make sense, especially when you are getting well compensated for taking on some additional risk; however, to do so based solely on a need for yield is a recipe for disappointment.

Bond investors therefore have a decision to make. Are the bonds in their portfolio meant to serve as ballast against adverse economic events? In that case, a focus on long-term Treasury bonds seems appropriate. In contrast, research indicates that investors can get more bang for their buck by avoiding the volatility of long-term maturities. There also seems to be some additional return to be gained by taking on some modest amount of credit risk, but this comes along with additional risks. These bond-related questions only make sense in the context of an entire portfolio. That broader viewpoint is the essence of portfolio management.

Key Takeaways

+ Bonds not only play an important role in investing, but bond yields also help link the financial markets and real economy.
+ Current Fed policies aside, the slope of the yield curve has served as a better forecaster of recessions than the consensus opinion of economists has.
+ Don't fight the Fed is a well-worn cliché on Wall Street, but there is ample evidence that the Federal Reserve can impact investors' willingness to take on risk.
+ Cash is an asset but not an investment. Cash represents a means for investors to ride out periods of uncertainty, but relying on cash equivalents to meet long-term goals is a losing proposition.
+ Bond funds are not bonds. Investors are well served by focusing on bond vehicles with definite maturities within the framework of an overall bond ladder strategy.
+ There are modest benefits to taking on some credit and maturity risk, but investors need to be wary of diluting the insurancelike aspects of bonds in their overall portfolios.

5

Portfolio Management

PORTFOLIO MANAGEMENT IS ALL ABOUT PULLING TOGETHER THE threads of risk and return. Balancing risk and return in a systematic fashion allows investors to best "stay in the game." We have seen that major asset classes can go down, and stay down, for longer than investors care to think about. Therefore, successful portfolio management involves moving portfolios intact from one period to the next. The secondary goal of portfolio management is to generate returns that help us in meeting our own unique investment goals.

Balancing risk and return is typically an exercise in mathematical abstraction. Instead let's break down portfolio management along the lines of things to do and things not to do. The things investors should focus on involve the basics of investment management: asset allocation, diversification, and rebalancing. And as important as the previous tenets are, maybe more important are things investors should actively avoid: ignoring performance, not understanding your investments, leveraging your portfolio, and embracing illiquid assets. The first section of this chapter focuses on the things investors do to generate returns. The second section is all about what not to do if you want to successfully manage a portfolio.

Diversification

The concept of portfolio diversification is one of the building blocks of modern finance. Simply put, diversification means spreading one's assets across a number of different securities and asset classes. Diversification is commonly called one of the only "free lunches" in finance because the risk of a diversified portfolio is less than the weighted sum of the risk of the underlying securities. An investor can expect to earn the same returns while experiencing less risk.

While other parts of modern financial theory have come under fire, there has been little evidence that the theory supporting diversification doesn't work. The financial crisis and its aftermath saw nearly every risk-bearing asset decline in unison, providing little benefit in this period of market stress. The irony is that diversification among risky assets failed to offer much benefit, but diversification into risk-free assets like Treasury bonds provided a great benefit. It wasn't the theory of diversification that failed, but rather its implementation.

Despite the theory backing up diversification, there has always been a vocal minority on Wall Street that eschews diversification in favor of holding concentrated portfolios in securities that the members of this group "know well." They feel comfortable holding an undiversified portfolio because it feels less risky. Diversification in this light seems like an admission of defeat. Fortunately a diversified portfolio is less an admission of defeat than a reflection of reality.

The reality is that no one can reliably foresee the future for any security or asset class. Diversification is therefore not an admission of ignorance; rather it is an admission that there are things we simply cannot know. The difference is subtle but real. There is nothing wrong with admitting "I don't know" in investing or in life in general. It is preferable to a glib or ill-informed response. Diversification simply recognizes our inability to forecast the future.

This view of diversification fits with the idea of trying to minimize the risk of ruin from any security or market, effectively wiping out a portfolio. As Peter L. Bernstein puts it, "Diversification works because owning more than one asset protects the investor from the contingency that everything will be lost in one fell swoop."[1] One way that investors can blow up their portfolios is through the use of excessive leverage. Another way is through a concentration in a single security. Unfortunately there are cases where employees in a company, like an Enron, had their entire retirement accounts wiped out due to a concentration in their employer's stock.

Luckily for investors, it is now trivial and inexpensive to create a well-diversified portfolio. Investors today have the ability to invest in broad-based portfolios of domestic and international stocks and bonds with the click of a button. A handful of funds can essentially provide exposure to all the global capital markets. Investors can now invest just as institutional investors did only a few short years ago. Investors these days have no excuses for an undiversified portfolio. We can therefore only explain concentrated portfolios as a conscious decision.

That is not to imply that diversification is perfect. In fact, most of the time diversification is going to seem like wasted effort. As Jason Zweig writes: "Likewise, whenever one sector of the stock market is hot, diversifying your money across other assets will always feel like a waste of effort—an umbrella you never seem to need...No matter how many times you carry an umbrella without needing it, you will be very glad indeed to be carrying one when a downpour finally hits."[2] In this regard, diversification is like other investment strategies that only shine during specific time periods.

The problem is that most investors decide to abandon diversification at the worst possible time. The diversification drag seems most acute during the height of a bubble when it seems like everyone else is profiting from the ongoing trend. As Meir Statman notes, we humans are always trying to balance the "desire for riches" with the "fear of poverty."[3] Because we are trying to balance these two goals, we create mental accounts in which we layer assets from the risk free all the way up to the risk seeking. This portfolio layering, while suboptimal in the strictest sense, works because it allows investors to undertake risky investments with the knowledge that there is a financial cushion resting underneath. The important thing is that investors need to resist the temptation to dip into their safety nets to further fund losing, often risky, bets.

Investors should recognize that diversification is not a magic bullet or panacea. Investments in risky assets are risky, and diversification can on the margin help mitigate risk but cannot eliminate it. Risk is an inherent feature of the financial markets and is unavoidable. Investors found this out in spades in the midst of the financial crisis. Losses incurred in the last bear market forced many investors to face up to the fact that they were likely taking more risk than they thought or could handle. This recognition has brought to the fore strategies aimed not at further diversification but at hedging. Hedging seeks to explicitly reduce risk through the use of a range of instruments including derivatives like options. These strategies are more complicated and costly to implement, but they do provide an additional avenue for investors not satisfied with the limits of traditional diversification.

We noted earlier that simply achieving mediocrity would be a worthy goal for the vast majority of investors. A broadly diversified portfolio helps serve the purpose of achieving acceptable returns over a lifetime of investing. Diversification is best not achieved in a haphazard fashion, but in fact requires thoughtful and purposeful action.

Asset Allocation

Once you recognize that diversification is important, asset allocation quickly follows as a way to implement a diversification process. Asset allocation is how a portfolio is apportioned across various asset classes and strategies. Asset allocation is the biggest decision that investors, large and small, have to make on an ongoing basis. And once you recognize that the performance of asset classes can greatly vary over time, it gives some sense for just how important asset allocation can be.

There has been an ongoing debate in academic and practitioner circles about just how important asset allocation is in explaining investor performance.[4] Luckily we can avoid this debate almost entirely. All we need to do as investors is focus on our own asset allocation plans and our own portfolios. How other people come up with their own plans is irrelevant. All that matters is that our asset allocation plans fit with our ongoing needs and goals.

In practical terms, asset allocation is worthy of a book unto itself.[5] Asset allocation in a sense is just a reflection of what investors are doing in their portfolios. Investors solely invested in U.S. equities have a 100% allocation to domestic equities. The complexity comes when you start adding asset classes and active strategies that are not easily characterized over time. A look back at 2008, when the world was in the midst of a financial crisis, highlights the importance of asset allocation.

In 2008 the S&P 500 declined 37%; the Barclays Capital Aggregate Bond Index, a broad measure of domestic bond performance, returned approximately 5%; and Treasury bills returned a touch over 1%. An investor solely invested in equities or bonds (or T-bills) in 2008 would have very different experiences. Most investors had some mix of these assets, among others, and experienced some middle ground. However, an investor wholly invested in equities at year-end 2008 likely had some serious soul searching to do, whereas an investor invested in bonds and cash was able to ride through the year intact and was able to hunt for opportunities in the new year.

Over the longer term, the importance of portfolio balance becomes clearer. The performance of a domestic portfolio 50% invested in bonds and 50% in stocks from 1926 to 2009 showed almost no difference in real returns between U.S. economic expansions and recessions.[6] All the work put into trying to forecast recessions and market timing should be put into context with this simply diversified portfolio.

When we talk about asset allocation as a conscious investment strategy, we aren't really interested in simply measuring an investor's portfolio exposures. That is easy to do these days. Asset allocation as a strategy is more about creating an ongoing plan for a portfolio. Asset allocation is also about making some conscious decisions on trading off potential risk and return.

Unfortunately the average investor has the asset allocation process backward. The average investor buys a handful of funds recommended by pundits, magazines, or portfolio managers seen on TV. The asset allocation just ends up being an amalgam of once-hot investment themes. Rarely, if ever, does the investor sort through these funds to sell off the losers. A true asset allocation plan starts first with a scheme to deliberately invest in certain asset classes. Then, and only then, does the investor begin selecting vehicles to fill out these asset-class targets. Simply turning a haphazard process into a deliberate one is an important step for investors.

Making precise asset allocations is less important than undertaking this deliberate process. Out of this process comes some sense both of the returns that investors have earned and of their stand relative to longer-term goals. Investors who have a well-defined asset allocation have a benchmark against which they can measure their performance, potential investments, or shifts in strategy.

For investors who invest solely in index funds, this process is almost trivial. For each asset class, they identify a fund that invests in that particular asset type. Things get more complicated when you start introducing actively managed funds. The managers of these funds often have the latitude to vary their portfolios in a number of ways. This introduces some uncertainty about where your true asset allocation actually stands.

So far we have been discussing the big strategic decisions investors make in their portfolios. In addition to these strategic decisions, some investors also actively manage their asset allocations. Active asset allocation is a conscious decision to overweight, and underweight, certain asset classes based on their expected future performance. At its extreme, it can be thought of as market timing, which implies large shifts in the portfolio. For most investors, designing a proper asset allocation in the first place is difficult enough; adding the challenge of trying to vary their asset allocation on an ongoing basis is likely to lead to regret and disappointment.

The fund management industry knows all too well that most investors do not do a particularly good job at asset allocation. In response the industry has designed what are called target-date funds that take the asset allocation decision out of the hands of investors and put it with a portfolio manager. The idea is that the asset allocation would evolve over time as the "target date," typically a retirement date, is reached. These funds are popular with retirement plans like 401(k) plans. Unfortunately, according to a recent survey, many investors were confused about what the goals of a target date actually are.[7] Investor misperceptions are one of the reasons that target date funds have their detractors. However, for individual investors, target date funds can represent a useful benchmark to compare their own portfolios.

As we have seen, asset allocation plans can be as simple or as complex as an investor desires. Above all, asset allocation is a guidepost investors can use to think about the big decisions they face on an ongoing basis. Investors cannot take an entirely hands-off approach to asset allocation. Markets move and push allocations out of line with their initial goals. Investors therefore have to have a process to bring their portfolios back into line with their stated asset allocation policy.

Rebalancing

Portfolio rebalancing really ties together a number of threads that we have introduced so far. Portfolio rebalancing is the periodic process in which investors bring their portfolio allocations back into alignment with their asset allocation. Unfortunately, few investors recognize the importance of portfolio rebalancing. Asset allocation is not a "set-it-and-forget-it" philosophy. Portfolio rebalancing enforces a discipline on a portfolio and has the additional benefit of enhancing returns.

As Scott Willenbrock writes: "Diversification is often described as the only 'free lunch' in finance because it allows for the reduction of risk for a given expected return. Diversification return might be described as the only 'free dessert' in finance because it is an incremental return earned while maintaining a constant risk profile. The contrarian activity of rebalancing, however, must be performed to earn the diversification return; diversification is a necessary but not sufficient condition. Although an unrebalanced portfolio generally has reduced risk, it does not earn a diversification return and suffers from a varying risk profile. The control of risk, together with the diversification return, is a powerful argument for rebalanced portfolios."[8]

The math behind the proof of the diversification return, or rebalancing bonus, is beyond the scope of this discussion. Any portfolio with assets with varying degrees of correlation with each other can earn a rebalancing bonus. This bonus is maximized when holding assets with low, or even negative, correlations. That is in part why the search for asset classes and strategies that are uncorrelated with equities and bonds is ongoing.

Two points from the prior quote are important to note. The first is that rebalancing is about maintaining, within limits, a constant risk profile. One of the strongest arguments for rebalancing is not that it generates higher returns but that it helps lower portfolio volatility.[9] Investors who let their portfolio weightings drift away from their strategy are implicitly taking on active risks whether they know it or not. The whole point is that it is useless to have an asset allocation strategy unless you adhere to it over time.

Second, rebalancing is a contrarian strategy. This means buying asset classes that have declined in value since the last rebalancing and selling those that have increased in value. Going back to our 2008 example, what that means is that investors who rebalanced at year-end would have been buying equities and selling bonds—this at a time when the world seemed like it was on the precipice of further catastrophe. Making those trades would have been a difficult, although ultimately profitable, decision.

Just because investors rebalance their portfolios on a periodic basis does not mean that their original asset allocation plans should stay in place indefinitely. An investor's asset allocation policy should change for any number of reasons. As we get older and we approach our goals, an asset allocation may need to change. Just as we evolve, so do markets. As new asset classes and strategies arise, it might very well make sense to include them in an asset allocation plan. Likewise it may make sense to remove certain assets from a plan as markets evolve. These are all conscious decisions to alter your asset allocation. What shouldn't happen is allowing market movements to shift your portfolio markedly away from your plan.

There is the practical question of how to go about portfolio rebalancing. A fair amount of debate has been generated about how often investors should rebalance their portfolios. But the frequency of rebalancing is far less important than an actual commitment to the process. For the vast majority of investors, rebalancing trades once a year is sufficient. For more adventuresome investors, a biannual approach may be worth looking into.

There is evidence that the stock market experiences seasonality based on investor mood. This observation of higher returns in the fall and winter and lower returns in the spring and summer goes by a couple of names including "Sell in May and go away" and the "Halloween indicator."[10] Mood, influenced by seasonal affective disorder, has a tendency to make investors more risk averse when daylight is waning and less risk averse when daylight is increasing. Researchers have also found evidence of this behavior in mutual fund flows.[11] An intrepid investor could use this observation to fine-tune a rebalancing program. If these seasonal tendencies hold over time, using the end of October and April to rebalance would tend to increase returns.[12]

Nor should investors feel like they need to rebalance down to the decimal point. Most investors use bands around which they let their portfolio weights drift without rebalancing. This simply cuts down on the amount of rebalancing that needs to occur. Another way to cut down on transactions is to infuse new cash into a portfolio as a means to bring underweighted asset classes back into balance. Rebalancing takes time, effort, commitment, and, maybe most important, the psychological determination to undertake contrarian trades. Making the process as infrequent and easy as possible makes sense.

An asset allocation strategy without a plan to rebalance is ultimately wasted effort. There are few good arguments against portfolio rebalancing. As David Swensen writes, "Ultimately disciplined rebalancing provides risk control, increasing the likelihood that investors achieve investment goals."[13] Achieving your investment goals is what this entire book is about, and rebalancing is an integral part of a well-constructed investment plan.

Investment Sins

Anyone who has read the Ten Commandments knows that most of the commandments begin with the phrase "You [or Thou] shall not." In this section, we focus on the things that investors do that get them in the most trouble when building and managing a portfolio. We can think of these things as investment sins—or things *not* to do.

Using the S&P 500 as Your Benchmark

Professional portfolio managers who are worth their salt will measure their portfolio's performance on a continuous basis. Individual investors don't need to be as performance obsessed as professionals do, but performance measurement is an important part of any portfolio process. As an investor, there are two components of performance measurement that you need to keep in mind. The first is that you have to measure (not ignore) your portfolio performance. The second is that your benchmark is not the S&P 500. Understanding where your portfolio stands relative to a relevant financial benchmark and where it stands relative to your own personal goals is key to keeping you on track.

It seems obvious that investors should measure their portfolio performance on a regular basis, but for many that is a difficult task. In other parts of our lives, we get measured. Schoolchildren get grades. Employees are reviewed on a regular basis. People on a diet weigh themselves. In short, everyone who wants to meet a goal first has to measure where he or she stands relative to that goal.

This used to be a complicated task involving account statements and spreadsheets. Now most brokerage firms and mutual fund providers offer personalized return measures to their clients. Seeing those performance figures in black and white is often a revelation for investors unaccustomed to calculating their own performance. The challenge for investors is to figure out what the appropriate benchmark should be.

We know for certain that it is not the S&P 500. The S&P 500 is the most popular and visible investment benchmark in the United States. The S&P 500 covers a majority of the U.S. stock market, and hundreds of billions of dollars are benchmarked against it. However, unless you invest solely in large-cap U.S. stocks, the S&P 500 is not your benchmark. The financial press does investors few favors by consistently comparing disparate investments, including hedge funds, against the S&P 500.

Most investors hold other assets, including cash, bonds, real estate, and international investments. All these asset classes are ill served by comparing them to the S&P 500. Creating a more realistic benchmark is more complicated, but it is a necessary part of any investment process. For investors who index, this process is relatively straightforward. For more active investors, this process becomes more complicated because it involves understanding the source of your own returns.

Ultimately your portfolio is there to serve your own personalized goals. Picking an inappropriate benchmark or choosing to ignore your portfolio will do little to help you meet your goals. What matters in the end is that over time you get closer to your own personal and financial goals. Knowing where you stand is a first step in any thoughtful investment process.

Using Leverage to Build Your Portfolio, Especially Unwittingly

Leverage kills. Leverage kills portfolios. Leverage kills institutions. Leverage is by far and away the most common theme that runs through the history of financial failure. Leverage is the act of borrowing money, knowingly or unwittingly, to increase the size of financial bets. In times of rising asset prices, leverage is a good thing; it magnifies returns to the upside. In times of falling asset prices, leverage can quickly turn falling prices into outright failure. Just ask Lehman Brothers or Long Term Capital Management.[14]

In our everyday lives, most of us are quite familiar with leverage even if we don't recognize it as such. Most people who own a home have a mortgage. That mortgage represents leverage because you were not required to pay the full price of the home on closing. Many people also have car loans or lease their car. Again these represent leverage. In most cases, people are able to handle this everyday leverage. Otherwise their house (foreclosure) or car (repossession) gets taken away from them.

Financial leverage acts very much the same way. It allows investors to control assets in excess of their original purchasing power. Just as in our everyday lives, when things go smoothly, leverage is a powerful thing. The challenge is that in the financial markets things often don't go smoothly. If your goal is to move your portfolio from point A to point B intact, then leverage can be an easy way to get off track.

The financial services industry is keen on getting investors to take on leverage. In many cases, that leverage is explicit. For example, a brokerage account that has margin privileges allows the investor to purchase assets in excess of his or her original equity. Leverage is also inherent in other types of financial instruments. Futures, by definition, do not require a trader to put down the full value of the contract. Margin covers only part of the total value of the instrument traded. In the world of retail foreign exchange trading, leverage is a part of the game as well. In all these cases, leverage serves to amplify, for better or worse, the returns earned from any particular strategy.

There is another type of leverage investors need to become aware of. Some financial instruments have leverage built in. In the case of leveraged ETPs, the leverage is right there on the label. These funds use instruments such as futures and swaps to magnify the returns of an index, oftentimes two times as much and sometimes as high as three times as much. The target market for leveraged ETFs is a trader with a short-term time horizon. Some long-term investors in these funds have had some nasty surprises over time as the leverage has worked against them.

There are other financial instruments with leverage built in. Many closed-end bond funds use leverage to boost their returns. When short-term interest rates are well below longer-term interest rates and when rates are stable or falling, this is a profitable strategy. The extra interest earned on the additional bonds outweighs the cost of the borrowings. When rates reverse course, the losses resulting from this kind of strategy can mount.

Options are another area where leverage is a way of life for traders. Option strategies come in nearly every kind of flavor, from conservative to wildly aggressive. Options are a tool that investors can use to sculpt the return profile of their portfolio. Leverage in the case of options comes about when investors take on larger positions than they could absent the options themselves.

While an understanding of the mechanics of leverage is important to adventuresome investors, there is a bigger risk than outright losses. The biggest challenge facing most investors is not the market itself, but their reaction to the market. When leverage is employed, it creates higher psychological highs when times are good and greater feelings of panic when times are bad. These mood swings tend to push investors to make precisely the wrong move at the wrong time. So, for most people, the biggest risk to leveraged investment is investor behavior.

From our everyday lives, we see how leverage can work to our advantage. From an investment perspective, if you feel like you need to leverage your portfolio to meet your financial goals, then you are already off track. Chasing returns with leverage is unlikely to make the situation better. Investment leverage is very much a two-edge sword: powerful but inherently dangerous. For the individual investor looking to sleep well at night, leverage is a nonstarter.

Investing in Illiquid Assets

Illiquid assets are investments that once purchased are either very difficult or very expensive to sell (or liquidate). The two most familiar illiquid assets we deal with on a daily basis are houses and small businesses. Anyone who has ever sold a house recognizes that it is often a long, complicated, and expensive process. Homes and businesses are necessary and desirable assets for many people, but here we are talking about our financial portfolios. In a portfolio, illiquidity is likely to provide headaches.

Most of the common financial assets we are familiar with, such as stocks, bonds, mutual funds, and ETFs, are by and large liquid assets. They are easily sold at a reasonable expense within a relatively short period of time. The challenge of illiquid assets is not necessarily the challenge of illiquidity. Rather it is everything else that comes along with an asset that the seller does not want you to sell any time soon.

We will see in a future chapter that both institutional and to a lesser degree individual investors have embraced so-called alternative investments. These include such alternatives as hedge funds, private equity, and venture capital. One of the selling points of these asset classes is that they require a longer-term time horizon than liquid market assets and that investors on average earn some return for taking on this illiquidity risk. However, for most individual investors, illiquid alternative investments are really not an option due to the high dollar amounts needed to invest in the vast majority of these funds.

For individual investors, most illiquid assets come along with the twin challenges of high costs and high complexity. Most illiquid investments sold to individuals are designed that way so that the salesperson can be paid a commission. These investments are sold to investors, as opposed to being purchased. Investment manager and blogger David Merkel makes three important points about illiquid investments: "Illiquidity means a loss of flexibility.... The costs of illiquidity are quiet. The extra yield seems free until there is a need for ready cash, whether to spend or to take advantage of investment bargains... [and illiquid investments] are hard to evaluate unless you have expertise greater than that of the seller."[15]

The challenge of illiquid assets comes not when they are purchased. Presumably the investor had ready cash to purchase them at the outset. Rather the costs, especially the opportunity costs, of illiquid assets only show up over time. Illiquidity prevents investors from taking advantage of better investment opportunities down the line. Since most illiquid assets are necessarily more complex than standard investments, they impose further costs on the investor. Illiquid assets sold to retail investors promise higher returns of some sort, but those returns come with real costs.

Luckily for individual investors, financial innovation is making it possible for investors to dip their toes in alternative assets without taking on the burden of illiquidity. Name an alternative asset and there is likely some sort of publicly traded vehicle that provides, at least on some level, exposure to that same asset class. These public vehicles are not perfect substitutes, but for the enterprising investor, there are opportunities to invest in alternative asset classes absent illiquidity.

Buying Something You Don't Understand

The close cousin of illiquidity is complexity. There is a very simple dictum investors should always follow. If you don't understand an investment, don't buy it. To repeat, there is no "must-own" investment you can make that should outweigh your ability to understand it. This is a simple and seemingly commonsense sort of thing to say, but investors who should know better purchase investments they don't understand all the time. When investors buy things they don't understand, bad things often occur.

For example, no one really understood how Bernie Madoff was generating the returns he was reporting to his so-called investors. Madoff's investment process was cloaked in all sorts of mystery and jargon but was ultimately a black box to people on the outside.[16] And that black box ended up being a disaster for his victims. While fraud is a rarity for investors, it highlights how not knowing how an investment works can lead to permanent losses.

Investors don't consciously buy things they don't understand. This is why investors need to have a heightened sense of self-awareness about their abilities. Complex investments always come with some feature that makes them seem particularly attractive to a particular set of investors. For example, retired investors who are in need of current income are often targeted with investments that purportedly throw off high yields. It is this hook on which complex investments are sold, and not bought.

Wall Street is largely built on the creation of products that its clients don't understand particularly well. Any time you see a product that offers current yields far in excess of those available on a plain vanilla product, you can be sure there has been some financial engineering involved. Somebody smarter than you has spent time devising this product in the hope someone on the other end will buy it and generate handsome fees in the process. Financial intermediaries, i.e., brokers, are like any other business in that they need to get paid or they go out of business. Selling Treasury bonds and selling stocks are not exactly high-profit-margin businesses. Wall Street firms feel compelled to create ever-more complex products because that is where the profits are generated.

Another reason why investors get sidetracked into complex investments is that they feel compelled to do so. They see other investors, either close by or far away, making money in complex investments. Investors of all stripes were speculating in Internet stocks at the height of the bubble. Very few of those investors actually understood what these companies did. Then again neither did the companies. It is important to understand your investments not when everything is going up, but when that inevitable turnaround rears its ugly head.

Avoiding complexity is a good reason for owning indexed investments. By tracking broad-based benchmarks, index funds are the epitome of low-complexity investments. By avoiding the active management game, the index fund calculus is pretty simple. Pick an index fund with the lowest fees and the ability to actually track the performance of its underlying index. The ETF industry has become, in the eyes of many, synonymous with indexing. We will discuss in a later chapter how the ETF industry has moved beyond plain vanilla index funds into far more complex products. So just because something is an ETF does not mean it is pegged to a well-designed index.

Index investors, by definition, are not trying to outperform the market, although in the end they do end up outperforming other investors who rack up fees and expenses in an attempt to beat the market. There is an important link between a simple index philosophy and the behavior of the best active investors. Investors, whether active or passive, do best when they keep things simple. We will see in the next chapter that in the complex world of trading and investing, a focus on simplicity is tougher than it looks to maintain.

Key Takeaways

+ Diversification works in theory and in practice. The problem is that investors often abandon diversification at the worst possible time.
+ Asset allocation should be a deliberate process of portfolio construction rather than a haphazard collection of funds.
+ Portfolio rebalancing through discipline and a contrarian approach works to lower portfolio volatility. There are a number of approaches to rebalancing, the only key being that it actually be done on a regular basis.
+ Measuring portfolio performance is an important feedback mechanism, but the S&P 500 is likely not the appropriate benchmark.
+ Portfolio leverage is the number one portfolio killer. Investors should avoid unwitting leverage.
+ Illiquid investments impose a reduction in portfolio flexibility and higher costs. They are most often sold to investors rather than purchased.
+ Investors should never purchase an investment they don't understand. There is no such thing as a "must own" investment.

6

Active Investing

BECOMING A COMPETENT INVESTOR IS A TOUGH TASK. IN THIS CHAP-
ter, we will focus on some of the lessons that hold for any investor
trying to achieve more than mere competence and actually "beat
the market"—or in more technical terms, earn abnormal returns.
Generating abnormal returns is, by definition, difficult, and it stands
to reason that becoming an accomplished investor or trader is an
even tougher task. (Throughout the chapter we will use the terms
trader and *investor* interchangeably to represent attempts to generate
abnormal returns, the only distinction being one of time frame.)

Active investing is the *attempt*, for lack of a better term, to beat
the market. Active investing comes in many forms. At one extreme,
it represents what professional traders, who rely on what they earn
from the market for their livelihood, do on a daily basis. At the other
end of the scale, it represents what individual investors are attempting when they buy a stock or two. Since there are few excuses left
to hold a broadly diversified portfolio, deviations from these benchmarks necessarily represent a form of active management.

Barry Ritholtz took a look at the odds that an athlete, high school
or college, is able to advance on to becoming a pro athlete. He found
that only a very small fraction of these athletes go on to the highest
levels. Ritholtz compares the odds of becoming a pro athlete with

those of becoming a professional trader: "Are the odds identical? Not precisely—there are many more people scratching out a decent living as semi-pro traders than there are semi-pro ball players earning enough to feed their families. And if you find you have a specific talent for it, and are willing to put in the long hours of work required, trading can be incredibly rewarding."[1]

It is easy to see why becoming a professional athlete or trader is so attractive and draws a steady stream of willing candidates. We just need to recognize that beating the market on whatever scale, professional trader or individual investor, is a tough task indeed.

Most Traders Fail

Most traders fail. That should not be an altogether surprising statement. Most small businesses, most prominently restaurants, fail. A trader takes inputs like capital, labor, knowledge, and skill and tries to generate profits. Trading in that regard is just another form of small business.

Mike Bellafiore, author of a popular book on proprietary trading called *One Good Trade,* looked at this very topic of the failure rate of proprietary traders: "Numbers abound about what the failure rate is. Some say 95 percent. Others claim 80. We had a college student fly across the country to visit us who was writing his college thesis on this very subject. He came in at 90 percent. At a big bank the whisper number is 55 percent."[2] If you look across trading and investing disciplines, a 90% failure rate is a reasonable number to work with.

Bellafiore notes the many ways a trader can fail, including not having enough training, not putting in the effort, or simply not being good enough. In that respect, a trading business is like all others that fail. Businesses usually fail for any number of reasons, including bad luck. There are ways to try and mitigate the chances of failure and the costs that come with that failure, but these are not panaceas.

Managing the financial and psychological challenges of trading is hard enough. Traders don't trade in a vacuum. In the end, they are trading against other traders, some of whom are quite literally rocket scientists. Increasingly these days, sophisticated computer programs are on the other side of a trade. The financial industry is filled with smart people, armed with sophisticated technologies, looking to do what every other active trader is attempting to do: beat the market.

So before putting hard-earned money into the market, aspiring traders need to think about whether they have what it takes to be successful. It is not enough to want to be a successful trader. Everybody who sets out wants to be a good trader. We cannot say in advance which 10% of traders are going to make it through the market gauntlet and find profits on the other side. We can say that the other 90% are going to experience some real costs in their attempt to become accomplished traders.

An issue largely overlooked in the trading literature is the concept of opportunity cost. The time and effort spent in trying to become an accomplished trader, by definition, come at the expense of other activities. The biggest cost to the 90% or so of traders who fail is not necessarily the financial costs, but rather the time lost to other opportunities. Money can be made in a number ways, trading only being one of them. However, time is not something any of us can get back. For this reason and this reason alone, aspiring traders need to recognize that the costs involved in failure are not always in dollars and cents.

Taken as a given that most traders fail, what constitutes success? The financial industry is awash with fund managers and newsletter providers quoting statistics that show them outperforming the market by wide margins. We know already that most professional investors underperform the market, so we should already be skeptical about these claims. The fact of the matter is that there is a speed limit on anyone's ability to outperform the market consistently over time.

One example of this is portfolio manager Bill Miller. He became arguably the most celebrated mutual fund manager in America by guiding the Legg Mason Capital Management Value Trust to a 15-year streak of S&P outperformance. That is no mean feat. However, subsequent to this streak, Miller's fund has underperformed the S&P 500 in 4 out of the past 5 calendar years (2006–2010).[3] The point is not to denigrate his efforts, but rather to show that becoming good and staying good is a challenge for even the most celebrated investors.

Let's look at this question another way. Warren Buffett is generally assumed to be the best investor of his or any subsequent generation.

A look at his performance over a 46-year period at Berkshire Hathaway can serve as a practical limit on just how much an individual could expect to outperform the market. From 1965 to 2010, Buffett was able to compound the per-share book value of Berkshire at a 20.2% rate. This far exceeded the 9.4% for the S&P 500, and in 8 of the 46 periods, Berkshire underperformed the index.[4] In so doing, Buffett has become one of the wealthiest men in the world.

It is likely not a coincidence that Buffett's performance is in line with what could be described as the theoretical limits on performance. Wesley R. Gray performed a thought experiment that put to the test just how rapidly individuals could compound their returns using the history of the U.S. stock market since 1926. Gray found that "earning 20%+ returns over very long horizons is for all intent and purposes virtually *impossible* (assuming the market experience of the past ~90 years is representative of the future)."[5] Gray's numbers show that if an investor had more rapid performance, that person would eventually end up owning the entire stock market.

Gray acknowledges the case of Buffett as an outlier and as a practical example of the limits facing investors. That is not to say that someone like a Bill Miller could not go on for an extended period of time beating the market. But it seems that for most investors these periods of exceptional outperformance eventually end.

The point of this discussion is not to discourage investors from trying to beat the market. This discussion should serve as a warning that much of the talk you hear from investment managers and research providers should be taken with a grain of salt. Outperforming the market by large amounts over extended periods of time is virtually impossible. Still, these numbers are not likely to discourage the most intrepid investors from trying to beat the market. So a look at some lessons can help provide some further insight into what it takes to be a great investor.

Trading Isn't Fair

Somewhere along the way, we all learn the harsh lesson that life isn't fair. For some this lesson comes earlier than for others. If life isn't fair, we shouldn't expect trading to be fair either. Anyone who has traded for even a short period of time will be involved in a situation or two that highlights the fact that the financial markets are not fair, and never were fair.

We have already demonstrated the long odds against becoming an accomplished trader or investor. No investors, however, can become great, let alone good or mediocre, without fully taking responsibility for their own trading. Great investors recognize that once they make an investment decision, the results are largely out of their control. They can have a plan about when to sell, but the market will ultimately dictate how that investment works out over time. Great investors recognize that they are going to end up taking losses even if their original thesis was airtight. Losses are simply part of the game.

Less accomplished, or immature, investors take these losses personally. They act as if the market somehow knew they were holding a particular position. The market does not know what you hold in your portfolio and, more important, does not care. You are the only one who really cares about your investment results.

Taking losses is difficult. It means that we have to admit to ourselves that we were wrong about a trade. It is ultimately easier to try and find someone else to blame for your losses than to own them. There is never a shortage of culprits out there. Investors used to blame the shadowy "market makers" for their losses; today high-frequency trading is the latest in a long line of market villains. The best investors do more than simply "own" their losses; they look at their losses in a constructive fashion. Research shows that the only way to learn from losses is to acknowledge them and not simply ignore them or explain them away.[6] Losses effectively become the tuition paid for a more complete market education.

Another thing individual investors also have a tendency to do is to rely on the crutch that if only they had the information or trading systems that the big institutional investors have, *then* they would be successful. The largest institutions pay large amounts of money to get news, data, and information as quickly as possible. Some firms are going so far as to move their servers as close as possible to the exchanges to minimize the time it takes for their trades to hit the market.[7]

There has always been an arms race to get an information edge on the rest of the market. In any race, there are going to be leaders and laggards. While the Internet has done a good job of leveling the playing field for individuals, there will always be haves and have-nots. Whining about what advantages the so-called big boys have is a waste of time. More so, it probably reflects the fact that you really are not ready to trade on your own. As Adam Warner writes, "There's not an even playing field out there. Learn to live within it or don't trade/invest, unfortunately it's that simple."[8]

Some strategies are better off left to the institutions. Short-term trading has largely become the province of the trading algorithms. The days of the SOES bandits are long gone.[9] Other complex strategies as well are likely off-limits to individual investors. Strategies that involve trading bonds like distressed debt or capital structure arbitrage are the province of institutional investors. Strategies that involve shorting individual stocks are also tough for individuals because the big institutions get first crack at available inventory. There is no doubt that institutions have very real advantages when it comes to the mechanics of trading and investing.

On the other hand, individual investors have some real advantages over institutions. For example, most institutions need to be acutely aware of their portfolio benchmarks. That is why many institutions require their managers to remain "fully invested" at all times. As an individual trader your performance benchmark is what best suits your style and risk tolerance. The performance of the S&P 500, for example, should be but a data point to an individual trader. Individual traders can happily go into cash knowing that they are preserving capital, or keeping their powder dry, for better opportunities down the road. Charles Kirk suggests that this is really the only way traders should go on vacation—in cash and with no positions to monitor.[10]

In many ways, size can be a real disadvantage for institutional investors. Many institutions cannot buy meaningful positions in small-cap stocks because they would move the stock price disproportionately getting in and out of the stock. An individual can usually get in and out of most stocks within seconds with relatively little price impact. Other strategies like those that involve options are often off-limits for institutions. But individuals can undertake options strategies at their own discretion. Maybe most important, individuals don't have clients breathing down their necks with unrealistic performance demands. As an individual investor, you are, for better or worse, your own client, and your only concern should be trying to attain your goals with the least amount of risk possible.

The bottom line is that in some very real ways individual investors have distinct advantages over institutional investors. If your strategy relies on perfect executions or institutional-grade information systems, then you are playing a game that you are likely to lose over time. Any advantage you think you have is likely unsustainable. Individuals, if they are going to actively invest, need to play an altogether different game than the institutions play.

Trading Plans

As a society, we don't let minors do a lot of things, including trading stocks, because we recognize they are not fully responsible for their actions.[11] With the ability to trade on our own comes an equal amount of responsibility. Responsible traders recognize that they need to have an overall trading plan, not unlike a business plan, to guide their daily trading.

One of the problems novice traders have is that they don't treat their trading with the same rigor and seriousness that they do any other sort of business endeavor. However, trading is just like any other business in that it has revenues, overhead, variable costs, etc. Trying to trade off the cuff without a plan or a means of measuring your performance is a recipe for disappointment.

Many traders balk at the idea of formulating a trading plan because they feel it might stifle their creativity or ability to react to rapidly changing market conditions. As well, in the wider world of startups, the detailed business plan seems to have gone into disfavor. In the world of trading, it never really seemed to catch fire. However, traders are well served to think about how they plan to go about generating profits. A trading plan that lays out what instruments they will trade, when they will trade them, and what methodology they will use to enter and exit trades is essential. Maybe even more important is a strategy to limit losses both on individual trades and in an overall portfolio. And as important as an overall trading plan might be, a trade-by-trade plan might be even more important.

Some traders find it useful to have a checklist they consult on an ongoing basis when they trade to ensure they are not missing anything along the way. As Atul Gawande, author of *The Checklist Manifesto,* writes: "In aviation, everyone wants to land safely. In the money business, everyone looks for an edge. If someone is doing well, people pounce like starved hyenas to find out how. Almost every idea for making even slightly more money—investing in internet companies, buying tranches of sliced-up mortgages—gets sucked up by the giant maw almost instantly. Every idea, that is, except one: checklists."[12] Checklists don't dictate what a trader does; rather they ensure that what a trader is supposed to do in a trade gets done.

The hallmark of a well-designed trading system may be the actuality that a checklist can be created. The more experienced and successful the trader, the simpler his or her trading system becomes over time. Many traders begin their education reading books on trading and come away with a jumble of ideas and techniques. Some of those ideas will resonate with a novice trader, while others will not. The challenge is that until those ideas are put into action, new traders really can't know what will work for them. Experienced traders have spent a lifetime whittling down ideas into a plan that works for them—and maybe nobody else.

Learning by Doing

As we have seen, the world of trading is an always unforgiving and sometimes paradoxical place. There are unfortunately few shortcuts to learning how to trade. The best way to learn is simply by doing. It is said that the worst thing that a new trader can experience is early success. This is because the important lessons of trading come from managing risk and minimizing losses, not from gaining profits. Trading losses represent the tuition the market is going to charge anyone trying to become a competent trader. Some novice traders think that engaging in paper trading is a way to avoid paying that market tuition.

Paper trading is an attempt to track what trades you would have made *if* you had the capital to trade. There are some real benefits to paper trading for beginning traders. These include being able to work through the mechanics of trading and the ability to try novel strategies absent financial risk. Another approach some traders use is to back-test their strategies. Back testing involves setting up a set of trading rules that one can use to look back at historical data to see how the rules would have performed over time. Both these approaches can accelerate one's learning without putting money at risk.

Paper trading and back testing are all well and good, but eventually traders need to put their money at risk. Don't be fooled into thinking that fantasy-trading contests like the CNBC Million Dollar Portfolio Challenge can simulate the real thing. The CNBC contest promises "No Risk. All Reward. Grand Prize $1 Million."[13] Unfortunately real live trading requires a completely different approach. The very best traders are laser-focused on risk and let the rewards take care of themselves.

There is simply no substitute for putting your own money on the line. Anyone who has had even the smallest bet down on a game, like the Super Bowl, recognizes the very different psychological and physiological effects the prospect of winning and losing can generate. For most traders, it isn't the analytical side of trading that trips them up; it is the psychological side. Novice traders can read books and blogs all day long, but learning by doing, even with small amounts of capital, is the only way to become a better trader.

The evidence indicates that in a very real way more trading equals more learning. Seru, Shumway, and Stoffman show that traders learn two important lessons from their trading experience.[14] The first lesson is that, for some traders, more trading leads to better results. The second lesson is that, for other traders, their trading skills are just not that good. It may make sense for people to trade even if they think they are not particularly skilled. Linnainmaa shows how traders "trade to learn" even if they are not confident about the outcomes.[15] Traders can only demonstrate their skills through trading. As with other things in life, there appears to be no substitute for experience.

The challenges of trading are many; the rewards are limited to a skilled (and lucky) few. Most investors would be well served by acquiring the skills to become competent, or even just mediocre, investors. Other investors are going to feel compelled to try their hand at trading despite the odds being against them. For them, learning by doing will be the only way to truly figure out whether they are suited for trading. Unfortunately most of these aspiring traders will have exhausted their capital before they had a chance to evolve into successful traders.

Survival and Adaptation

The science of evolution is, at its core, pretty simple. Those individuals and species that are able to adapt, evolve, and pass on their DNA or genetic information to the next generation survive; those that don't end up extinct. If they are lucky, like the dinosaurs, they become the object of fascination of preteen boys. Trading is in a certain respect like evolution. Those traders that are able to generate profits and minimize losses are able to survive and live to trade another day; those that don't will end up leaving the playing field or becoming extinct.

This section isn't about all the various strategies that investors and traders successfully use to beat the markets. It is beyond the scope of this book to properly introduce and explain these in any detail. What this section is about is losing. This is because to a large degree winning trades take care of themselves. What traders need to learn is how to lose effectively. In so doing, they can survive to trade another day.

A trader can't live on winning trades if the gains on those trades are offset by larger losses on losing trades. In trading, there is a concept called *expectancy*. It measures a trader's profitability by comparing the probability of a winning trade multiplied by the average win against the probability of a losing trade multiplied by the average loss. Expectancy therefore measures the expected profit from a typical trade. If positive, a trader should, on average, profit from trading and vice versa. Said more simply by Michael Martin, "Gains only look like gains only to the extent that you keep your losses small."[16]

In this framework, the percentage of time you are right is only part of the overall profit equation. In practice, traders can be right less than 50% of the time and still be profitable if they manage their trades well. However, if trading expectancy is negative, then a trader is on the path to failure. Traders need to recognize that a large percentage, maybe even more than 50% of their trades, are going to fail. Traders can sometimes get hung up on the idea that they need to profit from most if not all of their trades. The fact of the matter is that being right is only one part of what it takes to succeed in trading. Novice traders and the industry that sells trading systems want to believe that their win percentage matters a great deal. All that really matters for traders is making profits and generating those profits with a reasonable amount of risk.

Behavioral finance has found that investors have a seemingly irrational desire to sell winners quickly and hold on to losing trades indefinitely. The disposition effect seems to affect novice traders in particular. The desire to be right, or in the case of losses "get even," affects their better judgment. Research seems to indicate that changing our minds comes with a high psychological cost, even when the subsequent decision turns out to be correct.[17] In our minds, we want to be right all the time, but trading is one discipline in which being right is both impossible and overrated. Traders need to ask themselves whether they want to be right or whether they want to make money.

A focus on being right demonstrates a fundamental misunderstanding of trading. Being right may be a necessary component of trader profitability, but it is not sufficient. Proper money management techniques are required to turn trading decisions into trading profits. While it is sometimes difficult to take, being wrong—and accepting it—is a big part of being a trader. Don't let the need to be right prevent you from becoming a better trader.

The second great insight gained from using a framework built on expectancy is the importance for traders to cut short or minimize their loss per trade. Trading is in a certain respect less about being right or wrong and more about knowing when you are right or wrong and acting accordingly. It is far more important to take a loss on a losing trade and get to trade another day than it is to stubbornly try and turn a losing trade into a winning trade.

Tim Harford, in his book *Adapt,* talks about the importance of trial and error and explains how it is that great success often stems from failure.[18] Organizations that set up their operations to take advantage of trial and error ensure that no single experiment will wipe them out. In a trading framework, each trade needs to be of a size that won't torpedo your portfolio. On the face of it, this is a simple proposition for traders with a measure of discipline. Simply don't risk too much on any single trade. It is a cliché to say that you need to cut your losses short and let your winners run, but it is absolutely true. The mathematics of expectancy requires that the losses on losing trades be on average smaller than the profits on winning trades. However, the problem often doesn't lie in any single trade but rather in a series of trades.

The concept of drawdowns comes into play here. A drawdown is the percentage loss a security or portfolio experiences from peak to trough. Some traders devise rules based on portfolio drawdowns to prevent them from letting individual trades cascade into devastating results for an overall portfolio. Trades can often go wrong all at the same time because of a particular methodology a trader is using. So a focus on the overall portfolio is needed even if proper risk management techniques are used on each individual trade.

This stems from the mathematics of performance. If a portfolio declines 10%, it needs to return 11.1% to get back to the breakeven point. Similarly if a portfolio declines 50%, it needs to return 100% to get back to the breakeven. Large losses make it difficult for a trader to recover in any meaningful way. Some traders at this point simply quit. Others try to trade more vigorously to get out of the hole. On balance, this rarely works.

To minimize trading losses, traders need to have a system in place to recognize when a trade has gone bad. In the classic trading book *Market Wizards* by Jack D. Schwager, the idea of risk control is front and center. It was one of the common themes that great traders mentioned in their interviews. Schwager writes, "Rigid risk control is one of the key elements in the trading strategy of virtually all those interviewed."[19] Every trading plan should have risk control as an integral part of the trade management process. In fact, before any trade is entered, a trader should note what conditions will mark a trade as incorrect. Some traders use very simple rules to judge a bad trade, including rules such as any stock that declines 10% is a sell. Other traders use more sophisticated rules based on chart patterns, fundamental events, and even time. Despite the diversity in methods, the important point is that this recognition needs to be made *before* the trade is ever put on.

This is important because once a trade is under way, it changes the way you think about it. Once a trade is on, you are rooting for it to succeed. In a real sense, your ego is now wrapped up in its success. Losses, i.e., failure, now can affect how you react to the trade. Traders who confuse losses with being right or wrong are at risk of letting losing trades grow until they are of the size to ruin a portfolio. Some traders implement their plans for controlling risk with stop-loss orders. That is, stop losses are put in place when a trade is entered with a broker, and they become active if a stock reaches a certain price level (or loss). Stop-loss orders are more controversial than they seem on the face of things. Some traders swear by them; some are reluctant to leave their trade exits in the hands of the market. Both methods require discipline; the latter obviously requires even more discipline.

Nobody comes to the financial markets knowing how to trade. Novice traders can educate themselves in part on what they read in books and in blogs. Research and paper trading can be helpful as well. In the end, though, traders trade. There is no substitute for putting money on the line. It goes without saying that traders should only risk those funds that they can stand to lose. Some of the traders that went on to become legends often lost their entire initial stakes before going on to success. The lessons the market teaches us are going to be the most valuable lessons we learn. The best traders view their losses as tuition in the pursuit of a more thorough education in trading.

The fact is that every successful trader is a lifetime student for two very important reasons. The first is that markets change, especially in the area of technology. A trader from a couple of decades ago transported to today would be shocked at what even the most basic trading systems now have. Second, traders don't stand still either. Traders, it is hoped, embrace a lifetime of learning. This changes how we approach the markets. As traders age, what they want and can obtain from the markets changes as well.

Evolution happens in the natural world on a scale we cannot see happen. In the financial markets, the process of evolution occurs on a much faster time scale. The only thing traders can do is to first survive and second adapt. Survival is the most basic requirement of traders and something we have emphasized throughout this book. Adaptation to changing markets is also a necessity, but traders should also recognize that what they want (and need) from the markets is changing all the time as well.

Key Takeaways

◆ Most traders fail. The 90% of traders who fail will not only lose money but also experience the opportunity cost of time spent in the pursuit of trading success.

◆ Outperforming the market by large amounts over large periods of time is difficult. Don't get fooled by those who claim otherwise.

◆ Trading isn't fair. The best traders take full responsibility for their trades and treat their losses as tuition paid for a more complete market education.

◆ Every trader needs a trading plan. A checklist helps traders stay on track.

◆ Expectancy is an important framework for traders to understand. For traders, expectancy highlights the fact that being right is overrated and that there is a need to keep losses small.

◆ Markets are always changing, just as are the individuals who trade them. To thrive, traders need first to survive so that they can adapt to shifting market conditions.

7

Exchange-Traded Funds

ON JANUARY 22, 1993, THE SPDR S&P ETF LAUNCHED. THE investment world has not been the same since. ETFs are collective investment vehicles that combine the features of mutual funds and individual stocks. ETFs trade like other stocks on the exchanges, but because of their structure, they generally trade at or near their net asset value over time. Investors (and traders) can now trade broad baskets of stocks and other asset classes throughout the trading day.

The introduction of ETFs was revolutionary, but they did not cause a major transformation right off the bat. It took some time for ETFs to really take hold and begin changing the way investors invest. After starting off with a single ETF in 1993, the domestic ETF industry has grown steadily to where it now includes over a thousand ETFs with over $1 trillion in assets under management. Despite this growth, it was not until recently that investment advisors widely embraced the use of ETFs. ETFs are now also making inroads in products like 401(k) plans, where mutual funds had once ruled.

For decades mutual funds were the preferred investment vehicle for most Americans. There even was the aptly titled *Mutual Fund Magazine* that catered to the investor class. Mutual funds haven't gone away. As of October 2011, according to the Investment

Company Institute, the $11.66 trillion held in open-end mutual funds dwarfed the $1.055 trillion held in ETFs. But despite the numbers, interest in mutual funds has been edged out by interest in ETFs. Not too long ago, anyone who managed the Fidelity Magellan Fund was big news. Recently the firm changed portfolio managers, and the news was noted in passing by the media. The age of the star mutual fund manager is largely over.

Like all upheavals, the ETF revolution has both its benefits and its drawbacks. On the whole, ETFs have made investing easier, more diverse, and cheaper. On the other hand, the introduction of ETFs has changed the actual underlying nature of some markets, and the rapid introduction of new ETFs has diluted the benefits seen early on. Unlike many revolutions, we are not likely to see a counterrevolution unseating the ETF regime any time soon.

ETF Innovation

Innovation is rare in the investment world. If you think about it, investors continue to trade instruments like stocks and bonds that have been around for centuries. Open-end and closed-end mutual funds have been around since the 1920s. For investors there have been two big innovations in the past decades. The first was the introduction of listed options trading, and the second was the introduction of ETFs. Both options and ETFs caught on because they materially changed the way investors can structure and manage their portfolios.

The first ETF wasn't based on some new and novel asset class. As mentioned earlier, it was based on the most widely used investment benchmark, the S&P 500. It is not a coincidence that the SPDR S&P 500 remains the largest ETF based on assets under management. The striking thing about a current list of the largest ETFs is that it is so diverse. The list includes funds that invest in gold, emerging market equities, developed market equities, TIPS, investment-grade corporate bonds, and small-cap equities. In short, it looks a great deal like a balanced portfolio.

This access to a wide range of asset classes and strategies is one of the great advantages of the ETF revolution. Once investors became comfortable with the ETF structure, it was quickly adapted to include other parts of the investment world. Within the world of equities early on, we saw the major benchmark indexes covered. Soon thereafter, sector funds followed, and today seemingly every trendy theme has a dedicated ETF.

International equity was a natural extension for ETFs. One could argue that the introduction of ETFs based on single countries helped bring international investing more into the mainstream. By providing visibility, access, and transparency to the international investing process, ETFs accelerated the existing trend in global investing. Once most of the equity waterfront was covered, quite naturally the ETF industry pushed into other asset classes.

Fixed income was another logical extension. There are now well over a hundred fixed-income ETFs covering Treasuries, corporate and high-yield bonds, municipal bonds, and emerging and developed market bonds. There are also bond ETFs that target specific maturity dates. Essentially, the bond waterfront is pretty well covered. However, most, if not all, of these asset classes were accessible via open-end mutual funds. Where ETFs have really caught hold has been in the world of commodities.

At first, investors in ETFs had few good options to invest in commodities. They could invest directly in commodity futures or could buy and hold the actual commodity, for instance gold coins or bullion. But neither of these was a particularly cheap or easy solution. The introduction of commodity ETFs that either hold commodities directly or simulate the return via futures contracts really opened up the wider world of commodities—so much so that commodity ETFs now constitute some 10% of ETF assets.

ETF providers have not stopped at variations on various equity indexes. The frontier in ETF innovation is funds that follow novel strategies that include the currency carry trade, hedge fund replication, and other return factors. These are strategies that are either difficult or costly to implement for anyone other than large institutions. One can argue whether most investors need these funds, but the fact of the matter is they now exist.

While improved access to novel investment strategies is important, ETFs have had their biggest impact when it comes to costs. A constant complaint of mutual fund investors was that open-end mutual funds charged too high fees for too little performance. The one thing that ETFs have always had was a cost advantage over open-end mutual funds. This cost advantage directly translates into a performance advantage but has also struck fear into the traditional investment management industry.

ETFs are able to provide lower costs in part because their structure is simpler and more streamlined than that of traditional mutual funds. The biggest advantage may be that ETFs were introduced using passive indexes instead of being actively managed like most mutual funds. By following an index such as the S&P 500, ETFs can charge less because there simply is less work to do. This advantage has been sizable. For most of the life of the ETF industry, ETFs have had expense ratios that were 1% less than the ratios for open-end mutual funds.[1] In a world where equity market returns are hard to come by, this translates into real money. Indexing was available before the widespread introduction of ETFs from companies such as Vanguard Investments, but the visibility of ETFs has helped to mainstream the idea of using broad (and narrow) market indexes.

It wasn't the idea of low-cost indexing that initially brought attention to ETFs. It was the novel structure that provided investors, and, more important, traders, the ability to trade shares of ETFs throughout the day. Open-end mutual funds, in contrast, provide in and out access at the end of the trading day. The ability to trade minute by minute isn't something long-term investors really need, but it is comforting to know it is there, especially in times of heightened market volatility.

ETFs really caught on because traders embraced this flexibility. Prior to the introduction of ETFs, traders had to trade futures or index options for broad-based market exposure. The flexibility that ETFs provide goes beyond the actual trading mechanics. Now many of the largest ETFs also have options that trade alongside them. Investors interested in hedging their portfolios now have the ability to use inverse funds or simply sell short broad-based indexes.

ETFs also mitigate another big complaint with open-end mutual funds, and that is taxes. Because of their structure, ETFs are far more efficient in the way they handle taxable distributions. This is in stark contrast with open-end funds, which have a tendency to generate capital gains for investors even in years where the fund itself has lost value. The process by which this occurs is not magic, but simply represents a new way of doing business. This tax issue is one that is often downplayed relative to the benefits of ETFs, such as costs, access, and flexibility. Taxes are likely underplayed because the past decade hasn't generated net-net all that much in the way of capital gains to deal with.

If nothing else, our brief description of ETFs highlights the breadth of opportunities available to traders and investors. Like any other tool, ETFs can be used safely and intelligently or can be dangerous when abused. The challenge for investors is to recognize the difference.

ETFs Are a Tool

ETFs have in a very real sense democratized investing by making available to individual investors tools that were exclusive to institutional investors but a few short years ago. To boot, the ETF revolution has made these tools available at prices that were unheard of not all that long ago. Matt Hougan has been tracking what he calls the "world's cheapest ETF portfolio" for a few years now. Hougan assembled a globally diversified portfolio using six ETFs, with the goal of minimizing the expenses paid. From 2007 to 2011, this theoretical portfolio has seen its blended expense ratio drop from 16 basis points, or 0.16% per annum, down to 12.35 basis points, or 0.1235%.[2] Two findings are worth noting. First, 16 basis points was pretty low to start and is in line with what institutions paid not all that long ago. Second, the expenses keep coming down. Some of the new entrants into the ETF space have chosen to use price as a differentiating factor. If we stopped here, this analysis in and of itself would be a big advertisement for ETFs.

The story on costs gets even better. Within the past year, many of the major online brokerage firms have started programs that allow their customers to trade certain ETFs commission free. The one advantage no-load mutual funds had over ETFs was that investors avoided paying a commission, however small, to trade. Now, with commission-free trades, that advantage goes away. Commission-free ETF trades make strategies like dollar-cost averaging and rebalancing largely friction free. Free trades should be just a minor factor when it comes to designing and implementing a trading or investing strategy. Well-conceived trades are worth doing with or without a commission.

ETFs have become increasingly popular because they now provide access to asset classes and strategies that were previously off-limits to individual investors. ETFs can play an important role in helping investors implement an asset allocation strategy. What investors should be wary of is investing in a novel ETF if they don't understand the strategy as laid out by the fund manager. Complexity in and of itself is not an effective strategy. If you don't understand how and when an ETF is supposed to generate returns, then you should move on to the next one. There is no shortage of ETFs to choose from.

ETFs can also be helpful at tax time. We have already noted how ETFs are more tax efficient than open-end mutual funds. ETFs can be helpful in managing your tax bill from investing. Later we will discuss in detail the importance of tax-loss harvesting. For the time being, suffice it to say that investors can benefit by selling securities at a loss in the current tax year to offset any gains they may already have made. ETFs are useful because you can often find an ETF to swap into that is similar enough to maintain an exposure to a particular asset class or strategy without running afoul of the rules surrounding wash sales.[3]

Another area in which ETFs have made things easier for investors is portfolio hedging. ETFs have made it simple to get short exposure to either speculate outright or hedge your portfolio. There are now dozens of ETFs that provide inverse returns (−100%, −200%, even −300%) on broad equity indexes, sectors, and even bonds. Prior to the introduction of these inverse ETFs, investors had to short stocks or go to the futures or options market to gain some short exposure.

Using inverse ETFs to hedge your portfolio seems straightforward, but there are a few things to keep in mind. The first is that purchasing an inverse fund requires using up capacity in your portfolio. Second, these ETFs tend to have higher-than-average expense ratios. Third, and maybe most important, many of these inverse funds are leveraged. Historically these leveraged ETFs, both inverse and regular, have disappointed investors. These funds really are designed with short holding periods in mind. If held for longer periods of time, especially in volatile markets, the returns on the funds can diverge dramatically from their stated goals.[4] This occurs due to the way returns are compounded. So if you need to reduce your portfolio risk for an extended period of time, it makes sense to look for additional ways to get that done.

Like any other tool, ETFs can be used intelligently in the context of an entire portfolio. In the wrong hands, ETFs can be abused and cause immeasurable damage to your portfolio. The key to using any tool is to understand how it works and what its limitations are. This is a particular challenge with ETFs, where the label on a fund oftentimes falls short of being accurate and is sometimes misleading.

ETF Structure Matters

For a long time, the ETF industry has been the scrappy upstart taking on the established mutual fund industry. Therefore, criticism of the industry has been relatively muted, with cheerleaders outnumbering skeptics by a wide margin. The afterglow of innovation has made some investors less skeptical than they should be when it comes to looking inside the inner workings of novel ETFs.

We have already seen an example of how a class of funds like leveraged ETFs can work as promised but still disappoint investors. The mismatch between ETF returns and investor expectations occurs all the time. Most, if not all, of these misunderstandings occur because investors don't fully understand the structure of the underlying fund. Because when it comes to ETFs, structure matters a great deal.

When ETFs were first introduced, things were pretty straightforward. The funds held a broad basket of stocks that tracked widely followed indexes. In short, the components of the fund accurately reflected the label. As the industry has grown and spread into asset classes beyond equities, things have gotten more complicated. Indeed, the industry is now more properly called the ETP industry because that term covers structures that are far removed from the traditional fund format.

This labeling issue comes into play whenever you see a new ETF that invests in a very narrow sector or theme. Whenever you have one of these hot themes, it usually doesn't have much in the way of liquid, investable names. Therefore, fund sponsors can't construct a portfolio that is either diversified enough or liquid enough to pass muster. And so the ETF sponsors add bigger, more liquid names to the portfolio that are peripherally related to the trend in question to get around these restrictions. Unwary investors end up paying higher fees for a more diluted experience.

The introduction and rapid growth of commodity ETPs has been one of the great success stories of the industry. Yet commodity ETPs have also been one area where investors have been most disappointed by the promise of the funds and their actual performance. There are two ways in which commodity funds operate. The first is a physical model where the fund actually owns the underlying commodity. In the case of precious metals like gold, silver, and platinum, there are funds that own actual bars of metal in a warehouse. Investors pay the ETPs to hold and store these metals. The performance of these funds is therefore pretty straightforward, with changes in the price of the metal offset by the expenses accrued.

The other class of commodity ETPs relies on futures markets and swaps to replicate the returns on the underlying commodity. This derivative-based structure is used where commodity storage is more costly or complicated. This structure was widely used to create funds that attempted to track the returns of the energy complex, including crude oil and natural gas. The futures markets for oil and gas are some of the most liquid in the world and would seemingly represent a good opportunity for fund sponsors.

These funds were particularly popular in the run-up in energy prices in 2007 and 2008. Unfortunately for investors in these funds, they were not able to closely replicate the returns to spot crude oil or natural gas. Research shows that the flood of money, from ETFs and other index investors, fundamentally changed the nature of the oil futures markets.[5] Oil futures that usually were in backwardation flipped into contango. *Contango* is a technical term that denotes when futures contracts are trading above the price of the underlying commodity. The drag on returns from contango greatly diminished the returns to these ETPs. Investors who thought they were going to get the returns based on the headline prices of crude oil and natural gas were greatly disappointed.

Despite their flaws, these funds remain quite popular, especially with traders. Fund sponsors have come out with new funds that attempt to mitigate the costs (and risks) of contango; however, the fund sponsors cannot get around the fact that futures contracts on a commodity are not equivalent to the commodity itself. For investors who understand this distinction, these funds can represent viable trading vehicles. One way in which fund sponsors have tried to circumvent this issue of benchmark risk is to create products that directly track an underlying index. By issuing exchange-traded notes, or ETNs, fund sponsors promise investors the return on an index less any fees. The only problem is that ETNs are debt instruments, not actual funds.

Investors in an ETN don't have a claim on the underlying assets of a fund; rather they have a claim on the assets of the issuer, which is usually a large bank. Under normal circumstances, investors are willing to make the trade-off of index returns for credit risk. However, in 2008 the bankruptcy of Lehman Brothers brought to light the risk of the ETN structure. At the time of its bankruptcy, Lehman sponsored three, albeit small, ETNs, the holders of which had to go through the bankruptcy process like other Lehman creditors. While the risk of bankruptcy for most ETN sponsors, who are some of the world's largest banks, is hopefully remote, it is not zero. Investors who invest in ETNs should be aware that there is an additional layer of credit risk inherent in whatever index they are looking to track.

One other major issue comes along with the diversity of ETP structures, and that is taxes. There are five different tax structures, including ETNs, worth noting.[6] By and large the tax situation for each fund is driven by the nature of the underlying assets. However, each fund structure presents its own unique tax situation. For instance, commodity ETPs are often structured as partnerships and pass along the gains and losses from their underlying futures contracts via a K-1. These differences are material and worth noting. Investors therefore need to look past the name of the fund to get a better sense for how after-tax returns will be generated.

The bottom line for investors is that before you put one dime into an ETF, ETP, or traditional open-end mutual fund, you have to understand how that fund works. For most investors, this level of detail is neither fun nor interesting, but it is necessary. Going back to the analogy of ETFs as a tool, if you don't understand how a tool works, don't pick it up, let alone start using it. Said another way, "Know what you own." Complex fund structures are one of the main arguments for most investors sticking with traditional ETFs based on well-constructed indexes. This reduces the chance of surprises and mismatches between your expectations and actual returns. The pressure to invest in new, untested funds is only going to grow because that is where the ETF industry sees its future.

The ETF Business

The ETF industry has embraced a complex set of fund structures because it allowed for the rapid introduction of novel fund types. The ETF industry is on a 20-year growth path and is projected to continue taking share from traditional open-end mutual funds. To truly understand the ETF industry and its impact on the financial markets, you have to understand that ETFs are a business, a big business. The logic of the ETF industry only makes sense once you understand the desire, and need, for growth in assets under management.

The ETF industry has long since grown out of its humble origins. According to McKinsey & Company, from 2000 to 2010 assets under management in ETPs in the United States grew at a 31% annual rate compared with the overall fund industry that grew at a 6% rate.[7] Don Phillips calls the period from 2005 onward as the "ETF explosion."[8] During this period, we have seen over 1,000 ETPs launch in the United States. The ETF industry recognized that there were only so many broad-based, index-linked ETFs they could launch. To generate more assets under management with higher fees, they would have to embrace novel asset classes and more narrowly defined niches.

This strategy has worked. Don Phillips breaks down the development of the ETF industry into "three waves." The first wave reflects the introduction of ETFs based on broad-based equity indexes, the second wave reflects a broadening out of coverage, and the third wave is the explosion previously mentioned. According to Phillips, the industry was able to boost its average expense ratio from 0.17% for those funds launched in the first wave to 0.35% for the second wave all the way up to 0.63% for the current wave.[9] So the strategy of introducing more fund types has worked in increasing average fees. Along the way, this expansion has reduced the advantages ETFs held over mutual funds. Over time the fee spread has narrowed, portfolio turnover has increased, and volatility has increased as well. Despite this dilution, there is every reason to believe that the ETF industry is still poised for growth.

McKinsey & Company projects that through 2015 the global ETP industry should grow on the order of 16.7% on the low end and 26.7% on the high end.[10] This level of growth far and away exceeds anything expected for the overall asset management industry. The rapid growth is attracting an increasing number of asset managers interested in getting in on what is an important distribution channel. This competition has led to the side effect of fewer ETFs being able to reach critical mass. The McKinsey numbers show that back in 2003 nearly every (93%) new ETF introduction garnered $100 million in assets under management within two years of launch.[11] By 2009 that number had dwindled down to 26%. In short, new fund launches are now a much riskier proposition.

The rapid introduction of new and untested ETF types has led to a situation where an increasing number of funds are languishing with assets that make them unprofitable for the fund sponsor. These funds are sometimes described as "orphans," or more colorfully as "zombie ETFs." The fund sponsors keep them open in the hope that a particular niche will get hot and attract a viable amount of assets. Investors need to be wary of these funds not only because they are going to be more costly to trade, but also because they are more at risk of being liquidated in the future.

It is surprising to most investors whenever their ETF ends up in the zombie category. When one of these highly focused ETFs launches, it is often accompanied by a back test that shows the superior performance of the fund prior to the fund's launch. This is not altogether surprising because who wants to buy a new fund that has been underperforming? Narrow niches and novel strategies come with the increased chance that they simply won't perform up to their historical record. The introduction of a niche ETF often coincides with a peak in interest in the theme it covers. Investors who dabble in these funds should be prepared for disappointment.

We can liken the approach of the ETF industry to that of a supermarket. Retail analysts note that supermarkets frequently place the staples of our diets along the perimeter of the store. Here you will find fruits, vegetables, bread, meats, and dairy. These categories are the least processed and presumably healthiest products in the store. In the interior aisles of the store are the more highly processed, less healthy, and presumably higher-profit-margin goods. Some might call this "junk food." The ETF industry is similar in its approach by offering low-cost, broad-based funds alongside higher-cost niche funds. Consumers, or investors, have the choice among these different categories. Most investors would do well to stick with the basics and not waste their time and effort on "junk" funds. The ETF industry hopes that investors will push their cart into the middle of the store in search of more highly processed fare.

The ETF industry has succeeded in spite of a propensity to launch narrowly focused funds that fail to achieve critical mass. The industry has created so many hits that the misses fade in comparison. The industry's hits have become so popular that they have changed the nature of the markets they purport to track.

The ETF-ization of Everything

The ETF revolution has scooped up all manner of asset classes over time. Starting with domestic equities, international equities, fixed income, international fixed income, currencies, and commodities, the industry pretty much has the asset class scene covered. Within these niches, industries are now well represented alongside more narrow thematic plays, alternate-weighted indexes, and strategies that seek to replicate hedge fund returns and even plays on volatility. There are numerous examples that show that when one of these ETFs becomes popular, it can actually change how the underlying market trades.

This can occur when the ETF becomes so popular that in a certain sense it *becomes* the market. We saw this in the case of crude oil and natural gas ETFs, which were among the biggest buyers of futures on these commodities. Some market players believe that the complex of ETNs that tracks the CBOE Volatility Index (the VIX) now has a disproportionate effect on how VIX futures trade. The sponsors of these funds likely had little belief that their funds would become popular enough to influence markets, but they did. In a very real sense, these funds became the tail that wagged the dog. Not only do very popular niche funds risk changing the dynamics of the underlying market, but they also represent a warning sign to investors that the particular market has become overheated.

Another way in which ETFs can change a market is by making available an asset or strategy that was previously off-limits to the vast majority of investors. A prime example is the physical gold market. Prior to the introduction of the SPDR Gold Trust back in November of 2004, investors who wanted gold exposure were forced to go through the costly process of buying physical gold and storing it. Otherwise they could purchase futures contracts on gold or the shares of gold miners. The introduction of the SPDR Gold Trust, now the second largest ETF by assets, has changed the gold-buying calculus.

Exchange-traded gold funds have made it a trivial exercise to buy, sell, and trade physical gold. Anyone with a brokerage account can participate. This has been a boon to investors who have been in the fund from the time of its launch, since they have seen the price of gold increase from $444 to nearly $1,800 an ounce at present.[12] Gold has been viewed for ages as a store of value or safe-haven asset. The question for gold investors is whether having so much physical gold tied up in ETF-type structures has changed the way investors look at gold. Said another way, is gold simply another ticker symbol on investors' screens that investors now feel comfortable trading at a moment's notice?

One of the great tricks that ETFs have been able to accomplish is to generate liquid vehicles for assets that are generally less liquid. This has been the case with corporate bond ETFs that track investment-grade and high-yield bond indexes. The iShares iBoxx Investment Grade Corporate Bond Fund and the iShares iBoxx High Yield Corporate Bond Fund have become so big and liquid that active bond fund managers have started tracking these indexes more closely.[13]

Sometimes a simple index quirk can affect markets. For instance in 2010–2011, tech giant Apple constituted more than 20% of the popular PowerShares QQQ fund—this despite the fact that Apple's weighting in the underlying Nasdaq 100 index was much lower. After an index reweighting, Apple's weight came down well below 20%, but it reflects how simple decisions that index providers make when ETFs are small in stature can have big effects later on once assets have swelled.

If, as many expect, ETFs continue to take share from traditional fund types, then issues related to their size and market impact will become more common over time. The growth of the ETF industry has generated a number of funds that are likely to fail because they are unable to attract sufficient assets. The bigger issue for ETF sponsors, regulators, and investors will be funds that get too big for their own good and end up altering the markets they attempt to track.

Active ETFs

It used to be the case that ETFs were based on an index, either one that was already well known to the public, like the S&P 500, or one that was designed specifically for the purpose of the ETF sponsor. ETF sponsors have gotten increasingly aggressive in their desire to generate ever-narrower niches. ETF sponsors have now embraced indexes that are more dynamic in nature. These strategy ETFs seek to alter their exposure to the market based on various indicators. It is pretty much the case that if a fund sponsor can think of a strategy and categorize the rules involved, it can serve as the basis for an ETF. It's therefore not that big a step to go from custom-designed, dynamic indexes to ETFs that are actively managed.

Given the history of the ETF industry, this should not come as a shock. The rapid introduction of new ETFs has come along with a rise in expense ratios. Actively managed ETFs are the ultimate excuse to raise fees. The business of managing broad-based indexed ETFs is now highly competitive, and fees are beginning to approach the single digits in terms of basis points per annum. A rapid introduction of actively managed ETFs seems inevitable, but it is not clear than this is a boon for investors.

The push into active ETFs is not at present being driven by investor demand. Actively managed ETFs now make up less than 1% of U.S. ETF assets.[14] McKinsey & Company notes how active ETFs could, over the next decade, make up 10% of ETF assets. Given this potential, the current flood of applications by traditional managers to set up actively managed ETFs isn't surprising, albeit if they are doing it as a defense mechanism. Most of these managers have seen how the rise in ETFs has siphoned off assets and put pressure on fees. It is only logical that they would want to protect their core businesses. Some will try to accomplish this through fund conversions; others will simply launch ETF versions of their already existing funds.

People are going to look back at the introduction of the Pimco Total Return ETF as a watershed for the actively managed ETF business. The fact that Pimco, which is the largest bond fund manager in the world, is launching an ETF version of its most popular fund has put everyone on notice. The new Pimco ETF is essentially providing institutional-level pricing for this strategy in an ETF form.[15] This—along with the intraday liquidity, tax benefits, and transparency that come along with the ETF structure—should make for a compelling alternative to Pimco's already existing funds.

Other fund managers are working very hard to try and bypass one of the attractions of ETFs, and that is their transparency. The ETF structure works today because it requires fund managers to disclose their holdings so that participants can create or redeem shares as needed. Some active managers are unwilling to jump into the ETF fray if they have to manage their portfolios in an open fashion. They fear that their trades will be front-run by others to the detriment of their performance. Some managers are going to great lengths to create new structures that would allow them to sidestep the traditional, transparent ETF structure.[16] It isn't clear that the information is all that valuable, nor is it clear that investors have much interest in buying into a "black box" when alternatives abound.

It's ironic that the investment management industry would come to embrace the active ETF format. One of the main arguments for ETFs is that they provide investors a chance to trade intraday. The investment management industry has always preached a long time horizon for investors in actively managed mutual funds. Therefore, the liquidity of actively managed ETFs seems to be at odds with the standard industry line and will likely serve only to muddy the message to investors.

The convergence of ETFs and open-end mutual funds is a worrisome trend. The open-end mutual fund business has not served its clientele well. David F. Swensen wrote in an op-ed: "Too often, investors believe that mutual funds provide a safe haven, placing a misguided trust in brokers, advisers and fund managers. In fact, the industry has a history of delivering inferior results to investors, and its regulators do not provide effective oversight."[17] In that light, the prospect for an ETF industry that looks and acts more like the traditional mutual fund industry is not an altogether pleasant prospect.

Then again the ETF industry has been moving away from its original reason for being for some time now. Don Phillips writes: "The steady descent toward mediocrity of ETFs hasn't been pretty and will get worse. Still, investors have many great ETFs from which to choose, and we are seeing traditional funds finally lower their fees and marginally improve their practices in response to ETFs. In that sense, the ETF revolution will likely lead to lasting benefits for all investors."[18] On the whole, the ETF revolution has been a boon to those investors who have used ETFs in a thoughtful fashion.

Investors sometimes forget that just because the fund industry comes up with a novel fund type does not mean you need to embrace it. Active ETFs will succeed or fail based on their ability to outperform their benchmarks, not on the fact that they are ETFs. The vast majority of investors need not look beyond the most basic ETFs. For those that do, it is important to avoid faddish funds or ones that require complex replication strategies or entail taking on undue credit risk.

What investors need are "good ETFs" that are liquid and accurately track their benchmark. David Merkel, who writes on what a good ETF looks like, comments: "There are many ETFs that are closed-end funds in disguise. An ETF with liquid assets, following a theme that many will want to follow, will never disappear, and will have a price that tracks its NAV."[19] Good ETFs are therefore likely the minority of funds launched today. Selecting ETFs that meet the criteria of a good ETF becomes even more important when you look to diversify your portfolio internationally.

Key Takeaways

+ The introduction of ETFs was a real financial innovation providing access to novel asset classes, lower fees, and greater flexibility for investors.

+ ETFs are useful tools that have helped make life easier for investors, especially in lowering expenses. However, like any other tool ETFs can be misused and/or abused by inexperienced investors.
+ Structure matters for ETPs. For example ETNs are most definitely not ETFs. ETP structure can affect investment results in a number of ways, not least of which is taxation.
+ To understand the ETF industry you have to recognize that is a big business. In that light, the rapid proliferation of novel fund types makes sense for the issuer, less so for investors.
+ The popularity of certain ETFs has changed the underlying dynamics of the markets they attempt to track.
+ The ETF industry is intent on launching more actively managed ETFs. On the other hand, investors are well served by focusing on good, basic ETFs and avoiding most novel fund types.

8

Global Investing

THE ETF REVOLUTION HAS OPENED UP NUMEROUS OPPORTUNITIES for investors, especially in the area of global investing. Investors today have access to a wide range of vehicles for investing in foreign equities, bonds, and currencies. On the equity side, an investor can invest in ETFs that provide easy access to dozens of country, sector, and global themes. The bigger question is, to what degree do you want to take advantage of these opportunities?

All the evidence points to the fact that investors in the United States and elsewhere do not take full advantage of international diversification opportunities. This "home bias" flies in the face of the evidence from academic finance that supports the idea of globally diversified portfolios. In prior decades, there were real barriers to international investing, not the least of which was the high cost of investing overseas. Now the easy access to ETFs makes this argument largely moot.

For years, the idea of foreign diversification for U.S. investors was a secondary concern. And for decades, the United States was by far and away the largest equity market in the world, with upward of 90% of the world's market capitalization. The United States is still the largest equity market in the world, but its position has been greatly diminished. Recently the United States was estimated to have

40% of the global market capitalization.[1] By this measure, Japan is still the second largest stock market in the world.

It was the bull market, turned bubble, in Japan in the 1980s that really opened people's eyes to the potential of overseas investing. Another factor that helped along the way was the growing realization that the U.S. dollar was falling in value against other major currencies. One way investors could take advantage of this trend was by owning foreign securities.

Very few U.S. investors today have 60% of their equity portfolios overseas. The same is true for non-U.S. investors, only more so. Think about the case of Canada, which by last count had approximately 5% of world market capitalization. Very few Canadians have likely mirrored world market capitalization by having 95% of their holdings overseas. This psychological barrier is the home bias at work.

It is said that familiarity breeds contempt. However, in the world of finance, as Gur Huberman puts it, "familiarity breeds investment."[2] Huberman showed that investors were far more likely to invest in their local regional Baby Bell company than in any of the six other Baby Bells, this despite the fact that there were no real barriers to diversification. Maybe we shouldn't be all that surprised by these findings, because mere exposure has a powerful psychological effect.

Research shows that exposure to something that doesn't harm us actually changes our brains, hence the "mere-exposure effect." That's why we are more comfortable around familiar things. Jason Zweig writes, "Being in the presence of familiar things (even when we are unaware of them) simply makes us feel better."[3] It is not a big stretch to see how this effect would affect our own investment decision making. Zweig notes that this is why we feel more comfortable buying stocks in companies with products we are familiar with and use. Another way in which this manifests itself is in the realm of company stock. Because we are familiar, and presumably comfortable, with the companies in which we work, we are particularly comfortable holding company stock. A concentrated position in any single security, let alone the company you work for, is a situation rife with risk.

We have already discussed the virtues of portfolio diversification. If home bias is a barrier to achieving that goal, then the thoughtful investor needs to take steps to overcome this bias. There are two ways in which we can approach this problem. The first is a bit more analytical. For investors reluctant to invest overseas, we need to put in proper context the size of our domestic market relative to the world. Seeing that even the largest market, the United States, is well below half of the world market cap can help prod investors to look more closely at international investments.

The other approach stems directly from the mere-exposure effect. Simply exposing ourselves to news and information about overseas markets can help overcome that bias. It need not be a rigid, formal process. Merely spending more time on international coverage can help familiarize ourselves with the broader world around us. This serves not only our portfolios but also our general knowledge.

We have so far not discussed international bonds. In part this has to do with home bias. When it comes to foreign equities, at least we come across household names. In the realm of sovereign bonds, this is not likely the case. In that regard, diversification into foreign bonds is a higher hurdle. However, given our goals of broad diversification, considering foreign bonds as an investment is well worth doing. Like international equities, there are an increasing number of vehicles that invest in foreign developed and emerging market bonds. Given the turmoil surrounding the state of U.S. domestic finances, a trend toward more diversified fixed-income portfolios is likely to continue.

Most investors will never take a full market cap–type weighing to overseas markets. Indeed, a formal portfolio construction process would likely not recommend this large a weight anyway. All investors need to do is consciously overcome the home bias and approach international diversification without undue bias. Every trend in place points to a more globalized economy and financial system. Portfolios need to reflect that reality.

Global Shocks

On Friday, August 5, 2011, Standard & Poor's downgraded the sovereign credit rating of the United States from AAA, where it had been since 1941, down to AA+. This has important implications for the U.S. economy and financial markets. The following Monday, the global equity markets were in free fall, with every major equity index ending down substantially on the day. On this day, it wasn't surprising that the S&P 500 ended down more than 6%, but the MSCI EAFE index that tracks foreign developed markets was down even more.

You wouldn't think that a downgrade of the credit rating of the United States would affect the rest of the world's capital markets, but it did. We could spend pages trying to dissect the intricacies of what happens on a day like that, but it's sufficient to know that this is how our interconnected global markets operate. In an increasingly globalized world, what happens in one country, especially one like the United States, can affect the rest of the world. This incident was yet another example of how in times of stress the global financial markets have a tendency to trade as one.

In an ideal world, that isn't how international diversification is supposed to work. In an ideal world, the zigs of the U.S. market are supposed to be offset by the zags of the international markets. This global portfolio is supposed to provide a smoother ride for our port-folios. Unfortunately that isn't how things work these days—and this is why the idea of international diversification has come under fire. The experience of the financial crisis and subsequent bear market made it abundantly clear that as financial stress increases, the correlation on risky assets has a tendency to approach 1.0. Markets all begin to trade in unison on the upside and on the downside.

For this reason, some commentators have suggested that U.S. investors can get all the international exposure they need simply by holding stock in companies that do a substantial part of their business overseas. On the surface, this argument is very appeal-ing. Not having to diversify internationally tugs on our home bias. These same commentators likely recommend that investors diversify among large- and small-cap U.S. stocks. However, these two asset classes are far more correlated than the U.S. market is with any other foreign stock market. The point is that just because an asset class doesn't provide ideal diversification does not mean we should write it off summarily.

No one in this day and age should be surprised that the correla-tion between markets increases in periods of stress like bear mar-kets and economic recessions. For nearly two decades now, research has shown increased correlation in periods of market stress.[4] The big insight is that the correlation structure among countries is not, and frankly never was, static. The naïve case for international diversification has always rested on the idea that these correlations would hold up in difficult market times.

If anything, the phenomenon of rising correlations has only gotten more acute over time. It is clear that the global economy has become more globalized. A quick glance at our own spending would likely show that a significant portion of our consumption comes in the form of products produced, in part, overseas. So when a major earthquake hits in Japan, the supply chains across the world feel the pain.

Globalization is not limited to the production of goods. The service sector is increasingly opening up to trade across borders. This is occurring because the technological infrastructure is in place to allow for seamless communications across borders. This free flow of information affects how news and trends diffuse across the globe as well. Globalization will never be complete, because national identity is still important; but it cannot be dismissed as a reason for increasingly correlated financial markets in the short term.

Just as in the real economy, the financial markets have also become more integrated. It didn't used to be common practice to watch what was happening in overseas markets, but investors these days are paying increasing attention. Now that investors can easily trade these markets using ETFs, it is worth their time and effort to track them more closely. This sea change in attention affects how the markets work in practice. In periods of market stress, investors looking to reduce risk now can, with the push of a button, sell Japanese stocks just as easily as they can stocks in the S&P 500. Electronic trading in that sense has blurred the distinction between what is domestic and what is foreign.

Despite all this evidence that globalization is occurring in the real economy and financial markets, there is still a case to be made for investing globally. Despite the increase in correlations, a standard approach to building portfolios still puts a substantial weight on foreign assets. Chen, Goodwin, and Lin find that for a U.S.-only investor, any sort of international diversification makes sense in that it improves a portfolio's risk-return profile.[5] For investors already well diversified in large-cap developed and emerging market equities, there are but a few very limited additional diversification opportunities.

Despite the talk to the contrary, the benefits of global diversification are still real, albeit more limited in scope than they were. A more nuanced argument in favor of global diversification takes into account the fact that no country, including the United States, is free from a host of existential risks. Therefore, diversification is more than a simple portfolio tool; it is a concerted attempt to make our portfolios more real-world risk resistant.

Long-Term Thinking

Part of the confusion and controversy regarding international diversification really centers on the question of time frame. Investors want to believe that international diversification will work for them no matter what the markets are doing. When the U.S. market is up, we want our international investments to tag along for the ride. When the U.S. market is down, we would prefer that our international investments don't go down. In short, we don't want to be disappointed by our decision to diversify.

In a sense, disappointment is the essence of diversification. We have seen this at work with diversification among bonds and stocks. Bonds, by and large, are not going to provide outsized investment returns. However, in times of severe market stress, they can provide much needed portfolio ballast. Under normal market conditions, our bond investments are a nagging disappointment.

What investors need to avoid is faux diversification. Faux diversification occurs when new and novel asset classes turn out to have exposures that are roughly similar to those of already existing asset classes. The investment industry is always on the hunt for new investment products it can market as novel asset classes. This nomenclature tends to cement in investors' minds the unique nature of the new fund or strategy. The fact is that there are few truly novel asset classes whose returns are not affected by the risk factors common to most risky assets.

Like other many other approaches to investing, diversification is harder than it looks. One reason why recognition of the home bias is such a powerful phenomenon is that it forces us to think about our own country in a less than flattering light. Nobody wants to think that the United States, or any home country, isn't the best investment bet. That is in fact the very reason why international diversification is so important. We aren't talking about the zigs and zags of the current global economy. Rather we are talking about the big, secular economic shifts that occur over decades.

The Standard and Poor's downgrade of the sovereign credit rating of the United States, mentioned earlier, was a watershed event. The downgrade highlighted in a tangible sense just how far the United States had gone off track. As Fareed Zakaria writes: "Instead, we have demonstrated to ourselves, the world and global markets that our political system is broken and that we are incapable of conceiving and implementing sensible public policy."[6] This incident underscores how a country can lose its standing over time, or as Justin Fox writes, how the United States needs to come to terms with losing its status as the "world's dominant economy and has to learn to get by instead as *one of* the world's dominant economies."[7]

None of the problems that led to the S&P downgrade happened over night. The relative decline of the United States economy is something that investors should have been keenly aware of. This is exactly the reason why investors should think about international diversification with the long term in mind. In a really interesting paper, Asness, Israelov, and Liew posit a unique way to think about just what international diversification is supposed to accomplish.[8]

Asness et al. come to three main conclusions. The first is that the short-term benefits of international diversification are largely absent. As noted in the prior section, the global financial markets have the frustrating tendency to decline in unison these days, largely eliminating the benefits of international diversification. This "co-skewness" is unlikely to disappear any time soon. Over the intermediate term, the uncertainty inherent in international diversification comes via valuation. As noted earlier in the book, valuation plays a large role in how equity markets perform relative to one another even after taking into account economic growth.

Second, the authors note that over the long run it is specific economic performance that drives equity market returns. If this is the case, then there is the potential for countries and their equity markets to diverge over time. The risk for investors is that they are concentrated in a country that has exhibited, or is going to exhibit, relatively poor economic performance over a long period of time. As an example, we mentioned earlier the case of Argentina and how it spent much of the twentieth century losing its relative economic status.

Last, they note how international diversification over the long run can serve to mitigate some of these big risks. Asness et al. write: "Diversification protects investors against the adverse effects of holding concentrated positions in countries with poor long-term economic performance. Let us not fail to appreciate the benefits of this protection."[9] In this framework, global diversification serves as a hedge against the existential risk of local economic stagnation.

The point of this is not to denigrate the United States or somehow imply that the future performance of the U.S. economy is going to be markedly worse than its historical performance or poor compared with economies around the world. It simply means that investors, here and abroad, need to contemplate the possibility of an extended run of bad luck. Protecting against adverse outcomes is the whole point of diversification. Fortunately for investors in the United States and other developed countries, there is a growing pool of countries and markets in which we can look for additional investment opportunities.

Emerging Attractions

The term *emerging markets* is a bit of a misnomer these days because it covers a wide range of countries in both size (China and the Czech Republic) and level of development (Taiwan and Egypt). Emerging markets are best thought of as countries that still lag more developed countries in some important economic, political, or financial fashion. These markets are generally believed to be riskier than their more developed counterparts, hence the often bright lines drawn between the two camps. This distinction matters because of the importance of global benchmarks and the investments that flow from them.

There always seems to be some controversy about which markets should, and should not, be considered emerging markets. What is not in dispute is that emerging markets have been standout performers in the past decade. In the decade ended in 2010, emerging market equities and emerging market bonds were the two best-performing asset classes, racking up annual returns of 16% and 11%, respectively.[10] These returns stand out in comparison to the roughly 2% annual returns that U.S. stocks earned over this period. This outperformance has pushed the weighting of emerging markets in the MSCI All-Country World index up from below 4% at the start of the past decade to nearly 14% today.[11]

While this performance was impressive, the economic advances in the emerging markets were even more impressive. The emerging markets, especially the much-hyped BRIC nations of Brazil, Russia, India, and China, experienced rapid economic growth, particularly in comparison with the developed world. When Europe and the United States were going through their own debt crises, the emerging market bonds began to look and trade more and more like a safe-haven asset class.[12] This is a far cry from where the emerging market story began the decade.

The case for investing overseas was primarily built on the idea that foreign assets would provide diversification benefits. This idea was first applied to the developed markets and then naturally transitioned to the emerging markets. The challenge for investors is that along the way both economic and financial trends worked to reduce the benefit of global diversification. In a very real sense, the global economy became more integrated. The end of the cold war and decisions by the world's most populous nations (China and India) to become much more open economically helped push this process along. As trade and capital flowed across borders, the world's economies became more sensitive to what was going on in the rest of the world.

At the same time, the increasing sophistication of investors and the shift of trading onto electronic platforms brought globalization to the financial markets as well. International diversification used to be a much more costly and arduous process. In short, you had to want it. As markets became increasingly open and electronic, the practice of international diversification became simpler and cheaper. As we noted when talking about ETFs, international diversification today is just a mouse click away.

John Authers, in his book *The Fearful Rise of Markets,* talks about the "diversification paradox."[13] The paradox is that as investors increasingly bet on the benefits of noncorrelated assets, it made it more likely that the benefits would prove illusory. When the financial crisis hit, it did not matter to investors that one asset read Chinese equities and the other read U.S. equities. All that mattered was that they were both risky assets—and risk was something to avoid.

In this sense, emerging market diversification failed. That should not be all that surprising given our earlier discussion. What is surprising is that anyone believed that these markets would somehow decouple in the midst of a serious bear market. Nor has this experience stopped investors from looking for the next opportunity in the emerging markets. For some investors, their goal is a new combination of markets that can rival the past performance of the BRIC nations.

Other investors are looking to even smaller and less developed markets for opportunities. You can best think of these frontier markets, for example, Argentina, Romania, and Vietnam, as the minor leagues of the emerging markets. These frontier markets trade with a lower volatility and lower correlations to the U.S. market than more advanced emerging markets.[14] Despite the higher cost of investing in frontier markets, these markets represent a unique diversification opportunity.[15] Investors hope that these countries get a boost from the transition into full-fledged emerging markets. In short, getting called up from the minor into the major leagues.

Even though the idea of investing in emerging markets took a hit in the financial crisis, the search for opportunities overseas did not slow for long. One emerging asset class that did not take a major hit in the financial crisis was emerging market bonds. One could argue that the status of emerging market bonds has been enhanced by the financial crisis and the subsequent debt crises involving Europe and the United States. Emerging market bonds now represent to many investors a viable safe haven. This is due to the relatively strong fiscal position many of these issuers now find themselves in. Unfortunately for investors looking for additional yield, emerging market bond prices now reflect this positive news.

A significant reason why emerging market bond and equity markets performed so well in the past decade is that they saw an upward revaluation. Markets that were once shunned had become mainstream investments. Some will argue that these markets still have a marked growth advantage over the developed markets, which is likely true. Investors should not forget that the stock market is not the economy and vice versa. The same holds true for the emerging markets. The emerging markets will likely continue to grow as a part of the global markets, but that does not necessarily mean they will outperform.

For better or worse, the emerging markets have been caught up in the ETF wave as well. Fund sponsors have brought out all kinds of single-country equity ETFs and sector ETFs covering the larger emerging equity markets. On the bond side, there are now local currency emerging market bond ETFs and funds that cover specific geographic regions. This sort of granularity for traders is great. It gives them more opportunities to make specific bets. BRIC hype aside, research shows that it is difficult to forecast those emerging markets that are going to outperform.[16] For the vast majority of investors interested in gaining some exposure to the emerging markets, this level of granularity is unnecessary. It is hard enough picking what sectors will do well in the U.S. market, let alone trying to select winning sectors in Brazil or China.

That being said, investors are going to continue to optimize their exposure to the emerging markets. The opportunity is simply too large to ignore. If investors can no longer count on the easy benefits of diversification, then fund managers and investors will look for new ways to invest in the emerging markets. This might include approaches already used in developed markets, for example, low-volatility strategies. In any event, there is going to be no shortage of ways for investors in the future to invest in the emerging markets.

The coming decade for the emerging markets is not likely to be a repeat of the past decade. The biggest issue facing investors in the emerging markets is not the markets themselves but the high expectations for them. Despite the great strides many countries have made, real risks still exist in these markets. History tells us that the path to developed nation status comes with serious bumps along the way. Emerging markets are an important part of a globally diversified portfolio, but they no longer represent the easy diversification play they once did. Nor can, or should, investors count on their continued outperformance.

Currency Confusion

We have been discussing the nature and importance of global investing and have so far ignored a critical part of foreign investment returns: currencies. To gain access to any kind of overseas investment, stock, bond, or cash, it involves dealing in a foreign currency. From the outset, we should recognize that the foreign exchange (forex) markets are the largest financial markets in the world. By last count, some $4 trillion in currency changes hands every day, and that number seems only to be rising.[17] The Bank of International Settlements estimates that retail traders account for 8–10%, or $125–$150 billion, of forex trading.[18] No matter how you measure it, these are big numbers.

Before we go any further, we need to make a distinction between active currency trading and the passive exposure gained to currencies via an investment in overseas assets. Individual investors should recognize that currency trading is by all accounts a money-losing proposition for the vast majority of traders. In contrast, the diversification benefit of international investments comes in part from the exposure to foreign currencies.

There is no doubt that there is a great deal of activity on the retail forex front, but the question is whether the clients are generating any profits. On this question, the evidence is decidedly negative. Statistics compiled by the Commodities Futures Trading Commission, or CFTC, from the companies that provide retail forex services show that approximately 75% of customers lost money each quarter in the last year for which statistics were compiled.[19]

This should not be altogether surprising, because the deck is stacked against forex traders. First, traders are usually using a high amount of leverage (up to 50 times). Second, traders are dealing with firms that are acting as a principal and not an agent. In other words, they are trading against the house. Last, there are few limits placed on who can trade currencies, and so experience is no hurdle to opening and trading a forex account.

All these factors lead to very high customer attrition at the major forex firms. That means that a large fraction of their customers are dropping out of the game. As Joshua Brown writes: "The online currency trading shops are modern-day boiler rooms...I am not arguing that making money trading currencies is impossible, I am saying that most people who try are merely being taken advantage of."[20]

The lure of forex trading is easy to understand. Trading in the most liquid, visible markets in the world seems on the face of it to be a manageable proposition. However, once you mix in a high level of leverage, it turns forex trading into a losing proposition for the vast majority of people who try it. Avoiding situations where the odds are stacked against you is an important aspect in trying to keep your portfolio on track.

Institutional investors are not immune to the lure of foreign currencies. Many large investors have embraced currencies as a separate asset class. There is some evidence that these professional managers have been able to generate some gains above and beyond some already established benchmarks.[21] Even for institutional investors, forex profits are no sure thing. For example, there is some evidence that the profitability of trend-following strategies in well-established currencies seems to have eroded over time.[22] This is not surprising, since all markets evolve over time, and those managers who are fishing in the forex waters need to constantly search for new methods to generate profits.

This constant search for forex profits is at best a sideshow for long-term investors. We don't have to engage in hyperactive trading to benefit from currency exposure. We discussed earlier how international diversification should best be thought of as a long-term proposition. Gaining exposure to overseas markets implies a currency exposure as well. The whole point of this diversification is to offset the potential risk that your home market will turn out to be a negative outlier over the long term.

Another way to think about currency diversification is based on the idea of natural hedges. A natural hedge is an exposure to an asset class that also serves to hedge your ongoing consumption. We all recognize that a significant portion of the goods we buy comes from overseas. If the value of the dollar declines over time, which many believe to be the case, the cost of those imported goods will increase in dollar terms. Having an investment in foreign currency naturally helps offset this effect.

What investors can't do is invest overseas, hedge out the currency risk, and expect to get true international diversification. Foreign bonds and equities have lower correlations with domestic asset classes in part due to the currency returns. The process of currency hedging offsets some of the return benefits of global assets. If the whole point of international diversification is to gain long-term exposure to overseas markets, then currency hedging seems an unnecessary step.

Thanks to the financial services industry, exposures to foreign currency returns need not come only through equities or longer-term fixed-income instruments. Individual investors now have access to every major currency and many minor currencies in the form of exchange-traded instruments. Individual investors can also access specialized bank deposit accounts that provide exposure to foreign currencies. Investors can think of this as diversifying their cash holdings.

For a long time, and even today, foreign investments have represented an opportunity for investors to try to create more efficient portfolios. That task has become more difficult over time as markets have converged. That being said, investors who ignore the increasingly global nature of the economy and financial system are likely to get left behind. In a certain sense, international investing was one of the first attempts at alternative investing. The search for uncorrelated returns continues to this day in a number of different ways.

Key Takeaways

- Home bias prevents most investors from taking full advantage of the benefits of international diversification.
- An increasingly global economy and financial markets have reduced, but not eliminated, the benefits of global diversification.
- The greatest benefit of global diversification may come in the very long term in protecting investors from the existential risk of economic stagnation in their home market.
- Emerging markets are an important part of a globally diversified portfolio, but they no longer represent the easy diversification play they once did. Nor can, or should, investors count on their continued outperformance.
- Foreign currency exposure plays an important part of international diversification, but most individual investors should actively avoid forex trading.

9

Alternative Assets

THERE IS NO PERFECT INVESTMENT. ANYONE WHO TELLS YOU otherwise is trying to sell you something. Our discussion of the so-called standard asset classes like equities and bonds was filled with anecdotes about the many ways in which these asset classes can disappoint investors. It should not be surprising that investors are constantly on the lookout for novel investments that can provide a better risk-return trade-off than the old standbys.

Investors searching for a better mousetrap often do so in what most people call *alternative investments*. Alternative investments combine standard asset classes in novel ways or invest in companies or asset classes typically outside the purview of the public markets. Typically these vehicles are off-limits to most individual investors and are the province of institutional investors. Over the past decade, alternative investments have become an increasingly important part of the portfolios of pension and endowment funds.

Endowment funds in particular have embraced alternative investments over the past decade. Some, like John Bogle, might argue that this effort has been misplaced. In a speech to a group of university endowment managers, Bogle notes how a very simple portfolio made up of 50% domestic bonds and 50% domestic equities performed roughly in line with the average endowment fund over a 15-year period.[1] After taking into account risk, the simple indexed portfolio outperformed the machinations of the endowment funds. Bogle points out that for the smaller endowment funds that do have the resources of Ivy League institutions, a simple approach to investing may make more sense.

More so than in the standard asset classes, alternative investments rely far more on the performance of the fund manager. That is why larger institutions with larger budgets and staffs seem more adept at investing in alternatives. Alternatives are typically more costly, complex, leveraged, and illiquid than other investment vehicles. These are all things that we have cautioned investors to avoid in their investment journey. Despite that, alternatives are worth paying attention to for a couple of important reasons.

The first is that alternative investments are oftentimes accessible to individual investors via proxy. That is, there exist publicly traded vehicles that represent a good enough substitute for an alternative investment. For intrepid investors, these proxies may represent good diversification opportunities. Second, alternative investments often become mainstream investments over time. The ETF revolution is accelerating the process by which novel strategies and asset classes become available to the broader public.

Despite the hype, alternative investments are by no means perfect, but they are an important part of the financial landscape. In a certain sense, it is good that alternative investments are difficult to access. This keeps investors from venturing into areas in which they are not well versed. For intrepid investors, learning more about alternative investments makes perfect sense.

Hedge Funds

To say that hedge funds are an important part of the world of investing would be an understatement. Globally, hedge funds have some $2 trillion in assets under management, but that number likely understates their importance because many of these funds are often leveraged.[2] In addition to their size, they are also the most active market participants. One could argue that, on the margin, hedge funds set the price for most publicly traded securities.

Given this importance, hedge funds attract a great deal of attention from the media. It has long been the case that hedge fund managers are the stars of the world of investing. In many of the best books on investing of late, like *The Big Short* by Michael Lewis and *The Greatest Trade Ever* by Gregory Zuckerman, hedge fund managers are at the heart of the narratives. It wasn't always the case that hedge funds were so high profile. When hedge funds got off the ground in the 1950s, they were a mere curiosity. Not until the new century did hedge funds become an industry unto itself. The term *hedge fund* stems from that time, when the funds were run with "hedged" exposures in the hope of generating absolute returns. While hedge funds used to represent a particular investment strategy, now the name has more to do with the compensation structure than the actual strategy employed. The best managers today want to run hedge funds, and the biggest investors want to invest in hedge funds.

Hedge funds today are characterized more by their structure than their strategies. Hedge funds are loosely regulated, private investment partnerships that typically charge high fees in the hope that they generate high, positive, and uncorrelated returns. These funds often follow complex, opaque strategies and require investors to lock up their capital for an extended period of time. Hedge funds now follow every conceivable strategy, some of which are very highly focused on particular niches, whereas others range widely across asset classes and borders. Hedge funds are limited in that only accredited investors, i.e., wealthy individuals and institutions, can invest. Some of the largest and most accomplished hedge funds have been closed to new investors for some time now.

On the face of it, hedge funds have accomplished what they have set out to do. In a study, Ibbotson, Chen, and Zhu found that over a 15-year period the average hedge fund on average generated significant alpha in both bull and bear markets.[3] And on the face of it, the funds earned their very high fees. Other research shows hedge fund alpha declining over time and now nearing zero.[4] Another big problem is that hedge fund investors seem to have the same problem as individual investors. They buy high and sell low.

Using dollar-weighted returns, Dichev and Yu show that investors in hedge funds have historically earned much lower returns than previously thought.[5] A dollar-weighted measure of returns takes into account the actual dollar returns, not the percentage, that investors earn in hedge funds. When this measure is used, hedge fund returns no longer show any alpha and reliably lag the returns for the S&P 500.

These less-than-stellar results jibe with what Warren Buffett has been saying for some time now: "I think people who invest in hedge funds, in aggregate, are unlikely to do well. Hedge funds are in the midst of a fad. It's distinguished by an extraordinary amount of fees. If the world is paying hedge funds 2% and a percentage of the profits, and the losers fade away, then it won't be good for all investors. Obviously, some will do well, but not in aggregate."[6] It's not surprising that Warren Buffett entered into a highly publicized bet that the stock market, as measured by the S&P 500, would outperform a basket of hedge funds over a 10-year time period.[7]

Investors could likely live with this underperformance if hedge funds did a good job of protecting their returns during a market downturn. In the aftermath of the Internet bubble, hedge fund indexes were able to maintain positive performance. However, in the critical year of 2008, hedge funds experienced large losses, albeit smaller than the ones experienced by the overall stock market. This disappointing performance is largely a function of the popularity of hedge funds. One can see in the data that somewhere in the middle of the past decade hedge fund returns became more correlated with equity market returns.[8] The era of "hedged returns" has long since passed. Hedge funds are now, for the most part, mutual funds with good marketing and bloated fees.

Despite this evidence, there will always be a measure of hedge fund envy for some investors. The exclusivity of hedge funds and the media attention lavished on the very best managers will always make hedge funds seem like an opportunity that is just out of reach. The complexity, high costs, and illiquidity of hedge funds make them an inappropriate investment for the vast majority of investors. Given these very real hurdles to performance, most investors are fortunate that they cannot invest in hedge funds.

However, no one can deny the influence of hedge funds on the changing investment menu for individual investors. There are new ETFs that try to replicate the returns of various hedge fund strategies. In addition, a number of mutual funds now employ hedge fund–like strategies. Investors today can invest in strategies like merger arbitrage and long-short equity. Since these are mutual fund or ETF structures, individuals maintain a measure of liquidity, unlike hedge fund investors. Investors in these more public vehicles should not expect returns much better than that experienced by hedge fund investors themselves. Even if these funds avoid the problems of complexity and liquidity, they still run into the issue of higher-than-average fees and turnover.

One of the themes of this chapter on alternative investments is that for intrepid investors there are often publicly traded companies or vehicles that proxy for alternative investments. This sort of approach definitely adds portfolio complexity but can quench the desire of some investors to participate in this arena. So for investors who think that hedge funds will remain a preferred home for investor capital, there are some publicly traded companies whose main business is to manage hedge funds. In that respect, you can potentially earn the benefits of the hedge fund business model without the risk of actually investing in a fund.

Hedge funds have a certain mystique that is, despite the mixed performance record, not going away any time soon. Some argue that recent hedge fund performance shows that they are "morphing into long-only funds."[9] If that is the case, then individual investors need not give hedge funds a second thought. Investors today have easy and cheap access to all manner of long-only strategies while avoiding the high fees and complexity of hedge funds.

Private Equity and Venture Capital

Hedge funds are a much-sought-after alternative investment because they promise both exclusivity and an attractive risk-return trade-off. Hedge funds by and large use publicly traded instruments to try to create attractive returns. The other significant part of the alternative investment industry works outside the public markets. Private equity and venture capital generate returns with private companies. For many investors, the exclusivity of private investment drives their interest and clouds their judgment about the actual investment merits.

Many investors in the past decade became enamored with the so-called endowment model of investing. This model strives to replicate the portfolios of elite university endowment funds that emphasize alternative investments in an attempt to generate returns uncorrelated with the financial markets. In their book *The Ivy Portfolio*, Mebane T. Faber and Eric W. Richardson discuss the endowment fund model and its applicability to individual investors.[10] The financial crisis and subsequent bear market highlighted the dependence of this model on the health of the overall economy and financial system.

The challenge for most investors is that both private equity and venture capital represent leveraged bets on the equity market. What this means in practical terms is that the performance of private equity and venture capital relies on a strong stock market—more specifically, a stock market that is receptive to IPOs. In the case of venture capital, the IPOs are start-up companies operating in the broadly defined technology sector. In the case of private equity, the goal is to bring companies public that were once private and that are now carrying significant debt. While there is increasing merger and acquisition activity among private investors, the public markets still set the valuation of companies on the margin.

So in this regard, private investments don't really represent a way of reducing portfolio risk. By all accounts, these investments are riskier than the overall equity markets. This additional equitylike risk would be acceptable if it came along with enhanced returns. That is indeed what private equity investors say they are counting on.[11] The evidence is there for private equity outperforming public markets over long periods of time.[12] The problem is that once you take into account the liquidity risk that private equity investments face, their return premium is essentially eliminated. Franzoni, Nowak, and Phalippou find that this liquidity risk is the same risk facing investments in public markets. So not only does private equity not generate abnormal returns, but the perceived diversification benefits of private equity are also illusory.[13]

There is a bigger problem facing investors in private equity, and that is one we keep revisiting—high fees. Private equity and venture capital, like their hedge fund brethren, typically earn both a management fee on the funds they manage and performance fees on successful investments. These fees all add up over the typical life of a private equity or venture capital fund. Private equity and venture capital may represent some of the smartest investors around, but the investors in their funds ultimately pay for the privilege of investing alongside them many times over.

Kaplan and Schoar find that there is a great deal of heterogeneity in the returns to private equity, meaning the top firms tend to generate the highest return and repeat that performance over time.[14] The only sensible strategy for investing in private equity and venture capital seems to be to invest with the top firms that have a demonstrated track record of outperformance. The problem is that those firms are largely closed to new investors and never were open to individual investors.

The challenge in venture capital is even worse because in large part there is far less investment capacity for venture capital than there is for private equity. There is no shortage of investors who want to invest in venture capital to find the next Google or Facebook. The challenge is that the high-profile "wins" for venture capital usually mask a slew of lower-profile failures. This hindsight bias makes low-frequency, high-profile events like IPOs seem more likely than in reality. For intrepid investors, there are opportunities in the public markets to act like a private investor.

In the past few years, it has become increasingly popular for the large private equity managers to go public. For example, industry leaders like KKR and the Blackstone Group have chosen to become publicly traded. The reasons for this are many, including succession planning and a desire to become more diversified alternative investment firms. Whatever the motivation, they now provide investors with a way to play private equity without having to invest in an underlying fund. Other investors are focused on the niche of business development companies that act in many ways like private equity firms. In both of the above cases, there are even ETFs that allow for instant diversification. Venture capital is a bit tougher, but there are some public companies that act like venture capital firms. These proxy plays are not perfect substitutes for the real thing and require a level of research beyond the scope of most investors' skills.

David Swensen, who is a leading expert in endowment fund investing, has a message for individual investors when it comes to alternative investments like hedge funds, private equity, and venture capital. He recommends that "prudent investors avoid asset classes that derive returns primarily from market-beating strategies."[15] Swensen notes the difficult challenge that lies in trying to identify (and invest) in superior managers.

The firms engaged in private equity and venture capital play a key role in the functioning of the market economy. It would be hard to imagine the markets without them. In a very real sense, all investors benefit from the work of private equity professionals and venture capitalists. The challenge for average investors is that they don't have easy, inexpensive access to these asset classes. Whatever access they do have is mediated with layers of fees upon fees. As with most alternative investments, the allure of private investments is less than meets the eye.

Options

Alternative investments need not be limited to novel asset classes. Options are not novel in that they are based on or derivative of already existing securities. However, options-related strategies can generate novel returns not accessible in other ways. Most analysts would not include options-related strategies in a chapter on alternative investments. A quick survey of options strategies should show that the inherent flexibility of options makes them a unique approach to generating novel return streams.

Any survey of options strategies is going to be incomplete. Stated simply, options are contracts to buy or sell an asset in the future at a set price. Because an option's price is derived in part from the price of other assets, options are considered derivatives like futures contracts, which we will discuss later in the chapter. In the past decade, investors have really taken to options trading. According to data from the Options Clearing Corporation, the average daily options volume has gone up sixfold from 2001 to 2011.[16]

The malleability of options makes them good vehicles for experienced traders who are looking for novel ways to express market opinions. As Jared Woodard writes: "So what are options good for? Options allow you to say more, and to say it more precisely than you ever could with stocks or futures alone. Everyone implicitly thinks in terms of options...So one of the benefits of executing trades with options instead of just stock alone is that options allow you to say all the things you wanted to say already, but couldn't."[17]

The challenge for novice investors is to recognize that the inherent flexibility of options means that options can be abused as easily as they can be used thoughtfully. Earlier we noted how complexity, illiquidity, and leverage are three prime portfolio killers. For better or worse, options trading strategies hit all these danger zones. Options pricing is complex. A Nobel Prize in Economics was awarded for the creation of the theory behind options pricing. It is best to think of options and options strategies as a whole other language that needs to be learned.

By definition, options are less liquid than their underlying security. Many stocks and ETFs do not have listed options. For traders, illiquidity makes profiting from options strategies more difficult. One of the aspects most interesting to traders is that options and their lower prices make it possible to take positions not possible using the underlying security. This is also where novice investors get into trouble. Investors can unwittingly take on bigger, more leveraged positions without being fully aware they are doing so.

Despite these potential pitfalls, options are flexible and allow investors to create positions that can, not will, profit from different market conditions. An options trader has many more degrees of freedom than a trader who can only go long and short. Options pricing depends on implied volatility. Implied volatility is essentially the level of volatility that traders expect an asset to undergo during the life of the option. In effect, options traders aren't trading stocks; they are trading expectations about volatility.

To demonstrate just how meta markets can become over time, a "derivative of a derivative," the CBOE Volatility Index, or VIX, has become increasingly popular with market participants. This index tracks the implied volatility of options traded on the S&P 500. Among its many purposes, the VIX serves as a "fear index." When traders bid up options prices (and volatility), this is indicative of market fear. So the options market does more than serve as a means of trading; it provides market participants with further information as well. The VIX, and the futures that trade based on it, is also the basis for a number of popular ETPs. Thus, not only can traders track market fear; they can trade it explicitly.

One reason why options have become more popular over the past decade is that they provide investors a means of hedging their underlying equity position. The past decade has been a volatile disappointment to most investors, and options-related strategies have been one way investors have tried to cope. For example, the most common systematic options strategy that investors use is the covered call, often known as the buy-write strategy. A buy-write strategy involves writing (or selling) call options on an underlying equity position. In exchange for giving up further upside on the underlying position, the seller of the call receives a premium. Contrary to popular opinion, this stream of revenue is not income or a dividend. Call premiums are compensation for a trade-off for forgoing further profit on the upside. In an environment where stock prices have gone nowhere over a long period of time, a buy-write strategy has outperformed.

The disappointment of traditional portfolio management tools in the aftermath of the financial crisis has made many investors fearful of previously unrecognized risks. These so-called tail risks are often hedged by purchasing far-out-of-the-money options that will become valuable if markets fall dramatically. These strategies are costly to implement and are profitable only rarely. The cost of tail risk strategies derives in part from the need to constantly be buying options that largely expire worthless. The bigger question investors who feel like they need tail risk protection should ask themselves is whether they are taking on too much equity market risk to begin with.[18]

In contrast, there is reason to believe that options markets generally overprice risk, i.e., volatility. This volatility risk premium is pronounced in the market for equity index options.[19] One explanation is that investors demanding portfolio protection bid up the price of options beyond their fair value. This systematic overpricing is an opportunity for investors willing and able to sell options premiums. That is not to say that this sort of strategy is without risk. In fact, selling options is riskiest in times of severe market stress—exactly the time when most investors are craving safety, not additional volatility.

We have limited our discussion of options to systematic strategies in part because these are the only strategies we can define and analyze. Any discussion of options is, by definition, incomplete because the world of options is infinitely complex. In this complexity, however, lie a range of strategies that investors can use to literally sculpt returns. The use of options comes with costs, not least of which is the educational efforts needed to become competent in their use. However, options-related strategies do represent real alternatives to the returns available on standard asset classes.

Futures

Options and futures are lumped together in the world of finance as derivatives. Futures are more straightforward instruments than options. Futures contracts represent an agreement to buy or sell a commodity (broadly defined) at a certain price on a future date. Futures were once limited to commodities, but long ago they were extended to include financial instruments as well.

Recently, investors looking for alternatives have begun focusing on the commodities futures markets. A lot of this interest can be traced back to 2006 when a paper on commodities futures by Gorton and Rouwenhorst and another by Erb and Harvey documented the historical returns of commodities futures.[20] Investors and fund marketers quickly grabbed on to the results that showed commodities futures having equitylike returns along with a negative correlation with financial assets. This result was the holy grail for investors. Not surprisingly, the investment management industry took note. Many investment advisors responded to these findings by putting commodities futures funds into their recommended portfolio allocations. As a result, it is estimated that since 2006 the amount of assets under management dedicated to commodity investing has tripled.[21]

Unfortunately many investors misunderstood the more nuanced story in these results. Investments in commodities futures are not equivalent to investments in the underlying commodities themselves. The return on commodities futures is affected not only by changes in the spot price of the commodity but also by interest rates and what is commonly referred to as the roll return. As futures contracts expire, investors transitioning from one futures contract to the next will generate the roll return. The roll return historically had been positive for the commodity universe. However, the rush of capital into the commodities futures market greatly affected the pricing of these contracts and turned the roll return negative.

There is one approach to commodity investing that is based on the changing nature of the structure of commodities futures. A long-short approach to commodity investing that goes long commodities in backwardation and short commodities in contango has some interesting properties. Miffre finds that in comparison with other approaches, a long-short approach generates higher returns, lower volatility, and a lower correlation with equity markets.[22] Unfortunately for most investors, this approach was not widely followed. Only recently has an ETP launched that follows this sort of commodity indexing strategy.

This financialization of the commodities markets shows up in another way as well. Commodities now trade more like other financial assets than they did prior to this era. This negates some of the original attraction investors saw in an investment in commodities futures. The financialization of commodities played out in a prominent fashion in the world of ETPs. We already noted how investors in natural gas and oil ETFs were disappointed that their funds lagged the returns on the underlying commodities. Fund advisors have responded to this disappointment with new and modified products to try to offset the effects of negative roll returns. A more sophisticated approach to commodities futures selection can help in regard to the roll return, but it can do nothing about the increasing correlation between commodities and financial assets. The diversification paradox once again rears its ugly head. Not only do new investors in commodities not experience the returns they sought, but they ruin the game for early adopters as well.

While the commodities futures boom was going on, another approach to investing in the futures market also was being implemented—managed futures. Instead of trying to create static long exposure to commodities, managed futures managers try to generate active returns from the global universe of futures contracts, including both commodities and financial futures. In this light, managed futures can be thought of as the cousin of hedge funds. However, managed futures differ from hedge funds in a very important fashion.

Historically, managed futures have had a very low correlation with the equity market and with various hedge fund strategies. In fact, managed futures strategies shine in periods of equity market turmoil. In 2008, an index of managed futures strategies was up some 14% in a year when equity markets plunged and hedge fund strategies fell some 18%.[23] Research shows that almost all of the excess returns on managed futures come in periods when the equity markets are weak.[24] On the flip side, this also means that managed futures strategies can lag while other strategies prosper. Despite this relative volatility, investors continue to pour money into managed futures in the hope of finding some true diversification.

The performance of managed futures is not without controversy.[25] Many commodity trading advisors, or CTAs, charge fees that are similar to those charged by hedge funds. This means that a significant portion of these returns accrue to the manager and not the investor. Most CTAs can also be characterized as systematic trend followers. This makes sense given the performance of momentum-related strategies. However, this also means that their performance can be mimicked by indexes that do not require such high fees. The fact that these strategies are in a certain sense in the public domain has made vehicles available to the wider public.

There are now mutual funds and ETPs that track various indexes based on trend-following managed futures strategies, and investors should expect even more in the future. The question for investors is whether managed futures strategies will, like other popular strategies, fall victim to the diversification paradox. Managed futures strategies do have the historical weight of the momentum effect behind them. That being said, investors who buy into managed futures should do so for the promise of diversification and with a wary eye on too much money entering into the strategy.

Hard Assets

The desire of investors to diversify beyond financial assets is understandable. There is an almost primal urge on the part of investors to own tangible assets. These tangible, or hard, assets are best thought of as land or as products that are grown on or extracted from the land. Hard assets include investments in real estate, energy, metals, and agricultural products. We have seen that in many cases the futures market provides, at best, an approximation of the returns on some of these commodities. Investors interested in hard assets therefore have to turn to other means of getting this exposure.

Gold is one of the most discussed tangible assets and is in a certain way a special case. We will discuss gold further in the next section. Gold and other precious metals are the exception to the rule when discussing hard assets because investors today can get ready access to the commodity itself. Other hard assets are more difficult to access.

Institutional investors have the means to get direct access to hard assets. These institutions can invest in funds that hold oil and gas properties, timberland, farmland, and real estate. The rest of us have to be satisfied with indirect access to these hard assets through asset classes that include investments in real estate investment trusts (REITs), timber companies, oil and gas exploration companies, and miners. These asset classes are not a bad option. For instance, investors who gain exposure to hard assets via publicly traded vehicles can do so in an inexpensive fashion and have ready liquidity.

The other piece of good news is that an investor in the broad stock market already has some exposure to hard assets. For example, an investor in the S&P 500 already has a nearly 16% exposure to energy and materials companies. In light of this, some advisors recommend that investors need not have any additional allocation to hard assets. One hard asset class that is widely used is REITs. Real estate is a bit of an exception in the world of hard assets in part because of the size of the opportunity. According to the National Association of Real Estate Investment Trusts (NAREIT), the REIT industry at the end of 2010 covered companies with a value of some $389 billion. This fact and the higher dividend yield that REITs generate make it a popular asset class. Investors interested in real estate, both in the United States and overseas, have easy access to this asset class via funds and ETFs.

This easy access also highlights the problem with REITs as a portfolio diversifier. As REITs have become mainstream vehicles, their correlation with the equity markets has increased.[26] Research shows that since 2001, the correlation between REITs and the S&P 500 has steadily increased. In 2008 in the midst of the financial crisis, a NAREIT index of REITs generated a total return of −37%, largely matching the horrible performance of the stock market. Over the long run, the performance of REITs is generally going to match the returns to the underlying properties; however, in the short term, REITs can get caught up in market turmoil.

An investment in hard assets represents a natural hedge. We all consume various commodities, albeit in different proportions. A commodity like gasoline is one of the most visible prices we experience on a daily basis. Therefore, an investment in commodities and hard assets represents a hedge against inflation. But hard assets can only represent a hedge if investors choose to be disciplined and rebalance their portfolios over time. For some investors who already have a well-diversified portfolio, owning an asset that can provide some protection against commodity inflation can be a comfort.

The range of hard assets is dizzyingly wide: from the biggies like energy and real estate to more narrow niches like timber and rare earth metals. For intrepid investors, there exist ETFs or companies that proxy for this exposure. However, one hard asset stands alone, partly because of the media attention it receives and partly because it has played a prominent role in society for millennia, and that is gold.

Gold

Few investments are more controversial than gold due in large part to the fervor that many investors have for the shiny metal. For these investors, gold represents the one true money that has served as a store of value for thousands of years and is the perfect investment in any potential economic environment. In opposition, an equally boisterous camp notes that gold has no intrinsic value. These skeptics point out that gold cannot be valued by conventional financial models and is prone to booms and busts, depending on the collective psyche of investors.

Of late the psyche of investors has led them to gold. For a brief moment in August 2010, the SPDR Gold Shares passed the SPDR S&P 500 ETF in terms of assets under management.[27] In that same week, the polling firm Gallup reported that Americans had chosen gold over real estate and stocks as the "best long-term investment."[28] Companies that store gold bullion are running out of space as they try to keep up with demand.[29] Given the strong performance of gold, the uncertainty surrounding the U.S. economy, and the ongoing malaise in the real estate and stock markets, this result shouldn't be that surprising. Gold has become the ultimate "none-of-the-above investment." At the beginning of the new century, this result would have surprised everyone but the hard-core goldbugs.

This skepticism would have arisen from the fact that after a gold bubble popped in 1980, gold, had done very little pricewise for the next two decades. During the 1980s and 1990s, gold prices moved in a broad range while financial assets like equities and bonds took center stage. It is not a coincidence that gold began its decade-long bull market right around the time the Internet bubble was popping. Since 2001, the price of gold has moved higher every year for 11 years straight. This kind of run has not happened since 1920.[30]

For good reason, gold has held a role in commerce since biblical times. Kings and rulers have gone to great lengths, oftentimes to their own detriment, to obtain gold. One reason for this is the unique chemical properties of gold. A look at the periodic table of elements shows only five real candidates for a store of value, including gold, silver, and platinum. Unfortunately silver tarnishes, and platinum has too high a melting point, leaving gold as the only logical candidate for money.[31] While gold has been an obsession for millennia, it no longer serves in any meaningful way as money.

Another thing that has changed in the past 10 years is that gold has become a highly liquid and tradable commodity. The launch of the SPDR Gold Shares has altered the way in which investors hold and trade the precious metal. Gold is now accessible to investors both large and small and can be traded at the click of a mouse. Now that gold has been "ETF-ized," it will be interesting to see if, and how, gold pricing has changed. We will not likely find this out until gold experiences a true bear market.

For some investors, a gold ETF is a passing curiosity. For example, the Permanent Portfolio mutual fund has held and continues to hold some 20% of its assets in physical gold. Other investors are far more interested in being able to accurately value and trade gold. Unfortunately for investors, models that accurately forecast the price of gold based on either fundamental (supply and demand) or economic (inflation) factors are few and far between.

The one factor that does seem to play an important role in gold pricing is real interest rates. Eddy Elfenbein demonstrates that when real interest rates are low, the price of gold tends to increase and that as real interest rates rise, the price of gold tends to fall.[32] When real interest rates are low, the opportunity cost of holding gold is low, and investors give up little to hold the metal. However, when interest rates rise, then gold, with no yield to speak of, pales in comparison. This explains in part why the decades of the 1980s and 1990s were such a poor time for the owners of gold.

Gold represents only a very small fraction of world wealth; therefore, every investor can't meaningfully increase his gold holdings. There just isn't enough of it to go around. The question for investors is, what role should gold play, if any, in a broadly diversified portfolio? The answer lies somewhere in between what the gold skeptics and goldbugs would recommend. Gold still serves, even after its ETF-ization, as a decent portfolio diversifier. Diversified investors can pick a rebalancing bonus by holding gold since it often moves out of sync with financial assets.

Some investors like to hold the shares of gold miners in lieu of gold. In theory this makes sense because investors can often earn dividends from these companies. However, there are two big problems with this strategy. The first is that the price of gold miners can diverge from the price of gold for long periods of time. Second, among gold miners there is often political risk because their mines are often located in countries where the rule of law is tenuous, at best. Investors can look at gold miners, and other precious metals miners, as a substitute for gold bullion, but they should not expect a perfect correlation with gold or substantial outperformance.

In his book on the history of gold, *The Power of Gold*, Peter L. Bernstein writes that "gold reflects the universal quest for eternal life—the ultimate certainty and escape from risk." Bernstein notes that people have the tendency to fall for the illusion of gold when they "take the symbolism of gold too seriously."[33] Anyone having read this far should recognize that there is no escape from risk, not in gold or any other alternative investment. We should not discount the long world history and unique role of gold, nor should we place too much faith in gold. We are all seeking the perfect investment, but gold fails that test like all the other assets that have come in its wake.

Key Takeaways

+ There is no perfect investment, but investors are constantly searching for alternatives that can provide higher returns, lower risk, or both.

- Hedge funds play an important role in the financial markets, but their performance, weighed down by high fees and increased competition, has deteriorated and become more marketlike over time.
- Private equity and venture capital play an important role in the economy, but the return picture for them is mixed. In any event, individual investors have at best limited access to these investment vehicles.
- Options strategies allow investors to express all manner of market views, including hedging risks. However, options strategies come with a steep learning curve, higher costs, and illiquidity.
- Managed futures have historically been good portfolio diversifiers generating returns in times of market stress.
- Hard assets represent another diversification opportunity for investors, especially in light of their ability to partially hedge inflation risk.
- Gold has been an object of desire for millennia but, like other alternative assets, fails the test of a perfect investment.

10

Behaviors and Biases

NEARLY EVERY STUDY OF FORECASTING IN ECONOMICS AND FINANCE shows that we human beings are poor predictors of the future. Much of what passes for analysis on Wall Street is really just veiled, half-formed forecasts about the future. As Barry Ritholtz writes: "I wish an SEC-mandated disclosure accompanied all pundit forecasts: 'The undersigned states that he has no idea what's going to happen in the future, and hereby declares that this prediction is merely a wildly unsupported speculation.'"[1] Given our collective inability to forecast the future, why do we all persist in doing so?

Some believe like Philip Tetlock, who wrote a notable book on the topic of forecasting and prediction, that we humans have an innate need to feel that the world around us is in some fashion predictable.[2] Tetlock states: "There are a lot of psychologists who believe that there is a hard-wired human need to believe that we live in a fundamentally predictable and controllable universe. There's also a widespread belief among psychologists that people try hard to impose causal order on the world around them, even when those phenomena are random."[3]

It is because we humans hate randomness that many investors have a weakness for pundits with strongly held opinions about the future. The markets often feel like they are a messy, paradoxical place. A singular vision about where the markets are headed, even if it is of dubious value, feeds our need for a more predictable world. Investors can get especially sucked in when a market pundit actually gets a big market call correct.

Analysts who correctly called the market crash of 1987 have been living off that call ever since then. The irony is that research shows that those forecasters who get these "big calls" correct turn out to have the worst overall track records. Denrell and Fang show that this has to do in part with how forecasters take into account the full range of available information.[4] The trouble is that those forecasters who often take a more measured, probabilistic approach do not feed our need for certainty.

As James Montier notes, the problem is that the worst forecasters are oftentimes the most overconfident.[5] Overconfidence is a finding well documented in psychology and behavioral finance, based on the fact that people are routinely surprised by future outcomes. We humans have a persistent belief in our own skills, or that we are above average. Montier also notes that when forecasters are confronted with their erroneous forecasts, they are likely to choose from a list of excuses to avoid having to face up to their failures. Overconfidence is a prime driver of many ill-suited investing behaviors in part because it does not require us to be humble in the face of our own shortcomings.

There are better ways to forecast than to follow the advice of a handful of economists who are doing little more than spinning stories about historical results. Focusing on real-world indicators is a better approach. Earlier in the book, we saw how a simple economic forecasting model based on the slope of the yield curve outperformed economists' predictions. By focusing on indicators that take their cue from real-world decision makers, like the various purchasing manager indexes, we can do a much better job than the chattering classes.[6]

If forecasting the future is largely a waste of time, what should investors do? One approach is to spend more time preparing for unfavorable scenarios. We live a world that is generating all manner of surprises, both man-made and natural. Identifying those major risks and their potential costs is a big first step in creating a forecast-free approach to investing. This requires us to let go of the illusion that we can forecast the future and embrace a wider range of potential future outcomes.

We have already seen that stock and bond markets can go down and stay down longer than commonly believed. Investors should take into account scenarios in which the financial markets do not provide positive returns, but in fact generate negative returns. This kind of contingency planning focuses on the downside risks and lets the upside take care of itself. Above all, it meets our goal to move our portfolios, largely intact, from one period to the next.

As we have discussed, strategies like broad diversification and indexed investing have merit in part because they do not rely on forecasts. These strategies recognize our inability to predict with any great precision what certain asset classes or stocks are going to do. By saying "I don't know" to the question of future returns and by diversifying widely and indexing, investors follow a broad-brush approach to investing, capturing capital markets returns in an unbiased way.

The two main investment strategies discussed, value and momentum investing, do not use forecasts as a part of the process. Momentum investing is explicitly backward looking in that it uses past returns as a tool to rank potential investments; the only assumption is that recent past returns tend to persist. Value investing and the search for a margin of safety are necessarily backward looking. Value investors focus on the disparity between the current price of the stock and the true underlying value of the company. Because value and momentum investing both require analyzing the present much more than the future, they avoid the forecasting fallacy. In so doing, these two approaches to active investing are likely to be more consistent and sustainable.

The "prediction addiction," as Jason Zweig calls it, is a strong one.[7] We can, as Zweig suggests, take steps to restrict our ability to tinker with our portfolios, like setting up automatic investment plans. We can also try and test our ideas in a systematic fashion before we put them at risk in the market. Zweig notes how paper trading can be a way to test our capabilities in a lower-risk setting. More often than not, we will find that our ideas are not all that great in practice.

This idea of getting our portfolios largely intact from one time period to the next goes hand in hand with the need to avoid the folly of forecasting. A focus on the risks we face is far more important than making some one-time market call. It is not for nothing that *Abnormal Returns* has as its subtitle *A Forecast-Free Investment Blog*.

Skill versus Luck

Track records are the stuff of which Wall Street careers are made. The first thing potential investors want to know about a fund before they invest is the fund's past performance. Some managers have made careers off one or two good years of performance. Investors flock to hot performers despite the fact that the admonition "Past performance is not indicative of future results" appears on nearly every piece of fund marketing material. The truth is that in many cases we simply don't have much more in the way of information than past performance. The whole idea of active investment management revolves around the idea of identifying and paying for skilled managers. Nobody wants to pay a manager whose results are based solely on luck.

It is therefore difficult to distinguish the degree to which skill and luck play a role in investor performance. First, we should recognize that investing is a field in which both skill and luck do play a role. Investing is often compared to gambling and most often to poker, and for good reason. There is no doubt that chance, or the cards drawn, plays a role in poker outcomes. Recent research also shows, contrary to what the authorities say, that poker on the whole is a game of skill.[8] Unfortunately for investors, our ability to identify skilled investment managers is much more difficult than identifying skilled poker players.

Some argue that finding skill in the world of professional investors like mutual fund managers is like finding a needle in a haystack. Fama and French examine the performance of mutual fund managers and find that before expenses the top 5% or so of managers demonstrate some skill compared with chance.[9] The performance picture worsens dramatically once you take into account expenses, which largely wipe out the benefit of skill in the best managers. You can guess what it does for the rest of the mutual fund manager crowd. Anyone looking for skilled managers needs to recognize that identifying skill isn't enough. The challenge is identifying managers whose skill outweighs whatever fees they charge investors.

There is reason to believe that it has become more difficult over time to beat the market. There is little doubt that the investment management industry has become more sophisticated and professional over time. This professionalization also explains why it is so hard for fund managers to beat the market. This phenomenon is what Michael Mauboussin calls the "paradox of skill." Mauboussin writes: "The paradox of skill is one reason it is so hard to beat the market. Everybody is smart, has incredible technology, and the government has worked to ensure that the dissemination of information is uniform. So information gets priced into stocks quickly and it's very difficult to find mispricing. By the way, the standard deviation of mutual fund returns has been declining for the last 50 years or so, just as it has for batting averages."[10]

Just like in baseball, investing is awash in statistics. Unfortunately for investors, in most cases we simply don't have enough data to say with any statistical confidence whether a manager's performance was due to skill as opposed to luck. Baseball players get hundreds of at-bats in a single season. Investment managers need to be around nine years, using monthly returns, just to generate a hundred observations. As Aswath Damodaran writes, "One problem that we face in portfolio management and corporate finance is that we get to observe outcomes too infrequently, making it difficult to separate luck from skill."[11]

One measure that is appealing in its simplicity is streaks. Andrew Mauboussin and Samuel Arbesman demonstrate that streaks in fund performance indicate the existence of differential skill.[12] Streaks, and the consistency they imply, are a measure that appeals to our intuition. As any baseball fan knows, there is nothing more frustrating than a skilled but inconsistent baseball player. Streaks can occur in part by chance, but the existence of streaks can help investors distinguish among managers.

Just as the existence of streaks indicates skill, the existence of luck implies mean reversion. Mean reversion simply means that lucky streaks come to an end. There are few corners of the investing world that are not touched by mean reversion. Michael Mauboussin writes: "Importantly, reversion to the mean in the investment business extends well beyond the results for mutual funds. It applies to classifications within the market (small capitalization versus large capitalization, or value versus growth), across asset classes (bonds versus stocks) and spans geographic boundaries (U.S. versus non-U.S.). There are few corners of the investment business where reversion to the mean does not hold sway."[13] Given the importance of mean reversion, you would think that investors would be acutely aware of its role when making decisions. Research shows that investors overreact to recent performance, often to their own detriment.

One way in which investors can tamp down on their desire to overreact to recent performance is to become more informed, and comfortable, with an investor's investment philosophy and performance. Transparency plays a big role. Managers who are willing and able to communicate a clear investment process give investors some small comfort that the process is reproducible over time. As well, managers who are willing to acknowledge that luck plays an important role show that they recognize that the world of investing is a challenging place for even the most skilled.

In the end, we all need to be comfortable with our own investment decision making and to trust that a careful approach will yield positive results over time. Howard Marks says it well: "In the long run, there's no reasonable alternative to believing that good decisions will lead to investment profits. In the short run, however, we must be stoic when they don't."[14] We live in a world filled with randomness, and recognizing this is an important step in dealing with our investments in a more measured and mature fashion.

Confirmation Bias

We have seen that one reason why investors think it is easy to beat the market is that they don't recognize that both skill and luck play a role in investor performance. Another reason that investors believe they can beat the market is that they ignore evidence to the contrary. This issue is not limited to when we are dealing with investments but is a persistent mental model we access all the time. Simply put, "The confirmation bias is the tendency to seek information that confirms prior conclusions and to ignore evidence to the contrary."[15]

Confirmation bias is a persistent feature of the financial markets. All underperforming fund managers will point to the performance figures that put themselves in the best light. This is the case with individual investors as well. Earlier we discussed the necessity of keeping accurate records when tracking our own investment performance. This is important because as Meir Statman writes: "Investors who believe they can pick winning stocks are regularly oblivious to their losing record, recording wins as evidence confirming their stock-picking skills but neglecting to record losses as disconfirming evidence."[16] When it comes to our own skills, we are more than happy to delude ourselves by ignoring the hard truths.

It's not hard to see how our desire to focus on information that confirms our already existing beliefs could be a liability when it comes to investing. The fact is that even the very best investors are wrong a lot of the time. In a previous chapter, we saw that it is possible to be wrong most of the time but still be a profitable trader. Successful investors recognize that it is not a sin to be wrong, but it is a sin to stay wrong. Every trader will tell you that cutting your losses is the key to surviving in the markets. It doesn't matter why you are wrong, but recognizing you are wrong will save you from portfolio-killing events such as riding a favorite stock all the way down into bankruptcy.

The question is why are we stuck with this mental model that makes us so willing to overlook a broader reality. Michael Mauboussin notes how confirmation bias is really all about keeping the external world consistent with our own version of the world.[17] Constantly questioning every idea we hold with new data and information would not only be time consuming but also exhausting. Confirmation bias allows us to stop thinking about an issue and relieves us from the need to act or react. We humans simply don't have enough mental bandwidth to be constantly testing our core beliefs.

Not only is confirmation bias a flaw in the way we process information; it is also present in the way we take in information. With confirmation bias at work, we perceive information in a selective fashion. On one level, we make conscious decisions on what information to take in: we watch Fox News or MSNBC; we read the *Wall Street Journal* or the *New York Times*. On a subconscious level, we simply never perceive information that may not fit with our worldview. While the selective intake of information is dangerous enough, our increasingly electronic search for information can lead us astray.

With so much of information coming from online sources, we need to be aware of the ways that confirmation bias can happen without any action on our part. Eli Pariser in *The Filter Bubble* highlights the many ways in which online information providers tailor the things we see based on some profile they have of us. In some ways, this predictive search can be helpful. When we search for a pizza place, it is helpful to know where we are so as to generate geographically relevant results. The ultimate goal of this online profiling isn't necessarily to best inform us; rather it is designed to get us to click or interact with the site in question. As Pariser writes: "The filter bubble tends to dramatically amplify confirmation bias—in a way it's designed to. Consuming information that conforms to our ideas of the world is easy and pleasurable; consuming information that challenges us to think in new ways or question our assumptions is frustrating and difficult."[18]

Given all the internal and external forces working against us as investors, it is imperative that we work to try and offset the effects of confirmation bias. In a sense, we need to constantly be asking, "Tell me something I don't already know"—because there is a good chance the markets already know it. There are three ways in which we can try and work against confirmation bias.

The first is to be conscious of the risks of the filter bubble. Personalization on the Internet is a feature and not a bug. Pariser notes the best thing we can do is try to get outside our comfort zone and visit sites that stretch our thinking. A conscious effort to expand our influences can go a long way in opening up different ways of thinking.

Second, we need to actively search out discomfiting evidence. If we have a strong belief about a company, we need to consciously seek out evidence that is at odds with our view. This is admittedly hard work, but it is a necessary antidote to confirmation bias.

The third way is to expose our ideas to others. On the face of it, confirmation bias shouldn't exist. It is not a helpful adaptation. However, the argumentative theory posits that we have confirmation bias because it makes us more effective advocates for a position. That is why the first two remedies we recommend to combat confirmation bias may be of limited use. Hugo Mercier states: "On the other hand, when people are able to discuss their ideas with other people who disagree with them, then the confirmation biases of the different participants will balance each other out, and the group will be able to focus on the best solution. Thus, reasoning works much better in groups."[19]

We humans are beset with all types of biases, some that are helpful, some that are benign, and some, like the confirmation bias, that can be harmful at times. The best investors recognize that they are likely to be wrong on a pretty frequent basis and take steps to minimize the harm that comes when errors occur. The worst situation for investors to be in is to be wrong and not have the tools to turn their thinking around.

Invest More Like a Woman

If you were offered a way to increase your returns *while* lowering your risk, you would think it was some sort of cheap ploy. There are very few free lunches in the markets, but there is a very simple way to generate better risk-adjusted returns. Invest more like a woman. For the 51% percent of you who are women, this should be pretty easy. For the other 49% who professionally manage the vast majority of funds, it might be a more daunting task.

You wouldn't think this gender balance was the case when you look at the financial services industry in general and the money management business in particular. But even a cursory glance at the boardrooms or trading floors would show a lack of women. The numbers bear this out as well. Recent surveys show that women manage only 10% of mutual funds and only 3% of hedge funds.[20] Some argue that the evidence points toward a prejudice against females in finance.[21] No matter how you parse the data, this seems like a market failure.

This disparity is all the more confounding when research shows that women generate returns that are equal to if not greater than what men achieve. One study showed male fund managers trading more aggressively and not sticking to their investment mandate. However, this activity didn't translate into higher risk-adjusted returns for male managers.[22] According to these results, a female-managed fund is more likely to play nicely with other funds in a portfolio.

The danger of overconfidence and its impact on investing is a recurring theme throughout this book. Overconfidence manifests itself in overaggressive trading. A now classic study by Barber and Odean documented that men trade more than women, thereby reducing their returns.[23] This effect is even more pronounced among single men. Therefore, if men took a less frenetic approach toward investing, they could likely generate higher returns.

Taking a more measured approach may be more important in difficult markets. An index of hedge funds of which half were female-run outperformed dramatically a broader index of hedge funds in the turbulent market year of 2008.[24] This performance led in part to this conclusion: "The tendency of many women investment managers to be more patient and consistent, as well as their tendency to examine more conflicting data when making investment decisions, adds a moderating effect to highly turbulent markets and may be especially significant during market downturns."[25]

Maybe we shouldn't be so hard on men. It may simply be the case that their biology is working against them in some very fundamental ways. Research has shown a link between testosterone levels and risk taking. From a trading perspective, one could see how a little testosterone could help a trader. However, an overabundance of testosterone, which shows up after a series of winning trades, could lead to overly risky trades.[26] Another hormone-related effect is evident as well. Cortisol levels, which are associated with stress, show up during periods of market volatility. Over long periods of time, it seems that elevated cortisol levels can have real, negative effects on health and mood.

If you extrapolate this behavior to the markets as a whole, you could see how it could generate bull and bear markets. Researcher John Coates stated: "Maybe bubbles and crashes are coming from these steroids . . . maybe if more women and older men were trading, the markets would be more stable."[27]

We certainly can't legislate who trades in the markets or whom people hire to manage their money. The issue of gender equity in the financial services industry is beyond the scope of this discussion. However, we can highlight the ways in which female investors excel so that you can try to apply those ideas to your investment approach.

One author argues that female investors have a great deal in common with the way that Warren Buffett invests. LouAnn Lofton notes eight ways that the typical approach of female investors jibes with Warren Buffett's. She notes that female investors are more realistic in their investment expectations than men. Lofton also notes that women "put in more time and effort researching possible investments, considering every angle and detail, as well as considering alternate points of view."[28]

It is easy to get locked in to thinking about investments in a certain way. The important takeaway is that all investors, male and female, need to challenge themselves. Just as men are more prone to overconfidence, women are more likely to "consider every angle" in regard to an investment, which could very well lead to analysis paralysis. We are all flawed and filled with a range of biases. The challenge for men and women is to acknowledge these biases and try our best to combat them.

That being said, men probably have the most to gain from this sort of exercise. Jason Zweig's advice to men probably sums things up best: "Memo to men: Your household's investment portfolio will be less risky and more diversified if your wife helps manage it. She will share in what comes out of that portfolio down the road; shouldn't she share in what goes in to it? Chances are, her ideas and emotions will complement yours, and you will both end up wealthier. At least one of you will end up wiser."[29]

On the Benefits of Financial Counsel

Despite the many ways that investing has become easier and cheaper over time, it is still an area filled with complexity. As Lusardi and Mitchell write, "A larger array of available financial instruments does offer new opportunities for more tailored financial plans than available in the past, but these can also make poor decision-making more costly to the ill-informed investors."[30] The great thing is that your financial needs are likely not all that unique.

We have talked about some of the parts of a financial plan, including asset allocation, portfolio management, and investing in general. Any comprehensive personal financial plan would include not only investing, but also retirement planning, income taxes, insurance, and estate planning. No one is an expert in all these fields, and every one of them comes with its own costs and benefits. Unfortunately we are largely left to our own devices to navigate these fields.

Most people recognize that a do-it-yourself approach in *all* these areas is not realistic. Therefore, hiring qualified professionals to put together an estate plan or to counsel you in regard to insurance coverage seems like a prudent thing to do. The only thing worse is not undertaking those activities that serve to protect you and your family.

It is controversial to be against something as seemingly valuable as financial literacy, but this education does come with a cost. A paradoxical effect of financial literacy education is that it can create worse outcomes. Willis writes: "In reality, this education may do no more than increase overoptimism and the illusion of being able to control financial risks. Participants consistently self-assess as having learned a great deal and having gained confidence, but their poor performance on literacy exams indicates that their confidence is misplaced."[31] In short, participants do not really know what they think they know.

A worse sin that we all face is that we do not know what we do not know. We are all at risk of making decisions based not on faulty information but on a lack of knowledge of the issues at hand. For example, a majority of workers eligible for defined pension plans don't have much knowledge about what benefits they are eligible for.[32] We should all recognize the specialized areas in which we likely do not have enough knowledge or education to make decisions. In talking about investment education, it may seem an anathema to say that in many cases individuals would be better off with investment counsel than they would be doing it on their own.

The challenge comes not necessarily in education, although as we have seen, that could a problem. The investor's challenge comes down more to the issues of behavior. We know that one of the behaviors that can be detrimental to an investor is overtrading. While the explicit costs of trading these days are low, the implicit costs remain high. These costs are high because overtrading usually involves trades that occur emotionally rather than as a result of a rational calculation. In short, we buy high and sell low on a consistent basis.

One could think of all sorts of ways of preventing this type of behavior, but in the age of the online brokerage account, a potential trade is only a few mouse clicks away. One way of removing the temptation to click is to interject another party between you and your portfolio. This usually takes the form of some sort of financial advisor or investment manager.

No one who has looked at the evidence should expect to get consistently market-beating results by hiring an investment manager. Maymin and Fisher note that, given this middling performance, individuals who hire managers may be looking to them to serve some other function. They write, "Perhaps investors retain advisors to prevent themselves from making bad trading decisions—to help them navigate near-term emotions like fear, regret, and greed and make healthier, more-objective choices that keep them on track to meet their long-term goals."[33]

By tracking the "touches" an advisory firm had with its clients, Maymin and Fisher are able to demonstrate that individuals act consistently with this sort of approach. Clients eventually become more relaxed in their contacts with the firm. Not surprisingly, they become anxious in times of market volatility and seek out their advisor more often. So the value added in these client-advisor relationships comes not through the underlying performance of the portfolio but through the support of an advisor who acts as an emotional buffer. Maymin and Fisher write, "Therefore, we conclude that the advisor's role in helping investors stay disciplined and on plan in the face of market volatility, including dissuading them from excessive trading, is one that is highly valued by the individual investor."[34]

One of the challenges for investors is to find an investment advisor who can act in this capacity. The sexy part of the investment management business is in some of the areas we have already discussed—selecting securities, allocating assets, and managing portfolios. This is the ongoing challenge of "beating the market." These things have tangible outcomes that can be measured and monitored.

Yet this may be a misplaced effort. Charles D. Ellis, author of the investment classic *The Winner's Curse,* notes how clients would be better served by a focus on investment counsel as opposed to even more intensive investment management. He writes, "Our profession's clients and practitioners would all benefit if we devoted less energy to attempting to 'win' the loser's game of beating the market and more skill, knowledge, and time to helping clients recognize market realities, understand themselves as investors, and clarify their realistic objectives and then stay the course that is best for each of them."[35]

Ellis notes that this is easier said than done, in part because this requires a different skill set and mindset than that required for investment management. The point is a good one though. Putting together a globally diversified portfolio of index funds is now cheaper and easier than ever before. It should not be surprising that we are seeing new online services that want to manage your portfolio for a fee far less than what is commonly available from investment advisors. The difficulty does not lie in constructing the portfolio but rather in managing our inevitable reactions to its ups and downs.

Going further, financial advisors are in a prime position to help individuals make more informed choices about their financial future that have little or nothing to do with portfolio management. In commenting on the financial services industry, Dan Ariely writes, "It's still centered on the rather facile service of balancing portfolios, probably because that's a lot easier to do than to help someone understand what's worthwhile and how to use their money to maximize their current and long-term happiness."[36] These types of decisions are tougher and ultimately more important than the nuances of today's portfolio allocation. Unfortunately the vast majority of people in the financial services industry are not set up to provide this type of service.

Nothing in this discussion means you should, or should not, hire someone to manage your portfolio. Research shows that even when presented with an opportunity to receive free, unbiased investment advice, the vast majority of investors decline the offer. And those that do accept the offer don't follow through on the advice.[37] So we should not be complacent that availability of financial counsel is some sort of magic bullet. Some investors are competent in handling their finances. Others will never get comfortable handing the reins over to someone else. No matter the circumstances, we all need some strategy or structure to help buffer our portfolios from our worst instincts.

For some, that means hiring an advisor. For others, it may mean having some other trusted individual, perhaps a spouse or colleague, with whom they can discuss these matters. And still for others, it may involve using simple coping strategies that prevent them from making rash decisions in regard to their portfolio. It seems strange to talk about not going it alone in a book on becoming a more informed investor. The fact is that none of us have all the answers. We all need help in trying to make sense of an increasingly complex and noisy financial world.

Key Takeaways

* Despite a poor track record we humans are addicted to forecasting. Investment strategies based on accurate forecasting are likely doomed to underperformance.
* Investing is an arena in which both skill and luck play a role. Investors should seek managers who are transparent about their strategies and humble in their approaches.
* Confirmation bias prevents us from finding disconfirming evidence. Investors need to work actively to expose themselves to a wide range of information.
* Male investors would do well to take some cues from female investors, who achieve equal returns with less risk and less trading.
* No individual can be competent in all areas of personal finance. We all need some help and counsel, especially when it comes to avoiding rash decisions.
* True financial planning is less about portfolio management and more about the major financial dilemmas we all face.

11

Smarter Media Consumption

BY ALL ACCOUNTS, THE STATE OF FINANCIAL LITERACY IN THE United States is atrocious. A recent report by Annamaria Lusardi shows that Americans fail in large numbers to do even the most basic financial planning, such as saving for college or retirement. Even more troubling is that the majority of Americans fail to understand some of the most basic concepts in economics and finance.[1]

Maybe we shouldn't feel all that bad, because further research by Lusardi and Mitchell shows financial illiteracy is widespread in other developed markets as well.[2] The challenge is that in all these markets, where saving for retirement is a crucial function, many individuals are falling down on the job.

How we can better educate individuals is a public policy question, one that needs to focus on the educational system to help children learn the basic principles that will allow them to grasp the more complex questions they will face as adults. Still, some feel that this is not sufficient and that we need to better design financial products with widespread financial illiteracy in mind.[3]

The point is not to beat up on people for failing to become more literate investors. For better or worse, many Americans get their financial information and education from the media. To become a more literate investor, one therefore needs to become a more

163

discerning consumer of financial media. Unfortunately the financial media is largely filled with noise.

Noise

Noise has always been a part of the financial markets. We don't mean physical noise, because the days of the noisy trading floor are clearly numbered. Noise is chatter, in contrast with information. Around events both big and small there is a great deal of chatter and only a little bit of information. Years ago it required physical proximity to the markets to get in on market-related conversations. Today all it requires is access to the Internet.

Increasing access to market chatter has also made the markets increasingly noisy. One could assume that the rise in noise is detrimental, but financial markets would not exist without it. Fischer Black, in a famous article entitled "Noise," describes the ways in which noise makes trading possible and, by definition, makes possible the very existence of financial markets. However, increasing noise also makes it more difficult to uncover, for lack of a better term, the underlying reality.

The challenge is, as Black notes, that we often don't recognize when we are trading on noise and when we are trading on information. Black writes: "Why do people trade on noise? One reason is that they like to do it. Another is that there is so much noise around that they don't know they are trading on noise. They think they are trading on information."[4]

In a nutshell, that is the problem facing investors—distinguishing noise from information. Unfortunately for investors, the financial media is only tangentially in the information business, and so noise rules the day. There are two reasons for this. The first is that there is only so much in the way of information that the media can convey. Only so much changes from day to day. Second, information is boring. Noise is sexy. Noise sells.

This isn't news to anyone who has flipped through the so-called news channels these days. News and information have been displaced by talking heads engaged in faux debate, the point of which isn't to enlighten but rather to entertain. This is not necessarily a knock on these outlets. The news "business" is exactly that, a business. The powers that be are doing what they need to do to capture viewers and generate profits.

Nor should we assume that the financial media is somehow different from the broader media. Personal finance magazines have been running articles with titles like "10 Stocks to Buy Now" for ages. These articles are not much different from the "10 Ways to Drive Your Man/Woman Crazy in Bed" articles that festoon the magazine covers next to your checkout aisle at the grocery store. Both magazine covers appeal to our more base instincts: in one case greed, the other lust.

Distinguishing between noise and information is particularly difficult when it comes to financial television. This is due to the double-barrel blast of sensory overload we get from the video and the audio. The constant stream of information, opinion, and changing prices almost impels us to act, and by act in this case we mean trade. It is not for nothing that brokers are the bread and butter of financial television advertising. As Carl Richards writes, "Watching CNBC might be entertaining, but unless you fancy yourself some sort of day trader, it will not help you figure out what to do with your life savings."[5]

What should be clear from this is that the members of the financial media are not looking out for your best interests. Nor should we expect them to. In investing we talk about somebody having a fiduciary duty toward another person. This means the person with the fiduciary duty is legally obligated to act in your best interest. The members of the financial media have no such duty. They are there to entertain and by extension generate ratings, subscriptions, and page views.

In a certain respect, writing about personal finance, like investing itself, should be kind of boring. The principles that underlie sound personal finance practices don't change all that much. For instance, there are only so many ways you can tell people to save more and spend less. The financial media is compelled to try and make things more interesting than they actually seem.

Making tried-and-true principles seem sexier than they are is a pretty minor sin in the media landscape. Where the financial media goes wrong is when it ends up getting individuals to act in ways that they would not normally have. For example, CNBC now has a show focused on retail forex trading sponsored by one of the big retail forex brokers.[6] We have already reviewed the evidence that shows that the vast majority of retail forex traders lose money, and a lot of it. A slick show like this can only serve to induce individuals who really shouldn't be involved in the forex market to take the plunge.

On one hand, we can say that those who choose to get involved in forex trading are adults and should take responsibility for their own actions. Granted some people who begin trading forex will end up becoming accomplished traders. Given the statistics, though, the safer proposition would be to apply the principle of "do no harm" and recommend traders not get involved in the first place.

Forex trading is a great example to conclude our discussion of noise. Forex trading is dominated by technical traders. The fundamentals inherent in currency rates play out over long time horizons, leaving the short term filled with traders trading against other traders. To trade these markets effectively, in a sense you need to embrace noise trading. For the vast majority of investors, minimizing noise and maximizing information should be the goal instead.

In the end, there are really only two ways to approach the problem of noise. The first is to simply eliminate, or at least drastically cut back, on news consumption. If most news is really noise, then there should not be any cost in doing this. In fact, this should free up time for more worthwhile endeavors. The other option is to try and consume media in a smarter, more focused way. This admittedly has some up-front costs associated with it, but it is really the only way to deal with the onslaught of what we call news these days.

Going on a Media Diet

If today's financial media is awash in fake news, opinion, and noise, what is an investor to do? Think about the staple of the financial media—the daily market wrap-up. In the space of a short amount of time, a reporter is forced to try and put together a cohesive narrative on what happened in the trading day. As Felix Salmon writes, this is likely misplaced effort: "Market reports should not be an everyday staple of news coverage. Sometimes, occasionally, there are stories in the markets. And then those stories can be reported. But when there aren't any stories, there's no point in trying to invent them. And so the daily report—let alone the intra-day report—is at heart a stupid piece of journalism. Some are better than others, to be sure. But none of them are any good."[7]

Long-term investors with a multiyear time horizon should probably avoid the news altogether. It is said that one of the great advantages of ETFs is that they can be traded throughout the day. While true, one could also argue that for the long-term investor this only represents an unneeded temptation, which makes the case for actively managed ETFs all the more puzzling. Presumably anyone investing in an actively managed ETF has a time horizon that obviates the need for intraday liquidity.

A very small minority of traders trade (successfully) based on news flow. For them, continual access to news and opinion is important. However, trading on the news is a perilous endeavor. First, you have to get the news, next you have to analyze it correctly, and then you need to trade accordingly. The chances of a nonprofessional doing this on a consistent basis are slim at best. That is why computer algorithms now dominate short-term trading.

Some argue that the media, broadly defined, is not simply a neutral force in our lives but is something much more nefarious. Nassim Taleb writes in his now famous book, *Fooled by Randomness*, that "the problem with information is not that it is diverting and generally useless, but that it is toxic."[8] This is due in part to the incentives journalists have to increase attention and traffic. They do this by focusing on the sensational and graphic. Trying to cull a signal from this noise is difficult, if not impossible.

In the previous chapter, we discussed some of the biases that affect the way we make decisions and invest. Access to this news "fire hose" leads to overconfidence that can eventually lead to overtrading. If we use a signal-to-noise framework, we can see how increasing the noise (news) can potentially overwhelm our brain's ability to generate a meaningful signal. In any moment in time, it is difficult to weigh what information is important against the merely useless.

If we investors are at risk of being overwhelmed by the modern media onslaught, what are we to do? Increasing our time frame is key. The rise of algorithmic trading should convince us that we are playing a losing game at shorter time frames. This frees us up to take what is best described as a "media diet." A media diet, as practiced by Nassim Taleb, is a conscious effort to decrease the amount of media we consume. Most of what we consume is "empty calories." Most of it has little information value and can only serve to crowd out other more interesting and informative sources.

Dylan Grice, a prominent investment strategist, undertook this very exercise. He found that limiting his news intake to a select few, albeit delayed, sources made him neither ill-informed nor a less competent investor. Grice writes: "Treat the news for what it is. Read it, speculate about how stories will end, enjoy it. But be cautious about how much help it will be to you when investing."[9] In the end, we may simply not be able to filter the news effectively. As Vitaliy Katsenelson writes: "You may think you're able to filter the noise. You cannot; it overwhelms you. So don't fight the noise—block it."[10]

From an investor's standpoint, news is costly. As Rolf Dobelli writes: "News wastes time. It exacts exorbitant costs."[11] So not only does following the news eat up valuable time, but the vast majority of what we read in the news isn't really relevant to investing. Dobelli continues: "News consumers are suckers for irrelevancy, and online news consumers are the biggest suckers. News is an interruption system. It seizes your attention only to scramble it."[12] The cognitive costs of inveterate news reading may be greater than the time lost in trying to make sense of it all.

Despite the obvious benefits of a media diet, some investors will be unwilling to completely "unplug from the grid." For these inveterate news junkies, there is a middle course—aggregators.[13] As the word implies, aggregators seek to filter the news stream down into a more relevant and digestible amount of news. While some people attempt to do this algorithmically, the ones we are focusing on here are "hand-crafted." That is, an individual or team scours the news stream for themes and actionable information.

By relying on aggregators, you take the risk that they will miss relevant information. The bigger risk is that the aggregator has a very different idea of what is important news and what is not. This is due in part to differing time horizons, but also has to do with the subjective nature of what is important and what is merely passing trivia.

Aggregators represent a trade-off, but if you recognize the value of a media diet, then it is not a difficult trade-off to make. In our investing lives, we are faced with trade-offs all the time. Some we explicitly recognize; others pass without conscious thought. So an obvious benefit of a news diet is that it frees up time that would be spent reading news that has little or no relevance to our investing. By removing these temptations, we are likely to avoid making impulsive trades with little prospect for profits. Trading noise for additional time seems like one of the better trades we can make.

The news itself is often less important than the reaction to the news. By disconnecting from the often entertaining and always enticing news flow, we can better see the crucial interplay between what happens and how markets react. This perspective is difficult to achieve under the best of circumstances. If you are inundated with the noisy media, it is nearly impossible.

Expertise and Evidence

If the mainstream media is filled with noise, what about blogs? The great virtue of the blogosphere is that anyone can get started blogging or tweeting literally within minutes. This breaks down the artificial barriers among journalists, bloggers, and investors. For many in the mainstream media, this is viewed as a threat. Just the same, there is increasing evidence that shows that news is just as likely to break on Twitter as in the mainstream media and at as fast a pace or even faster.

One of the great complaints from the mainstream media is that what goes out on Twitter and blogs isn't vetted by an editor. Oftentimes we don't even know if the people sending this information out are who they say they are. There is a now famous cartoon from the *New Yorker* showing a dog at the computer, talking to another dog, saying, "On the Internet, no one knows you are a dog."[14] The attitude of some of the mainstream media remains stuck in this mindset.

In this age of the Internet, anonymity is a scarce resource, and so the issue of identity seems to resolve itself. Anonymous writers don't remain anonymous long if they become very popular. Frankly, it is in their interest to have this happen. Movie studios and book publishers don't generally give deals to anonymous writers.

The issue is less about identity and far more about quality. In the blogosphere, Sturgeon's law applies as well. Sturgeon's law states that "90% of everything is crap."[15] What this means is that most content, whatever the medium, isn't really that good. In that regard, the blogosphere is no different from any other form of media. The blogosphere can be just as noisy as the mainstream media.

The bigger challenge for someone coming to the blogosphere is one of expertise. Do the people who are writing about various issues know what they are talking about? There are two ways to approach this issue. The first is to simply zero in on the credentials people claim they have—work experience, degrees, etc. The second is to let the market do some of the work for you.

To a certain degree, the blogosphere is a meritocracy, an imperfect one for sure, but a meritocracy nonetheless. In general, the blogs that are consistently updated will find a growing readership. Keeping a blog up and running is no easy task. As mentioned earlier, it is deceptively easy to start a blog, but keeping it relevant is an altogether tougher task.

Many blogs have come out of the gate gangbusters but quickly peter out. It could be the case that the writer had nothing else to say. A stronger possibility is that, after a period of time, the blogger recognized the hard work involved in running a successful blog. In either event, the blogs that stick around likely have something to say and at least a big enough audience to keep the blogger motivated.

So if you accept the assumption that the blogosphere is a meritocracy, then the most successful blogs should also be of relatively high quality. In the blogosphere, as in any other business, there are real first-mover advantages. That is, the people who started blogging first are more likely to have well-established readerships. That is not to discount the role of taste. Some blogs appeal to a very specific readership that often is willing to overlook facts in the service of some stylized market agenda.

A willingness to disregard certain facts is a staple of commentary, be it political, economic, or financial. The challenge for new readers of the blogosphere is to try to ferret out these biases. For instance, if a site has "gold" somewhere in the title, you can be reasonably confident that the site is an advocate of gold, no matter the environment. In cases like this, the bias is explicit.

The subtler problem is when fact and opinion get all scrambled. In economics a distinction is made between "positive" economics and "normative" economics. In positive economics, the focus is on "what is." In normative economics, the focus is on "what ought to be."[16] Milton Friedman notes that positive economics is ultimately about its ability to explain things today and make predictions about the future. Normative economics is much more subjective in that it focuses on how the economy should be structured relative to where it is at present.

The same distinction could be made about the blogosphere. Some blogs have a "positive" outlook by their focus on data, trends, etc. Much of the blogosphere really has a "normative" viewpoint, focusing on how things should be as opposed to where they are today. The danger is that blog readers will spend their time and energy focusing on opinion as opposed to fact. And what would be even worse would be the inability to distinguish between the two.

This is all the more true because there is no room for ideology or politics in investing. The markets do not generally care what party is in power. While the best investors may have a very specific political worldview, they do their best to not let those opinions cloud their judgment. Think about it; if you let your political views cloud your judgment, there is a good chance you will be making poor decisions whether your preferred party is in or out of power. Investors simply don't have the luxury of time to waste on political biases and beliefs.

In the end, it may not be fact or opinion that is the best feature of the blogosphere. The most compelling content gets you to think in a novel fashion about your biases and investment philosophy. As we said, there is no shortage of viewpoints in the blogosphere; what is more rare is a piece that gets you to really think differently about investing. In the end, the care and feeding of our investment philosophy is more important than the latest meme that recently passed through the blogosphere.

Everybody Talks His or Her Book, Everybody

If people didn't talk their book, the entire talk show industry would have to close up shop. The staple of the talk show, be it daytime, late night, or news, is built on bringing on guests to talk about their projects and causes. People wouldn't go on these shows if they didn't get a chance to publicize themselves, their firms, and their work.

First, let's define our terms here. *Talking your book* occurs when fund managers, analysts, and others discuss the merits of one or more of their holdings. The assumption is that the managers have done their own research into the name and have a position in it. We see this play out all the time on financial television, in articles, and at various conferences.

The Ira Sohn Conference in particular draws a great deal of press attention because of the high-profile nature of its speakers. Katie Benner describes the conference that raises money for pediatric cancer research thusly: "Ira Sohn feels a little like the church where people gather to renew their faith in the gospel of hedge fund managers as truth tellers, soothsayers and heroes."[17] All this attention brings out criticism of the managers for talking their book.

Then again, what's the alternative? As Joshua Brown writes, "What else should they talk about, someone else's book?"[18] Talking your book has been playing out over time and across industries and has some real benefits. Brown notes that someone who goes on record with a pick will now have some accountability for that idea. The manager will presumably profit if that idea turns out to be a good one.

Don't always assume that is the case, however. Some of the people you see on TV recommending a stock may not have put their money in it. James Altucher writes, "Most of the big financial pundits I know out there have all of their money in municipal bonds but will never admit to that publicly."[19] So even when you hear some commentators suggest a certain stock, don't necessarily assume they have a vested interest in the pick.

It goes without saying that no one should buy any stock or investment based solely on the recommendation of some fund manager, no matter how successful the person or how stellar the person's reputation. The best investors have developed their own investment strategies through trial and error over time. These strategies fit their unique needs and personality. It does not necessarily follow that their picks are the best fit for your portfolio.

One would assume that a large-fund manager would have the same goals as you—picking stocks that go up. However, these managers are operating on a very different playing field, not only from an informational standpoint but also from a risk standpoint. The fact is that these managers may have a different time horizon and risk tolerance. There is nothing worse than buying a stock, seeing it languish, selling it, and later seeing it climb higher. This can happens when your thesis was correct but your time horizon was too short.

In certain respects, a large institutional fund manager is at a disadvantage to an individual investor. Individuals, if they choose, can flit in and out of stocks without much fear of moving the stock price. For this very reason, some managers must avoid small-cap stocks. Managers might also mention situations, like distressed debt or some overseas stock, that the individual investor would have a difficult time accessing in any event.

Rather than focus solely on the stock pick itself, it makes sense to get behind the manager's reasoning for the pick. Anybody can throw a stock pick out there, but actually being able to explain and defend that pick is far more valuable. If we don't know the reasoning behind a pick, how will we know when it is time to sell? As the proverb goes, it is more valuable to teach a man to fish than to actually give him a fish. The same is true for stock picks. At its most useful, the financial media provides insight into the thought processes of knowledgeable investors.

The rise of social media has made many investors, but not all, more willing to share their ideas in public. Sites have sprung up that allow institutional investors to share their ideas with colleagues. The blogosphere is filled with investors and writers willing to air their analyses and picks. The ultimate question is, why are investors willing to give away their insights for free? There are two main reasons for this. First, by publicly stating their views, they expose them to criticism. This (sometimes) constructive criticism can help hone an idea and ferret out potential errors. Second, it may very well pay off in terms of a higher stock price for the pick in question.

Some research into the idea of talking your book shows that releasing an idea on an investing forum was followed, on average, by abnormal returns for the stock.[20] The effects are small but notable. Authors Gray and Kern suggest that this process helps drive the "price discovery process." Publicity makes the disparity between a stock's price and its true value shrink. Sounds like a win-win situation. Don't be surprised if we begin to see more of these types of sites spring up over time.

Some investors have taken the further step of systematically tracking the stock picks of high-profile managers. Investors use this information to help screen for new investment ideas. Some investors have taken it to the next logical step to build portfolios based on the favored stocks of highly successful hedge fund managers.[21] There are both pluses and minuses to this sort of approach, but at least it has some basis in the data. Furthermore this is a systematic strategy that eschews individual stock picking.

Admittedly the process of talking your book is likely to lead to more rather than less noise. To that end, most investors should give the stock picks of the rich and famous wide berth. However, for those who are interested in learning more about the thought processes of high-profile managers, this will be an interesting area to investigate. Don't for a minute forget that everyone is talking his or her book, and we do mean everyone.

On the Value of Reading Widely

Warren Buffett is famous for giving some very simple advice to anyone asking how to become a great investor. Buffett says, "Read everything you can."[22] Buffett's taste in reading material ranges from industry periodicals to company reports. His penchant for reading both in his youth and through to the present is well known and provides us with a clue about how to become a well-rounded investor.[23]

This penchant for reading widely brings to mind the discussion about the multifaceted challenge of becoming a well-rounded investor. Great investors get that way following two parallel tracks. The first is actually investing. The most salient lessons any investor learns are from the profits and losses generated on actual trades, no matter how big or small.

On that other track are other education efforts. Many great investors have a formal education in business of one kind or the other. It is not clear how much value we should put on this education in light of the failures of academic finance. Even before the financial crisis, Michael Mauboussin writes, "Trillions of dollars are exchanged in global markets every day. Yet despite the high stakes and considerable resources researchers have committed to understanding markets, there is much we do not grasp."[24] In light of the financial crisis, our understanding of the markets is even less comprehensive than previously thought.

We have already touched on some of the skills a well-rounded investor should possess. Our discussion in the previous chapter on the many biases we are afflicted with highlights the importance of an understanding of psychology. The fact that every actor in the financial markets is talking his or her book highlights the need to be able to parse arguments based on statistics, accounting, or good old-fashioned hucksterism. Last, our discussion of financial bubbles underscores the importance of being able to put today's markets into some sort of historical context.

The skills cited above by no means make for a comprehensive list. In periods of relative market calm, one could argue that these skills might be sufficient. For better or worse, the world and the markets are undergoing changes at what seems like an accelerating rate. These changes often create structural breaks where tried-and-true principles no longer hold. Investors who have the ability to put into context these changes have a big leg up on investors who are solely focused on the next trading day, week, or quarter.

One of the challenges of reading the financial media is the focus on finding some explanation for each and every market move. We humans are pattern-recognition junkies and demand an explanation even when there is none. This coverage should be viewed as being more entertaining than educational. It is only with the passage of time that we can put into proper context today's market action. This focus on the short term is simply a symptom of a much larger phenomenon.

It seems that as technology has progressed and markets have become more automated, they also have become more myopic, i.e., focused on the short term. This manifests itself in a number of ways. It shows up in ever-more trading volume and, by extension, ever-shorter holding periods for equities. Stocks around the world are now held by investors for, on average, less than a year.[25]

This should not be all that surprising, as modern society has evolved. Andrew Haldane notes the many ways in which increased information loads have changed the ways we actually process data and make decisions. This also can have a profound effect on the financial markets. Haldane and Davies write: "Capital market myopia is real. It may be rising."[26]

If so, it can have a profound effect on the way in which securities are priced. It can also have a broader societal impact in that investment is misallocated across companies. And it has implications for the way we invest as well. We have already touched on the difficulty that individual traders have in trying to trade against computerized algorithms. In short, it is hard for individuals to beat the machines at their own game.

For individual investors to succeed in any sort of active investment endeavor, they need to play an altogether different game. As markets trade in unison, it seems logical that opportunities would arise in the valuation of individual companies. We have already noted the folly of stock picking for all but a small minority of investors. But this argument is a profound one. If the markets are so short-term oriented that long-term trends are overlooked, this makes for a now favorably unlevel playing field for real investors. Ang and Kjaer argue that "long-horizon investors have an edge."[27] Indeed this edge may be growing as markets undergo increasing levels of turmoil.

In many regards, institutional investors have the advantage over individuals with their access to data, information, and trading systems. However, those investors who possess a "liberal arts education" in investing can offset those advantages at these longer time horizons. A focus on long-term investing takes into account not only economic and financial considerations; it is also likely to include technological, demographic, and cultural trends that lie outside mainstream Wall Street thinking. So we have returned to the importance of reading widely and crossing disciplines.

The idea of *consilience,* or "the linking together of principles from different disciplines especially when forming a comprehensive theory,"[28] is an interesting way of putting this idea into context. Investing in its highest form is a creative activity. Finding and exploiting patterns across time and disparate disciplines is a rare challenge, one that has been drawing people to the markets since the markets began.

Key Takeaways

+ The state of financial literacy in the United States is abysmal. The financial media does not help by emphasizing noise over information.

+ The financial media sells noise because it is exciting. The fact is that the principles of personal finance and investing are pretty boring.
+ Most investors would do better to think and act in longer time frames. Unplugging from the grid via a "media diet" can help free up time better used in research and analysis.
+ The investment blogosphere is an imperfect meritocracy where investors should be careful to avoid confusing fact and opinion.
+ Everybody talks his or her book. Just because a star fund manager gives out a stock pick does not mean it is right for everyone. Understanding a manager's thought process is more important than the actual pick itself.
+ The best investors take a "liberal arts" approach to investing, embracing insights from a wide range of fields. As markets have become more myopic, having a longer-term focus becomes more important for investors.

12

Lessons from a
Lost Decade

To say that the past decade has been a difficult one for investors is a gross understatement. The S&P 500 has essentially spent the past 13 years treading water. That is not to say that the market has stood still. Investors have been treated to the deflation of two major bubbles with ensuing bear markets. Many analysts describe this as a "lost decade for stocks." We are at present living through what we described earlier as an extended drawdown for the U.S. stock market. And so the past decade should not come as a complete shock, but it is disturbing nevertheless.

Admittedly if we widen our focus, we can see that things are not nearly as bad as the story told by the S&P 500. Carl Richards notes that the lost decade is in part a myth because it focuses on this narrow slice of the investable universe.[1] Every other major asset class during the past decade outperformed large cap domestic equities. An investor who was widely diversified over the past decade in bonds, small-cap domestic equities, foreign equities, emerging markets, REITs, and commodities would have weathered the past decade with solidly positive, roughly 5%, but not spectacular returns.[2] The lesson of the lost decade for stocks provides us with support for a strategy that focuses on a widely diversified portfolio.

Even more significant than the financial fallout of a lost decade is the psychological fallout of living through an extended period of market volatility. Floyd Norris describes all of the market moves that add up to little progress as "excess volatility."[3] Investors are by all accounts feel beaten down. Jason Zweig writes, "People seem to feel like bystanders in their own financial lives—almost as if they were spectators at a racetrack equally incapable of stopping an impending car crash and of tearing their eyes away from it."[4]

Andrew Haldane notes that financial crashes and car crashes have similar causes—an underestimation of risk. After a crash, investors subsequently have a tendency to then overestimate the risk of further financial trauma. Haldane writes: "Memories of financial disaster are now fresh, as after the Great Depression, causing an over-estimation of the probability of a repeat disaster. In these situations, psychological scarring is likely to result in risk appetite and risk-taking being lower than reality might suggest. Risk will be over-priced."[5]

For some this past decade is the logical conclusion of what has been the financialization of our economy. Satyajit Das, in his book *Extreme Money,* notes how this increasingly financialized economy came to be and how we ended up with too many people, companies, and governments laden with too much debt.[6] Maybe even worse was that a great deal of talent was siphoned off into the financial sector. Talented people were attracted to the high pay of finance and spent their time coming up with ever-more-exotic financial instruments instead of doing things that in the end actually matter for the economy. The end game for the financialized economy was the financial crisis. The subsequent support of the financial sector proved to many to be a last straw. The very industry that brought the global economy to its knees, for better or worse, got bailed out.

This past decade has turned many investors off equities as an investment for some time to come. These investors are then likely to turn to a fixed-income market that is at the moment particularly inhospitable. At least prior to the lost decade for stocks, the bond markets provided some measure of prospective returns. Unfortunately we are now in the fourth year of what can best be described as a "war on savers." Since 2007, the Federal Reserve has kept short-term interest rates at or near 0%. As of today, that policy looks to remain in place for some time to come. So investors looking out over the horizon do not have the solace of further declines in interest rates to cushion another tough decade for equities.

The next decade will not only have to deal with traumatized investors; it will also have to deal with a very real demographic challenge. The much-hyped baby-boom generation is entering into retirement age, and with that comes the potential for a headwind for domestic equities. Research has shown that equity markets thrive when the bulk of the population is in its prime earning and savings years. That is not what is happening now. A model using U.S. demographics shows continued pressure on market P/E ratios for another decade or so.[7] Demography is not destiny, and the stock market could rebound based on any number of other factors, but this potential demographic drag is worth keeping an eye on.

Nobody knows what the coming decade will bring. The past decade highlights the importance of everything other than financial market returns. Before you ever invest dollar one in the financial markets, it makes sense to understand what other factors can play an important role in generating real gains both in and out of the market.

Savings Is the Best Investment

One way the coming decade is likely to differ from the prior decades is in how Americans approach debt. The two decades leading up to the mortgage and financial crisis were filled with Americans taking on ever-increasing levels of consumer and mortgage debt. That era ended leaving the global economy on the brink of financial disaster.

Unfortunately there is no magic button to push to bring down debt levels. The only way to climb out of debt, absent foreclosure and bankruptcy, is to start living within your means. This is a difficult transition for many to make. A more conscious approach to spending seems an appropriate response when the economy and markets no longer generate ample returns. A focus on savings and debt reduction really just reflects a return to an age where credit was not so readily available.

The first step in increasing savings should be focused on reducing debt. In an age of 0% short-term interest rates, it makes little sense for families to be carrying high-interest debt, i.e., credit card debt. A sure reduction in interest expense beats the risky return in the financial markets any day. In that sense, paying down debt becomes the best available investment on the table for most investors.

We have talked about how it is essential to focus on risk when building portfolios to ensure that those portfolios survive the rough patches and allow us to reap the benefits of more favorable market environments. The same idea holds in our personal finances. We can think of living within our means, with a minimal amount of debt, as a way to withstand the shocks that life throws at us. Individuals and families that are leveraged to the hilt are vulnerable to small shocks and are unable to make the investments necessary to achieve long-term goals.

In one respect, a focus on saving diminishes the importance of investing. A dollar saved through a more conscious spending plan is a far more certain return than the uncertain return on an investment. Said another way, savings is the best investment an individual can make. In that sense, increased savings achieved through expense reduction is a sure thing. Another way of saving, without any additional hardship or risk, is through your employer's 401(k) plan. Many retirement plans offer a matching contribution in cash or in company stock. In either case, it represents a way to bolster your savings in an easy, automatic fashion. Or viewed another way, company matching represents a way to enhance the return on your 401(k) investments.[8]

There are very few sure things in investing. Expense reduction seems to be one of them. Research into mutual fund returns universally shows that funds with low expense ratios, on average, outperform funds with high expense ratios. The math is pretty simple. Gross investment returns are uncertain by definition. On the other hand, expenses are pretty stable and represent a one-for-one reduction in returns. As Russel Kinnel writes: "If there's anything in the whole world of mutual funds that you can take to the bank, it's that expense ratios help you make a better decision. In every single time period and data point tested, low-cost funds beat high-cost funds."[9] Costs matter. They matter in our personal lives and our investment lives. We shouldn't need a lost decade for stocks to convince us of that simple fact.

Just because our capacity to purchase goods may have diminished doesn't mean that our demand for new goods has waned. Luckily for consumers, there is a movement afoot that aims to enhance the opportunity to share goods and services. Lisa Gansky, author of *The Mesh,* writes: "The credit and spending binge has left us with a different kind of hangover. We need a way to get the goods and services we actually want and need, but at less cost, both personal and environmental. Fortunately, we're quickly gaining more power to do so. A new model is starting to take root and grow, one in which consumers have more choices, more tools, more information, and more power to guide these choices."[10]

This so-called sharing economy is being fueled by the rise of technology that allows us all to stay connected on a continuous basis. Gansky notes that it is no longer just information industries that are getting disrupted. Now all manner of physical goods are becoming fair game in this new sharing economy. Investors like Steve Case are at the forefront in funding companies that look to provide "access over ownership."[11] For consumers trying to do more with less, the sharing economy allows us to live within our means without sacrificing consumption opportunities. So while investors come to grips with the potential for a lost decade, there is the hope that a new consumption model will help us with this transition.

When Losses Hurt Less

We have already discussed loss aversion, or how it is we feel losses more acutely than gains. However, there is one saving grace to losses. Smart tax planning makes good use of losses, somewhat easing the pain of paying taxes on April 15. Uncle Sam gives investors a number of ways to lessen their tax burdens, but for most investors taxes are at best a tertiary concern.

Part of this disinterest in taxes comes from the lack of media coverage on the investment management industry. Given our earlier discussion of the financial media, this is not altogether surprising. In terms of sex appeal and an ability to attract viewers, taxes ranks right down there at the bottom with a discussion of generally accepted accounting practices.

Much of the investment world is built on the peculiarities of tax law. For example, vehicles such as REITs and master limited partnerships exist in large part because of favorable tax treatment. Another example of this is the admittedly unique tax treatment of futures contracts. This list goes on, but suffice it to say that not much happens in corporate America or in the investment world that doesn't include a discussion of taxes.

By definition, investors interested in generating real, after-tax returns need to focus on taxes. In a certain respect, it is easier to try and generate incremental returns from careful tax planning than trying to generate higher pretax returns on a portfolio through smarter investing. The IRS gives us all a road map, admittedly a convoluted one, on how to lower our tax bills. To the after-tax investor, a dollar saved on taxes is just as valuable as a dollar earned on investments.

A quick note: This discussion is focused on the philosophy behind generating after-tax investment returns. Tax laws change on a frequent basis, and contemplated tax law changes are a fixture in Washington. Taxes are an area where an investor should have access to competent advisors, because the decisions made surrounding taxes are irreversible. There is no substitute for expert advice when it comes to making high-stakes decisions like those involving retirement accounts and estate planning.

The one challenge that even tax experts face is the desire to try and forecast future changes in tax laws. Having perfect foresight on what tax rates will look like down the road would be quite valuable in tax planning. Tax experts are like any other expert in that their ability to forecast the future is not all that great. Investors are usually better served by focusing on the here and now and letting future taxes play out on their own time.

Given that we can't see very far into the future, a simple principle regarding taxes makes sense. Defer taxes as long as you can. This principle is particularly important when it comes to equity investing. There is one key variable investors can control that helps minimize taxes, and that is portfolio turnover. You want to minimize it. The faster you turn over a portfolio, the greater the amount of gains that will be taxed, and they will be taxed at the higher rates prevailing for short-term capital gains. This explains one of the great attractions of index funds. Well-designed equity index funds have the benefit of having low turnover. In that sense, index funds are tax efficient by design.

The investment industry has rolled out tax-aware funds that use various strategies to try and reduce turnover and ensure that gains are long term in nature. Unlike plain vanilla index funds, these tax-aware strategies have not caught on with investors. Some analysts argue that the existence of ETFs makes tax-managed funds largely superfluous.[12] Trying to minimize the tax bite from investing is far less sexy, and far less lucrative for the manager, than trying to shoot the lights out with high headline returns.

One area where equity investors have ultimate discretion is their timing in selling a stock. *When* you sell that stock, assuming you have a gain, can make a big difference in the tax rate you pay. Simply waiting to sell a stock after holding it more than a year currently allows for a lower capital gains rate. Likewise, selling a stock before the end of the tax year allows for those losses to offset other capital gains, or in the case of capital losses, against other income.

We have already discussed how rebalancing can help generate a better risk-return profile. Rebalancing also provides the tax-aware investor with a framework to harvest losses and defer gains. Wesley R. Gray did a simple exercise showing that a maximally tax-efficient portfolio rebalancing process could add surprisingly large incremental returns. He writes, "Stop reading this blog to try and find alphas…go out there and find a great tax attorney and CPA!"[13]

If you know that future tax rates are going to be higher, then it might very well make sense to defer losses to a future date. While this case is unusual, it is not out of the question. In this case heed Jason Zweig's advice: "Before you harvest a loss, make sure you or your adviser have thought through whether it will be treated as long-term or short-term and what kind of income you can offset with it. Ask for proof that by lowering your basis today you haven't raised your tax bill tomorrow."[14]

The opportunity to limit taxes on fixed-income investments is generally more difficult. There are few ways to think about this dilemma. High-income investors have, for some time, used municipal bonds in their portfolios, especially those that avoid the alternative minimum tax, to limit their tax bite. This can make sense provided that investors are not taking on additional credit risk to do so and that the breakeven calculation between munis and comparable taxable bonds makes sense. Then there is the issue of where to hold certain asset classes.

Having tax-deferred accounts allows investors to make smarter decisions on where to house certain assets. The general principle is that investors should hold high-tax-cost assets, like corporate or Treasury bonds, in a tax-deferred account. The flip side is that investors should hold assets that can take advantage of low, long-term capital gains rates in taxable accounts. The writer Christine Benz describes this as the "art of asset location."[15] So simply by being tax aware and holding certain assets in the right place, investors can minimize the overall tax the IRS takes.

From this discussion of "asset location," we can see the importance of taking full advantage of tax-advantaged plans like retirement accounts. It is beyond the scope of this book to discuss the intricacies and trade-offs of retirement saving schemes, including 401(k)s and the many flavors of IRAs. Suffice it say that if Uncle Sam lets you defer taxes to a future date, often retirement, you should take him up on the offer. The frequent argument given against this idea is that tax rates are going to be markedly higher in the future. Therefore, it doesn't make sense to defer taxes to a time when rates will be higher. Nobody has a crystal ball on where tax rates will be 2 years from now, let alone 20 years from now. Unless you have perfect foresight, the principle of deferring taxes makes the most sense for investors today.

Behavior and Taxes

While most investors pay little attention to the topic of taxes, for a smaller subset taxes become an unhealthy obsession. Some investors, to their own detriment, try to avoid taxes at all costs. For example, some investors are reluctant to sell a stock that has greatly increased in value for the simple reason that they do not want to write the IRS a big check.

Nobody likes paying taxes, but a sensible focus on taxes can reduce their impact on investment returns. Generating returns from the financial markets is difficult enough, and so taking advantage of what the government provides is sensible decision making. Smart tax planning won't make you rich in the absence of outsize returns, but in the world we live in, every little bit of incremental return helps.

No discussion of taxes is complete without at least touching on the topic of estate planning. Investors spend a lifetime working hard, saving, and investing. To ignore the final disposition of this lifetime of effort seems foolish. However, the majority of Americans do not take the important step of creating a will and setting up an estate plan in a timely fashion.

The recent EZLaw Wills & Estate Planning Study shows that 60% of Americans recognize the importance of having an estate plan in place. However, only 44% of Americans have such documents in place.[16] There are several reasons why these numbers are all not 100%. Financial illiteracy certainly has a role to play here. So does the reluctance of individuals to face up to their own demise, which is not particularly surprising. In addition, Americans today have a number of more pressing economic issues that crowd out long-term planning.

For individuals with dependents or with estates of sufficient size that estate taxes come into play, an estate plan is essential. The best way to think about estate planning is to think about who actually benefits. Ultimately estate plans are for the living. Putting forth the effort to assemble an estate plan can seem insurmountable, but once in place, it provides a measure of comfort. The costs, both financial and emotional, of time spent in probate court far outweigh the emotional effort required to put together a sensible estate plan. We have spent a book highlighting the fact that there are no sure-thing investments. Estate planning, on the contrary, is a win-win investment.

Opportunity Costs

We have already seen how costs matter in our personal and our investment lives. There is another cost that does not show up directly in our financial statements: time. If there is any resource in short supply in today's society, it is time. Managing our investment portfolios takes time. This time spent represents an opportunity cost in that it takes time away from family, friends, leisure, or even our careers—things that for most of us represent time better spent. When investors think about their portfolio, not only do they need to think about the results they achieve and the costs incurred, but they also need to think about the time required to achieve those results.

If you hire an advisor to manage your portfolio, the time spent can be reduced on an ongoing basis. However, the time required to identify, research, and monitor an investment advisor should not be underestimated. Individuals who choose to manage their own portfolio need to be cognizant of the time involved. Active strategies require substantial time commitments. Along with these time commitments also comes the psychological stress involved in trying to keep up with the markets. Actively managing a portfolio is ultimately an ongoing series of decisions.

The twin challenges of modern society are the lack of time (which we just discussed) and the sheer volume of decisions that need to be made, decisions about investments being just one of them. These decisions can cause us stress, in large part because of the stakes involved. This constant stream of decisions can fatigue us as well. Social psychologist Roy F. Baumgartner describes this condition as "decision fatigue," and the ensuing fallout tells us a great deal about our behaviors.[17] Research shows that we have a limited store of mental energy, and when that energy is depleted, our ability to exert self-control and make rational trade-offs is greatly diminished. The implications for investing are obvious, but the solution to decision fatigue is not. According to John Tierney, Baumgartner's research suggests "that people with the best self-control are the ones who structure their lives so as to conserve willpower... and they establish habits that eliminate the mental effort of making choices... so that it's available for emergencies and important decisions."[18]

Investing is difficult enough even without falling prey to decision fatigue. There are a couple of ways investors can reduce the amount of decisions that they need to make. The first is to automate as much of their investment process as they can. Banks and brokers these days have a number of tools that allow investors to automate some of their routine decision making. The second way to combat decision fatigue is to adopt strategies that require fewer decisions. It sounds trivial, but avoiding strategies that require frequent monitoring and transactions will reduce this mental load. Even the simplest active investment strategies require a steady stream of decisions that for most investors represent potential land mines.

Our lives are filled with plenty of stress before we ever get to the question of investing. Research shows that those individuals who best manage stress arrange their lives to minimize the amount of potentially stressful encounters.[19] For the great majority of people, investments are a stress-inducing activity. Structuring our lives so that investments become a less frequent stressor can make for less stress, fewer decision-making opportunities, and simply more time to spend on the things we enjoy.

Invest in What Matters

In the end, all this effort in saving and investing should work to our advantage. We have already discussed the importance of the ultimate disposition of our assets. In the meantime, the purpose of our investments is to help us better achieve our own life goals. Our investments should be working for us, not the other way around.

For some people, investing becomes an avocation in and of itself. For this crowd, investing is an intellectual challenge that has, as a side benefit, the potential for financial gain. This avocation could simply be a hobby, or for some it could become a career. However, for the vast majority of others, investing is, at best, another one of those adult responsibilities we have a difficult time staying on top of.

In that light, maybe we need to define investing a little more broadly. People who have started investing recognize that they have some goals that they are trying to meet. Obvious ones include saving for a down payment on a house, paying for college, or providing for a comfortable retirement. These are all worthy goals, but these goals should not preclude us from making what may be even more meaningful investments along the way.

For instance, for most people the most valuable asset is their human capital and the income their careers generate. The transformation of the economy over time from one of stable lifelong careers into a "freelance economy" highlights the importance of obtaining and maintaining a skill set. And so an investment in your own education and skills may be a much more valuable investment than any portfolio investment ever could be. An investment in yourself, or others, could include additional education or professional certifications, or for the more adventuresome, it might be going into business for yourself.

There is ample reason why many people over the past decade have gotten off the corporate track to strike out on their own. Being a solo operator admittedly has its challenges, but the benefits are not solely financial. Furthermore, people who work for themselves experience a level of intrinsic motivation that is very rare in traditional career paths. It is cliché to say that you spend most of your waking hours at work, but it is true. Therefore, trying to maximize the monetary and psychic benefits from one's career is an investment well worth making.

Some of the dissatisfaction with our current work lives has to do with the fatigue many consumers now feel after the past decade. Having gorged on debt to acquire ever-more-expensive goods and services, many now recognize that the benefit of "stuff" is admittedly fleeting. How we spend our limited resources, including time and money, becomes an important determinant of how we spend our lives. Umair Haque notes: "The 'best' investment you can make isn't gold. It's the people you love, the dreams you have, and living a life that matters."[20] Haque admits that this is an idealistic approach to trying to create a new economy out of one that is so centered on acquiring "stuff." This sentiment does provide an antidote to anyone who is hung up on the investment performance game. An additional 1% here or there is not likely to meaningfully impact your life.

Your investments are important, but they are not more important than other aspects in your life. Haque continues: "As the never-ending global economic crisis has intensified, we've had plenty of what economists call 'capital flight' to 'safer' financial assets, whether gold, bonds, or blue chip stocks. But perhaps the safest investments of all are the human, social, and emotional ones. They're what give human life texture, depth, resonance, and meaning."[21] We have spent a great deal of this book talking about financial risk and returns. There are things in life that we cannot quantify. We should never let our pursuit of investment gains overshadow those things in life that can never be lost or traded.

Losing the Lost Decade

The lost decade has been a rough time for many Americans. The poor performance of the U.S. economy, equity market, and housing market has been challenging for many. The lost decade has served as a useful exercise in stress-testing our assumptions about finance and investing. Even if you have gotten through this past decade with your portfolio largely intact, it has likely dampened your expectations about the future. Said another way, the lost decade served as a reality check on our innate sense of optimism.

Researchers have gone so far as to coin a term for the belief that the future will be better than the past—they call it the "optimism bias."[22] Research shows that optimism is a necessary ingredient in our ability to move forward after having made a decision. In fact, it is argued that this optimism bias is inherent in our brain structure, the theory being that optimism increases our odds of survival in a wide range of environments.

However, an overabundance of optimism can be dangerous. Naïve optimism can lead us to make poor decisions. We have discussed a number of biases we humans have, and we can add the optimism bias to the list. Our discussion of the lost decade is a useful antidote and planning exercise. By planning for the worst and hoping for the best, we can combat our inherent optimism while still taking concrete steps toward a better future.

Tali Sharot writes: "Once we are made aware of our optimistic illusions, we can act to protect ourselves. The good news is that awareness rarely shatters the illusion. The glass remains half full. It is possible, then, to strike a balance, to believe we will stay healthy, but get medical insurance anyway; to be certain the sun will shine, but grab an umbrella on our way out—just in case."[23] That sounds like advice all investors who are looking at a lifetime of investing can take to heart.

Key Takeaways

+ The past decade, filled with popped financial bubbles and economic recessions, has traumatized investors. A highly diversified approach to investing, however, avoided the "lost decade for stocks."
+ Savings is the best investment. A focus on reducing expenses makes generating high but uncertain returns on your investments less critical. The so-called sharing economy is making it easier for consumers to have experiences without the cost of ownership.

- In pursuit of real, after-tax returns, investors often neglect the effect of taxes. Taking full advantage of current tax laws provides a far more certain return than any investment strategy.
- After a lifetime of working, saving, and investing, it makes no sense for individuals not to have an up-to-date estate plan in place.
- Successful investing requires time—time that for many is better spent in other pursuits. Arranging our financial lives to minimize the number of decisions we make can result in better outcomes.
- For many, the best investment may not be a financial one but rather an investment in the things in our lives that cannot be quantified.
- The lost decade provided us with many lessons, not the least of which is a check on our innate optimism. Planning for the worst and hoping for the best is a sensible approach for a lifetime of investing.

Conclusion

We decided to finish the book with a discussion of what a lost decade for stocks meant for investors. During the summer and fall of 2011, when the bulk of this book was written, it seemed like the lost decade was going strong into its second decade. Markets have been exceedingly volatile, finding reason to move a couple of percentage points a day based on, among other things, pronouncements coming out of the capitals of Europe. In the United States high and persistent unemployment, tepid economic growth, poor consumer sentiment, the hollowing out of the middle class, giant fiscal deficits, and a gridlocked political system all seem to point to continued tough times ahead. The visibility for the global economy and financial markets is, to say the least, foggy.

Nor do things look much better for investors. The war on savers is still ongoing. The yield on short-term Treasury bills is essentially 0%. The yield on a 10-year Treasury note hovers just below 2%. After inflation (and taxes), this yield is almost guaranteed to lose purchasing power over time. The upside of the lost decade for stocks is that it leaves stocks, as measured by the S&P 500, in the enviable position of having a higher yield than the 10-year Treasury note for an extended period not seen since the 1950s![1] It remains to be seen whether this unique situation represents a return to post–Depression era thinking when equities were viewed to be so risky as to require a dividend yield in excess of Treasuries. In contrast, it might represent a time when equities will once again generate a return over and above risk-free assets.

Maybe that is all that long-term investors can really hope for at this point: a return to some measure of normalcy. Poor financial and economic performance of late makes it easy for us to extrapolate the poor recent past into the distant future. Historically, poor decades for stocks in general have been followed by better times. For some that may not be enough to go on, but in a certain sense that is all we have. Carl Richards writes: "In some regard, investing based on the weighty evidence of history is the most prudent thing we can do. So far it has always proven to be correct. Every time someone has predicted the death of the stock market, they have been wrong. Given this record, isn't it reasonable to assume that stocks will continue to be better than bonds, and that bonds will continue to be better than cash?"[2]

That does not mean we should have some naïve faith that the future will hold nothing but good times. A prudent approach to investing always recognizes that risk is inherent in the process. There always is a wall of worry that can prevent us from investing. Then again, what is the alternative? As Jack Bogle said in response to a question about the tough times facing investors: "But the problem is that we must invest. We can't stand back. If you don't save anything, I guarantee you will end up with absolutely nothing."[3] In an ideal world, many more financial decisions would be taken off our hands via automation.

Of late we have seen some tentative steps taken to provide investors with algorithmic investment services. This represents a natural evolution for the investment business because much of the everyday work inherent in investing can be done algorithmically. And it represents another way in which algorithms have become a part of our lives, oftentimes without our knowledge. More sophisticated, automated investment plans will make life easier for a wide swath of American investors who would be happy to take routine, everyday investment decisions off their plate. Automation or not, investors need to educate themselves along the way. It will allow us to spend more time thinking about the bigger, more weighty questions surrounding money.

You can think about investing the way you might about exercise. Before you can run, you have to jog; before you jog, you have to walk; before you can walk, you have to get off the couch. The first step for potential investors is to learn how to walk. In a financial sense, that includes getting your financial house in order. No one should be putting money in the stock market before his or her other financial obligations are in good stead. As blogger and investment advisor David Merkel writes, "Until someone can meet all cash needs easily, including small disasters, he should not be investing in stocks."[4]

The next step up from walking is jogging. In the realm of investing, this is the ability to create, monitor, and manage a portfolio. At the very least, this means being an educated consumer of financial services should you choose to outsource this task. The great thing for self-directed investors today is that it has never been easier or cheaper to manage your portfolio. Assembling a broad, globally diversified portfolio of low-cost funds now rivals what institutional investors were able to do just a few short years ago. Leaving aside poor market conditions, there has never been a better time to be an individual investor.

Some will argue that a regularly rebalanced, well-diversified portfolio managed with risk, low costs, and taxes in mind is a suboptimal strategy. They will point to research showing a particular strategy that outperforms what amounts to a simple, boring portfolio. They will be right in the strictest sense. The great challenge for investors isn't putting together a strategy; it is putting together a strategy that they can follow over time. Every strategy will require some future tweaking, but investors almost always get into trouble when they adjust their plans during periods of market stress. It is always better to be proactive, rather than reactive, and avoid making major decisions when we are under stress and suffering decision fatigue. In the end, we are better off with a suboptimal strategy that we can follow, rather than one we don't fully understand and will abandon at the first sign of trouble.

Some investors will try to switch from jogging to running. Unfortunately, many do so without any real plan. Trading and active investing should be treated with the same seriousness that you treat any other business. Taking on market risk is one thing; taking a risk on yourself is something altogether different. The fact of the matter is that most investors that try to outperform the market will fail, sometimes spectacularly. Trading is a challenging game played by some of the smartest people (and machines) in the world. There is no shame in failing, but the one thing traders can't do is let trading put their entire portfolio at risk. In trading, you have to protect yourself not only from the markets, but most of all from yourself.

It is impossible to say what the markets will do over the next decade. The tailwinds of falling interest rates and rising valuations are likely gone, and another lost decade is a possibility. Market returns are guaranteed to no one. At its core, sound investing is not all that complicated. Nor are your investing needs unique. Assessing and managing risk, diversifying, rebalancing, keeping costs low, and minimizing taxes are things that everyone can do, and they should be a part of an educated investor's toolkit. Given the uncertain environment in which we live, it is important that we take advantage of all the tools that are available to us.

Investing is hard. It is hard for everyone, including the most successful investors in the world. Nevertheless, investing is one of those adult responsibilities we all need to come to terms with. The hope is that this book has made the basics of investing a little easier to understand. A humble approach to the markets is an essential step in bringing our investing lives into balance, because for most of us investing isn't really what matters. Our investments are there to serve our goals, not the other way around. What matters are the opportunities that those investments ultimately provide us to live richer, more fulfilling lives.

Notes

Introduction

1 Dan Gardner, *Future Babble: Why Expert Predictions Are Next to Worthless, and You Can Do Better*, New York: Dutton, 2011.

2 Peter Cohan, "Five Reasons Why Investing Is Dead," Forbes.com, December 5, 2011, http://www.forbes.com/sites/petercohan/2011/12/05/five-reasons-why-investing-is-dead/.

3 Nathan Hale, "Why You're Not as Unique as You Think You Are," *CBS Moneywatch*, June 4, 2011, http://www.cbsnews.com/8301-505123_162-37640645/why-youre-not-as-unique-as-you-think-you-are/.

4 Barry Ritholtz, "On Investing: The Many Hats of Great Investors," *Washington Post*, May 21, 2011, http://www.washingtonpost.com/business/on-investing-the-many-hats-of-great-investors/2011/05/17/AFN02c8G_story.html.

5 Robert Hagstrom, *Investing: The Last Liberal Art*, Texere: Independence, KY, 2002.

6 Michael J. Mauboussin, *More Than You Know*, New York: Columbia University Press, 2006, p. 207.

7 William J. Bernstein, *The Investor's Manifesto*, 2010, Hoboken, NJ: John Wiley & Sons, p. xv.

8 "Primum non nocere," Wikipedia, http://en.wikipedia.org/wiki/Primum_non_nocere.

Chapter 1

1 Merriam-Webster.com, http://www.merriam-webster.com/dictionary/risk.

2 This is a gross simplification of the CAPM, where the risk of any individual security is actually measured by the degree to which it covaries with the market portfolio.

3 Those interested in reading further about the history of risk and the academic construction of risk should check out three books by the late Peter L. Bernstein. These include *Against the Gods*, Hoboken, NJ: John Wiley & Sons,

1996; *Capital Ideas*, New York: Free Press, 1992; and *Capital Ideas Evolving*, Hoboken, NJ: John Wiley & Sons, 1997. An excellent recent addition to the literature is Justin Fox, *The Myth of the Rational Market*, New York: HarperCollins, 2009.

4 Anti Ilmanen, *Expected Returns: An Investor's Guide to Harvesting Market Rewards*, Hoboken, NJ: John Wiley & Sons, 2011, pp. 3–4.

5 James Montier, "The Seven Immutable Laws of Investing," GMO White Paper, March 2011, http://www.gmo.com/America/default.htm.

6 Seth A. Klarman, *Margin of Safety*, New York: HarperCollins, 1992.

7 Howard Marks, *The Most Important Thing: Uncommon Sense for the Thoughtful Investor*, New York: Columbia Business School Publishing, 2011, p. 66.

8 Amir Barnea, Henrik Cronqvist, and Stephan Siegel, "Nature or Nurture: What Determines Investor Behavior?" (February 3, 2010). Fourth Singapore International Conference on Finance 2010 Paper, available at SSRN, http://ssrn.com/abstract=1467088.

9 FDIC website, http://www.fdic.gov/deposit/deposits/insured/basics.html.

10 Eddy Elfenbein, "Happy 115th Birthday Dow Jones Industrial Average," *Crossing Wall Street*, May 26, 2011, http://www.crossingwallstreet.com/archives/2011/05/happy-115th-birthday-dow-jones-industrial-average.html.

11 The definitive history of Enron's rise and fall is Bethany McLean and Peter Elkind's *The Smartest Guys in the Room*, New York: Portfolio, 2003.

12 The lack of a risk-free asset poses a problem for modern asset pricing theory. See Aswath Damodaran, "Into the Abyss: What If Nothing Is Risk-Free?," New York University, July 2010, http://www.stern.nyu.edu/~adamodar/pdfiles/papers/nothingisriskfree.pdf.

13 Carl Richards, "Investors Are Still Behaving Badly," *Bucks Blog*, August 5, 2011, http://bucks.blogs.nytimes.com/2010/08/05/investors-are-still-behaving-badly/.

14 Philip Z. Maymin and Gregg S. Fisher, "Past Performance Is Indicative of Future Beliefs," *Risk and Decision Analysis*, vol. 2, no. 3, 2011, pp. 145–150.

15 Danny Yagan, "Why Do Households Chase Stock Market Returns? Long-Term Extrapolation, Not Market Timing," Harvard University, 2010, http://www.people.fas.harvard.edu/~yagan/papers/Chasing_Returns.pdf.

16 S&P/Case-Shiller Home Indices, September 27, 2011, http://www.standardandpoors.com/indices/articles/en/us/?articleType=PDF&assetID=1245321043147.

17 Barry Ritholtz, "The Bubble in Bubbles (Reflexive Version)," May 30, 2011, http://www.ritholtz.com/blog/2011/05/the-bubble-in-bubbles-reflexive-version/.

18 The classic text on bubbles is Charles Kindleberger, *Manias, Panics and Crashes*, 4th ed., Hoboken, NJ: John Wiley & Sons, 2000.

19 John H. Cochrane, "Why Identifying a Bubble Is So Much Trouble," *Bloomberg*, September 22, 2011, http://www.bloomberg.com/news/2011-09-22/why-identifying-a-bubble-is-so-much-trouble-john-h-cochrane.html.

20 "News You Can (Almost) Use," *The Economist*, July 20, 2011, http://www
.economist.com/blogs/johnson/2011/07/journalistic-language.

21 Meir Statman, *What Investors Really Want*, New York: McGraw-Hill, 2011, p. 69.

22 Daniel Gross, *Pop! Why Bubbles Are Great for the Economy*, New York:
HarperCollins, 2007.

23 Stephen P. Utkus, "Market Bubbles and Investor Psychology," Vanguard
Group, February 2011, https://institutional.vanguard.com/VGApp/iip/site/
institutional/researchcommentary/article/InvResmktbubbles.

24 Jason Zweig, "Why Spotting Bubbles Is Harder Than It Looks," *Wall Street
Journal*, November 5, 2011, http://online.wsj.com/article/SB100014240529
70204621904577017960729384948.html.

25 Merriam-Webster.com, http://www.merriam-webster.com/dictionary/
panic?show=1&t=1317931214.

26 Bob Ivry, Bradley Keoun, and Phil Kuntz, "Secret Fed Loans Gave Banks
$13 Billion," *Bloomberg.com*, November 27, 2011, http://www.bloomberg
.com/news/2011-11-28/secret-fed-loans-undisclosed-to-congress-gave-banks-
13-billion-in-income.html.

27 Mebane Faber, "When Things Go on Sale, People Run out of the Store,"
World Beta, March 12, 2001, http://www.mebanefaber.com/2011/03/12/
when-things-go-on-sale-people-run-out-of-the-store/.

28 Guy Kaplanski and Haim Levy, "Sentiment and Stock Prices: The Case of
Aviation Disasters," *Journal of Financial Economics*, vol. 95, no. 2, February
2010, pp. 174–201, available at SSRN, http://ssrn.com/abstract=1084533.

29 Peter L. Bernstein, *Against the Gods: The Remarkable Story of Risk*, Hoboken,
NJ: John Wiley & Sons, 1996, p. 220.

30 Marks, *The Most Important Thing*, p. 44.

31 Nassim Nicholas Taleb, *Fooled by Randomness*, New York: Random House,
2005, p. 192.

32 Edward Glaeser, "What Happened to Argentina?," *Economix*, October 6,
2009, http://economix.blogs.nytimes.com/2009/10/06/what-happened-
to-argentina/.

33 Felix Salmon, "Recipe for Disaster: The Formula That Killed Wall Street,"
Wired Magazine, February 23, 2009, http://www.wired.com/techbiz/it/
magazine/17-03/wp_quant.

34 Mike Shell, "The Essence of Investment Management Is the Management
of Risks," *Asymmetric Investment Returns*, June 2, 2011, http://www
.asymmetricinvestmentreturns.com/asymmetric-investment-returns/
the-essence-of-investment-management-is-the-management-of-risks/.

Chapter 2

1 Claude B. Erb, Campbell R. Harvey, and Tadas E. Viskanta, "Inflation
and World Equity Selection," *Financial Analysts Journal*, vol. 51, no. 6,
November/December 1995, pp. 28–42.

2 Michelle L. Barnes, Zvi Bodie, Robert K. Triest, and J. Christina Wang, "A TIPS Scorecard: Are They Accomplishing Their Objectives?" *Financial Analysts Journal*, vol. 66, no. 5, September/October 2010, pp. 68–84.

3 Warren E. Buffett, "How Inflation Swindles the Equity Investor, *Fortune*, May 1977, http://features.blogs.fortune.cnn.com/2011/06/12/warren-buffett-how-inflation-swindles-the-equity-investor-fortune-1977/.

4 Aswath Damodaran, "Equity Risk Premiums (ERP): Determinants, Estimation and Implications—A Post-Crisis Update," October 22, 2009, available at SSRN, http://ssrn.com/abstract=1492717.

5 Pablo Fernandez, Javier Aguirreamalloa, and Luis Corres Avendaño, "US Market Risk Premium Used in 2011 by Professors, Analysts and Companies: A Survey with 5.731 Answers," April 8, 2011, available at SSRN, http://ssrn.com/abstract=1805852.

6 There are some doubts about these survey results. See Eric Falkenstein, "Equity Premium Survey Doesn't Register My Vote," *Falkenblog*, June 6, 2011, http://falkenblog.blogspot.com/2011/06/equity-premium-survey-doesnt-register.html.

7 Pablo Fernandez, "The Equity Premium in 150 Textbooks," November 16, 2010, available at SSRN, http://ssrn.com/abstract=1473225.

8 Elroy Dimson, Paul Marsh, and Mike Staunton, *Credit Suisse Global Investment Returns Yearbook 2011*, p. 51.

9 Ibid., p. 52.

10 Jason Zweig, "Does Stock Market Data Really Go Back 200 Years?" *Wall Street Journal*, July 11, 2009, http://online.wsj.com/article/SB124725925791924871.html.

11 Eric Falkenstein, *Finding Alpha*, Hoboken, NJ: John Wiley & Sons, 2009.

12 Eric Falkenstein, "Is the Equity Risk Premium Actually Zero?," *Falkenblog*, July 13, 2009, http://falkenblog.blogspot.com/2009/07/is-equity-risk-premium-actually-zero.html.

13 Ilia D. Dichev, "What Are Stock Investors' Actual Historical Returns? Evidence from Dollar-Weighted Returns," *American Economic Review*, vol. 97, no. 1, pp. 386–401, 2007.

14 David Merkel, "The Equity Premium Is No Longer a Puzzle," *The Aleph Blog*, July 15, 2009, http://alephblog.com/2009/07/15/the-equity-premium-is-no-longer-a-puzzle/.

15 Howard Marks, *The Most Important Thing*, New York: Columbia Business School Publishing, 2011, p. 107.

16 Dimson, Marsh, and Staunton, *Credit Suisse Global Investment Returns Yearbook 2011*, p. 8.

17 James Montier, "A Value Investor's Perspective on Tail Risk Protection: An Ode to the Joy of Cash," GMO White Paper, June 2011, http://www.gmo.com/America/default.htm.

18 James P. O'Shaugnessey, *What Works on Wall Street (Fourth Edition)*, New York: McGraw-Hill, 2011, p. 443.

19 Anti Ilmanen, *Expected Returns*, Hoboken, NJ: John Wiley & Sons, 2011, p. 301.

20 Clifford S. Asness, Tobias J. Moskowitz, and Lasse Heje Pedersen, "Value and Momentum Everywhere," AFA 2010 Atlanta Meetings Paper, March 6, 2009, available at SSRN, http://ssrn.com/abstract=1363476.

21 Mebane T. Faber and Eric W. Richardson, *The Ivy Portfolio*, Hoboken, NJ: John Wiley & Sons, 2008.

22 Michael W. Covel, *Trend Following: Learn to Make Millions in Up or Down Markets*, Upper Saddle River, NJ: FT Press, 2009.

23 Ilmanen, *Expected Returns*, p. 295.

24 "Trading against the Trend Followers," *FT.com*, June 26, 2011, http://www .ft.com/intl/cms/s/0/11867b3a-9b3f-11e0-a254-00144feabdc0.html.

25 Werner F. M. De Bondt and Richard Thaler, "Does the Stock Market Overreact?," *Journal of Finance*, vol. XL, no. 3, July 1985, pp.793–805.

26 Jay R. Ritter, "Equilibrium in the Initial Public Offering Market," *Annual Review of Financial Economics*, vol. 3, 2011, forthcoming, http://bear .warrington.ufl.edu/ritter/AnnualReviewofFinancialEcon_July22011.pdf.

27 Katy Burne and Kellie Geressy-Nilsen, "Investors Peg Some Triple-A Corporate Debt as Safer Than Treasurys," *Wall Street Journal*, July 19, 2011, http://online.wsj.com/article/SB10001424052702303795304576456092212 511916.html.

28 Eugene F. Fama and Kenneth R. French, "The Anatomy of Value and Growth Stock Returns," *Financial Analysts Journal*, vol. 63, no. 6, November/ December 2007, pp. 44–54.

29 David Swensen, *Pioneering Portfolio Management: An Unconventional Approach to Institutional Investment*, New York: Free Press, 2000, p. 95.

30 Ibid., p. 98.

31 Marks, *The Most Important Thing*, p. 105.

32 Asness, Moskowitz, and Pedersen, "Value and Momentum Everywhere."

33 David Blitz, "Strategic Allocation to Premiums in the Equity Market," October 25, 2011, available at SSRN, http://ssrn.com/abstract=1949008.

Chapter 3

1 Charles Roxburgh, Susan Lund, and John Piotrowski, "Mapping Global Capital Markets 2011," McKinsey Global Institute, August 2011, http:// www.mckinsey.com/Insights/MGI/Research/Financial_Markets/ Mapping_global_capital_markets_2011.

2 Bradford Cornell, "Economic Growth and Equity Investing," *Financial Analysts Journal*, vol. 66, no. 1, January/February 2010, pp. 54–65.

3 Peter Bernstein and Robert Arnott, "Earnings Growth: The Two Percent Dilution," *Financial Analysts Journal*, vol. 59, no. 5, September/October 2003, pp. 47–55.

4 Jay Ritter, "Economic Growth and Equity Returns," *Pacific-Basin Finance Journal*, vol. 13, 2005, p. 501.

5 Ibid., p. 494.

6 See Vitaliy N. Katsenelson, *The Little Book of Sideways Markets: How to Make Money in Markets That Go Nowhere*, Hoboken, NJ: John Wiley & Sons, 2010.

7 Elroy Dimson, Paul Marsh, and Mike Staunton, *Credit Suisse Global Investment Returns Yearbook 2010*, p. 17.

8 Malcolm Baker, Brendan Bradley, and Jeffrey Wurgler, "Benchmarks as Limits to Arbitrage: Understand the Low-Volatility Anomaly," *Financial Analysts Journal*, vol. 67, no. 1, January/February 2011.

9 Andrea Frazzini and Lasse Heje Pedersen, "Betting against Beta," NBER Working Paper Series, vol. w16601, December 2010, available at SSRN, http://ssrn.com/abstract=1723048.

10 Eric Falkenstein, "Low Volatility and Beta 1.0 Portfolios," *Falkenblog*, September 21, 2010, http://falkenblog.blogspot.com/2010/09/low-volatility-and-beta-10-portfolios.html.

11 Gregory V. Milano, "Is Cash Still King?" *CFO*, February 4, 2011, http://www.cfo.com/article.cfm/14554467.

12 Dimson, Marsh, and Staunton, *Credit Suisse Global Investment Returns Yearbook 2010*.

13 Ibid., p. 21.

14 Robert D. Arnott and Clifford S. Asness, "Surprise! Higher Dividends = Higher Earnings Growth," *Financial Analysts Journal*, vol. 59, no. 1, January/February 2003, pp. 70–87.

15 Owain ap Gwilym, James Seaton, Karina Suddason, and Stephen Thomas, "International Evidence on the Payout Ratio, Earnings, Dividends, and Returns," *Financial Analysts Journal*, vol. 62, no. 1, January/February 2006, pp. 36–53.

16 Ping Zhou and William Ruland, "Dividend Payout and Future Earnings Growth," *Financial Analysts Journal*, vol. 62, no. 3, May/June 2006, pp. 58–69.

17 Michael W Covel, *Trend Following*, updated ed., Upper Saddle River, NJ: FT Press, 2009, p. 331.

18 Ibid., p. 332.

19 Eric Crittenden and Cole Wilcox, "Trending Stocks Drive the Stock Market," Blackstar Funds, 2007, http://michaelcovel.com/pdfs/TrendingStocks DriveTheMarket.pdf.

20 Michael Mauboussin, *More Than You Know: Finding Financial Wisdom in Unconventional Places*, New York: Columbia University Press, 2006, pp. 178–179.

21 Joshua Brown, "Shorting Is a Blood Sport," *The Reformed Broker*, August 15, 2011, http://www.thereformedbroker.com/2011/08/15/shorting-is-a-blood-sport/.

22 Eddy Elfenbein, "Will They Ever Learn?" *Crossing Wall Street*, August 11, 2011, http://www.crossingwallstreet.com/archives/2011/08/will-they-ever-learn.html.

23 Bill Alpert, "Even Short-Sellers Burned by Chinese Shares," *Barron's*, June 18, 2011, http://online.barrons.com/article/SB5000142405311904113704576383892664177456.html.

24 David Swensen, *Pioneering Portfolio Management: An Unconventional Approach to Institutional Management*, New York: Free Press, 2000, pp. 214–215.

25 Ekkehart Boehmer, Zsuzsa R. Huszar, and Bradford D. Jordan, "The Good News in Short Interest," *Journal of Financial Economics*, vol. 96, no. 1, 2010, p. 81.

Chapter 4

1 David Swensen, *Pioneering Portfolio Management: An Unconventional Approach to Institutional Investment*, New York: Free Press, 2000, p. 171.

2 Cornell Eddings, "Say What? In 30-Year Race, Bonds Beat Stocks," *Bloomberg.com*, October 31, 2011, http://www.bloomberg.com/news/2011-10-31/bonds-beating-u-s-stocks-over-30-years-for-first-time-since-19th-century.html.

3 Charles Roxburgh, Susan Lund, and John Piotrowski, "Mapping Global Capital Markets 2011," McKinsey Global Institute, August 2011, http://www.mckinsey.com/Insights/MGI/Research/Financial_Markets/Mapping_global_capital_markets_2011.

4 Arturo Estella and Mary R. Trubin, "The Yield Curve as a Leading Indicator: Some Practical Issues," Federal Reserve Bank of New York, *Current Issues in Economics and Finance,* vol. 12, no. 5, July/August 2006, http://www.newyorkfed.org/research/current_issues/ci12-5.html.

5 Cullen Roche, "Yield Curves Don't Lie," *Pragmatic Capitalism*, June 24, 2011, http://pragcap.com/yield-curves-dont-lie.

6 Glenn D. Rudebusch and John C. Williams, "Forecasting Recessions: The Puzzle of the Enduring Power of the Yield Curve," Federal Reserve Bank of San Francisco, July 2008, http://www.frbsf.org/publications/economics/papers/2007/wp07-16bk.pdf.

7 Kavan Kucko and Menzie David Chinn, "The Predictive Power of the Yield Curve across Countries and Time," January 11, 2010. La Follette School of Public Affairs Working Paper no. 2010-002, available at SSRN, http://ssrn.com/abstract=1536211.

8 Simon Gilchrist and Egon Zakrajsek, "Credit Spreads and Business Cycle Fluctuations," NBER Working Paper Series, vol. w17021, May 2011, available at SSRN. http://ssrn.com/abstract=1833158.

9 Bruce G. Resnick and Gary L. Shoesmith, "Using the Yield Curve to Time the Stock Market," *Financial Analysts Journal*, vol. 58, no. 3, May/June 2002, pp. 82–90.

10 Norman Fosback, *Stock Market Logic: A Sophisticated Approach to Profits on Wall Street*, Chicago: Dearborn Financial Publishing, 1991.

11 Scott B. Beyer, Gerald R. Jensen, and Robert R. Johnson, "Don't Worry about the Election," *Journal of Portfolio Management*, vol. 30, no. 4, Summer 2004, pp. 101–109.

12 Ben S. Bernanke and Kenneth N. Kuttner, "What Explains the Stock Market's Reaction to Federal Reserve Policy?," *Board of Governors of the Federal Reserve System*, Finance and Economics Discussion Series 2004-16, http://www.federalreserve.gov/pubs/feds/2004/200416/200416pap.pdf.

13 Ben S. Bernanke, "Remarks by Governor Bernanke: Monetary Policy and the Stock Market: Some Empirical Results," speech given at the Fall 2003 Banking and Finance Lecture, Widener University, Chester, PA, October 2, 2003, http://www.federalreserve.gov/boarddocs/speeches/2003/20031002/default.htm.

14 Elroy Dimson, Paul Marsh, and Mike Staunton, *Credit Suisse Global Investment Returns Yearbook 2011*, p. 50.

15 Jonnelle Marte, "Beyond the Money Market," *Wall Street Journal*, July 2, 2011, http://online.wsj.com/article/SB10001424052702303763404576418172992611898.html.

16 Eric G. Falkenstein, "Risk and Return in General: Theory and Evidence," June 15, 2009, p. 133, available at SSRN, http://papers.ssrn.com/sol3/papers.cfm?abstract_id=1420356.

17 James Montier, "A Value Investor's Perspective on Tail Risk Protection: An Ode to the Joy of Cash," GMO White Paper, June 2011, p. 2, http://www.gmo.com/America/default.htm.

18 Meir Statman, *What Investors Really Want: Discover What Drives Investor Behavior and Make Smarter Financial Decisions*, New York: McGraw-Hill, 2011, pp. 144–145.

19 Ibid., p. 145.

20 David Merkel, "On Bonds in Retail Accounts," *The Aleph Blog*, January 25, 2011, http://alephblog.com/2011/01/25/on-bonds-in-retail-accounts/.

21 Russel Kinnel, "New Bond Funds Act Like Bonds Only Better," *Morningstar.com*, June 27, 2011, http://news.morningstar.com/articlenet/article.aspx?id=385213.

22 Kenneth L. Judd, Felix E. Kubler, and Karl H. Schmedders, "Bond Ladders and Optimal Portfolios," (June 17, 2009). Swiss Finance Institute Research Paper No. 08-32, available at SSRN, http://ssrn.com/abstract=1289257.

23 More information can be found at http://www.treasurydirect.gov/.

24 Floyd Norris, "At Schwab, Unkept Promise to Investors," *New York Times*, January 13, 2011, http://www.nytimes.com/2011/01/14/business/14norris.html.

25 Andrea Frazzini and Lasse Heje Pedersen, "Betting against Beta," NBER Working Paper Series, vol. w16601, December 2010, available at SSRN, http://ssrn.com/abstract=1723048.

26 Dimson, Marsh, and Staunton, *Credit Suisse Global Investment Returns Yearbook 2011*, p. 9.
27 Falkenstein, "Risk and Return in General: Theory and Evidence."
28 Dimson, Marsh, and Staunton, *Credit Suisse Global Investment Returns Yearbook 2011*, p. 9.
29 Samuel Lee, "Does Lower Risk Mean Higher Returns?," *Morningstar .com*, June 27, 2011, http://news.morningstar.com/articlenet/article .aspx?id=385320.

Chapter 5

1 Peter L. Bernstein, *Capital Ideas: The Improbable Origins of Modern Wall Street*, New York: Free Press, 1992, p. 49.
2 Jason Zweig, *Your Money & Your Brain*, New York: Simon & Schuster, 2007, p. 211.
3 Meir Statman, *What Investors Really Want*, New York: McGraw-Hill, 2011, pp. 108–110.
4 Roger G. Ibbotson, "The Importance of Asset Allocation," *Financial Analysts Journal*, vol. 66, no. 2, March/April 2010, pp. 18–20.
5 A worthwhile read in this regard is: William Bernstein, *The Investor's Manifesto*, Hoboken, NJ: John Wiley & Sons, 2009.
6 Joseph Davis and Daniel Piquet, "Recessions and Balanced Portfolio Returns," *Vanguard Group*, October 2011, https://personal.vanguard.com/ pdf/icrrbp.pdf.
7 Kelly Greene, "'Target Date' Doesn't Equal 'Guaranteed'" *Total Return*, November 7, 2011, http://blogs.wsj.com/totalreturn/2011/11/07/target-date-doesnt-equal-guaranteed/.
8 Scott Willenbrock, "Diversification Return, Portfolio Rebalancing and the Commodity Return Puzzle," *Financial Analysts Journal*, vol. 67, no. 4, July/August 2011, pp. 42–49.
9 Hubert Dichtl, Wolfgang Drobetz, and Martin Wambach, "Testing Rebalancing Strategies for Stock-Bond Portfolios: Where Is the Value Added of a Rebalancing Strategy?" September 15, 2011, available at SSRN, http:// ssrn.com/abstract=1927764.
10 Ben Jacobsen and Sven Bouman, "The Halloween Indicator, 'Sell in May and Go Away': Another Puzzle," July 1, 2001, available at SSRN, http://ssrn .com/abstract=76248.
11 Mark J. Kamstra, Lisa A. Kramer, Maurice D. Levi, and Russ R. Wermers, "Seasonal Asset Allocation: Evidence from Mutual Fund Flows," August 1, 2011, available at SSRN, http://ssrn.com/abstract=1907904.
12 For more on using seasonality in portfolio rebalancing, see Charles Rotblut, "Use April Strength to Rebalance?," *Pragmatic Capitalism*, April 2, 2011, http://pragcap.com/use-april-strength-to-rebalance.

13 David Swensen, *Pioneering Portfolio Management: An Unconventional Approach to Institutional Investment*, New York: Free Press, 2000, p. 138.

14 The definitive books on Lehman Brothers and LTCM are, respectively, Lawrence G. McDonald and Patrick Robinson, *A Colossal Failure of Common Sense: The Inside Story of the Collapse of Lehman Brothers*, New York: Crown Business, 2009, and Roger Lowenstein, *When Genius Failed: The Rise and Fall of Long-Term Capital Management*, New York: Random House, 2000.

15 David Merkel, "The Costs of Illiquidity," *The Aleph Blog*, July 13, 2011, http://alephblog.com/2011/07/13/the-costs-of-illiquidity/.

16 A compelling version of this story can be found in Harry Markopolos, *No One Would Listen: A True Financial Thriller*, Hoboken, NJ: John Wiley & Sons, 2010.

Chapter 6

1 Barry Ritholtz, "How Hard Is It to Become the Michael Jordan of Trading?," *The Big Picture*, July 14, 2011, http://www.ritholtz.com/blog/2011/07/how-hard-is-it-to-become-the-michael-jordan-of-trading/.

2 Mike Bellafiore, "The Failure Rate of a Proprietary Trader," *SMB Training*, January 29, 2010, http://www.smbtraining.com/blog/the-failure-rate-of-a-proprietary-trader.

3 Performance figures for the Legg Mason Capital Management Value Trust—C Shares via *Morningstar.com*, http://quote.morningstar.com/fund/f.aspx?t=LMVTX. See also Allan Sloan, "Bill Miller Had a Great Run. But Did His Investors?" *Fortune.com*, December 7, 2011, http://finance.fortune.cnn.com/2011/12/07/bill-miller-legg-mason-returns/.

4 Warren Buffett, "Shareholder Letter to Berkshire Hathaway Shareholders," 2010, http://www.berkshirehathaway.com/letters/2010ltr.pdf.

5 Wesley R. Gray, "Mission Impossible: Beating the Market over Long Periods of Time," *Turnkey Analyst*, June 30, 2011, http://turnkeyanalyst.com/2011/06/mission-impossible-beating-the-market-over-long-periods-of-time/.

6 Jonah Lehrer, "Why Do Some People Learn Faster?" *The Frontal Cortex*, October 4, 2011, http://www.wired.com/wiredscience/2011/10/why-do-some-people-learn-faster-2/.

7 Kristi Oloffson and Stephen Gandel, "High-Frequency Trading Grows, Shrouded in Secrecy," *Time*, August 5, 2009, http://www.time.com/time/business/article/0,8599,1914724,00.html.

8 Adam Warner, "Kristin Did It," *Daily Options Report*, July 28, 2009, http://dailyoptionsreport.com/2009/07/28/kristin-did-it/.

9 Themis Trading, "SOES Bandits Revisited," July 23, 2010, http://blog.themistrading.com/?p=1189.

10 Charles Kirk, "How to Trade While Away," *The Kirk Report*, June 29, 2011, http://www.kirkreport.com/2011/06/29/how-to-trade-while-away/.

11 Richard Knox, "The Teen Brain: It's Just Not Grown Up Yet," *NPR.org*, March 1, 2010, http://www.npr.org/templates/story/story.php?storyId= 124119468.

12 Atul Gawande, "'Airline Pilot' Protocols in Finance," *Financial Times*, January 16, 2010, http://www.ft.com/intl/cms/s/2/86d97610-00ab-11df-ae8d-00144feabdc0.html; see also Gawande, *The Checklist Manifesto: How to Get Things Right*, New York: Profile Books, 2010.

13 "CNBC's Million Dollar Challenge," *PRNewswire*, August 22, 2011, http://www.prnewswire.com/news-releases/cnbcs-million-dollar-portfolio-challenge-128175463.html.

14 Amit Seru, Tyler Shumway, and Noah Stoffman, "Learning by Trading," *Review of Financial Studies*, vol. 23, no. 2, February 2010, pp. 705–739.

15 Juhani T. Linnainmaa, "Why Do (Some) Households Trade So Much?" *Review of Financial Studies*, 2011, vol. 24, issue 5, pp. 1630–1666.

16 Michael Martin, *The Inner Voice of Trading*, Upper Saddle River, NJ: FT Press, 2011, p. 33.

17 Geir Kirkebøen, Erik Vasaasen, and Karl Halvor Teigen, "Revisions and Regret: The Cost of Changing Your Mind," *Journal of Behavioral Decision Making*, 2011, forthcoming, http://onlinelibrary.wiley.com/doi/10.1002/bdm.756/abstract.

18 Tim Harford, *Adapt: Why Success Always Starts with Failure*, New York: Farrar, Straus and Giroux, 2011.

19 Jack D. Schwager, *Market Wizards: Interviews with Top Traders*, New York: NYIF Corp., 1989, p. 439.

Chapter 7

1 Don Phillips, "You Say You Want a Revolution?" *Morningstar Advisor*, August 4, 2011, http://www.morningstar.com/advisor/t/45786557/you-say-you-want-a-revolution.htm.

2 Matt Hougan, "The Cheapest ETF Portfolio Gets Cheaper," *IndexUniverse*, February 17, 2011, http://www.indexuniverse.com/sections/blog/8821-the-cheapest-etf-portfolio-gets-cheaper.html.

3 Abraham Bailin, "Tax-Loss Harvesing: A Tactical Strategy to Add Incremental Value," *Morningstar.com*, November 2, 2011, http://news.morningstar.com/articlenet/article.aspx?id=439379.

4 Matt Hougan, "How Long Can You Hold Leveraged ETFs?," *Journal of Indexes*, March/April 2009, http://www.indexuniverse.com/publications/journalofindexes/joi-articles/5421-how-long-can-you-hold-leveraged-etfs.html.

5 James Hamilton, "Changing Behavior of Crude Futures Prices, " *Econbrowser*, September 21, 2011, http://www.econbrowser.com/archives/2011/09/changing_behavi.html.

6 Dennis Hudachek, "The Complete Guide to ETF Taxation," IndexUniverse .com, November 3, 2011, http://www.indexuniverse.com/sections/white-papers/10172-the-complete-guide-to-etf-taxation.html.

7 McKinsey & Company, "The Second Act Begins for ETFs," August 2011, p. 4, http://www.mckinsey.com/App_Media/Reports/Financial_Services/ ETF_SecondActFINAL.pdf.

8 Phillips, "You Say You Want a Revolution?"

9 Ibid.

10 McKinsey & Company, "The Second Act Begins for ETFs," p. 5.

11 Ibid., p. 10.

12 Liam Pleven and Carolyn Cui, "Behind Gold's New Glister: Miner's Big Bet on a Fund," *Wall Street Journal*, November 25, 2010, http://online.wsj.com/ article/SB10001424052748703628204575618602535514506.html.

13 Howard Simons, "ETFs Change Corporate Bond Behavior," *Minyanville .com*, June 9, 2010, http://www.minyanville.com/businessmarkets/articles/ bonds-corporate-bonds-etfs-credit-default/6/9/2010/id/28617.

14 McKinsey & Company, "The Second Act Begins for ETFs," p. 19.

15 Olivier Ludwig, "Pimco Total Return ETF to Cost 0.55%," *IndexUniverse .com*, July 7, 2011, http://www.indexuniverse.com/sections/features/9521- pimco-total-return-etf-to-cost-055.html.

16 Jackie Noblett, "Eaton Vance Takes the Wraps Off Its Active ETF Patent," *Financial Times*, August 16, 2011, http://www.ft.com/intl/cms/s/0/ fc24d7a8-c809-11e0-9501-00144feabdc0.html.

17 David F. Swensen, "The Mutual Fund Merry-Go-Round," *New York Times*, August 13, 2011, http://www.nytimes.com/2011/08/14/opinion/sunday/the-mutual-fund-merry-go-round.html.

18 Phillips, "You Say You Want a Revolution?"

19 David Merkel, "The Good ETF," *The Aleph Blog*, October 9, 2009, http:// alephblog.com/2009/10/09/the-good-etf/.

Chapter 8

1 Ron Lieber, "Resisting the Urge to Run Away from Home," *New York Times*, August 5, 2011, http://www.nytimes.com/2011/08/06/your-money/stocks-and-bonds/resisting-the-urge-to-run-away-from-home.html.

2 Gur Huberman, "Familiarity Breeds Investment," *Review of Financial Studies*, vol. 14, no. 3, Fall 2001, pp. 659–680.

3 Jason Zweig, *Your Money & Your Brain: How the New Science of Neuro-economics Can Help Make You Rich*, New York: Simon & Schuster, 2007, p. 95.

4 Claude B. Erb, Campbell R. Harvey, and Tadas E. Viskanta, "Forecasting International Equity Correlations," *Financial Analysts Journal*, vol. 50, no. 6, November/December 1994, pp. 32–45.

5 Chun-hung Chen, Tom Goodwin, and Wenling Lin, "What Matters in International Equity Diversification?" July 23, 2011, available at SSRN, http://ssrn.com/abstract=1894346.

6 Fareed Zakaria, "The Debt Deal's Failure," *Time*, August 15, 2011, p. 32.

7 Justin Fox, "The End of American (Economic) Exceptionalism," *Harvard Business Review*, August 8, 2011, http://blogs.hbr.org/fox/2011/08/the-end-of-american-economic-e-1.html.

8 Clifford S. Asness, Roni Israelov, and John M. Liew, "International Diversification Works (Eventually)," *Financial Analysts Journal*, vol. 67, no. 3, May/June 2011, pp. 24–38.

9 Ibid., p. 34.

10 James Picerno, "What a Year...What a Decade!" *The Capital Spectator*, January 3, 2011, http://www.capitalspectator.com/archives/2011/01/what_a_yearwhat.html.

11 "Are Emerging Markets the Next Developed Markets?" Blackrock Investment Institute, August 2011, https://www2.blackrock.com/webcore/litService/search/getDocument.seam?contentId=1111146576&Source=SEARCH&Venue=PUB_INS.

12 Cynthia Lin, "Emerging Trend: Seeking Safe Havens beyond Treasurys," *Wall Street Journal*, August 29, 2011, http://online.wsj.com/article/SB10001424053111904875404576532852868190550.html.

13 John Authers, *The Fearful Rise of Markets: Global Bubbles, Synchronized Meltdowns, and How to Prevent Them in the Future*, Upper Saddle River, NJ: FT Press, 2010.

14 Lawrence Speidell, *Frontier Market Equity Investing: Finding the Winners of the Future*, The Research Foundation of CFA Institute, 2011, Charlottesville, VA, pp. 48–50.

15 Ben R. Marshall, Nhut H. Nguyen, and Visaltanachoti Nuttawat, "Frontier Market Diversification and Transaction Costs," October 11, 2011, available at SSRN, http://ssrn.com/abstract=1942592.

16 Christopher Philips, Roger Aliaga-Diaz, Joseph Davis, and Francis Kinniry, "Individual Country or Broad-Market Exposure?" *Journal of Indexes*, September/October 2011, pp. 18–21.

17 Michael R. King and Dagfinn Rime, "The $4 Trillion Question: What Explains FX Growth since the 2007 Survey?" *BIS Quarterly Review*, December 2010, p. 27, http://www.bis.org/publ/qtrpdf/r_qt1012e.pdf.

18 Ibid., p. 39.

19 Nathaniel Popper, "Foreign Currency Trading Is Easy—an Easy Way to Lose Money," *Los Angeles Times*, April 3, 2011, http://articles.latimes.com/2011/apr/03/business/la-fi-amateur-currency-trading-20110403.

20 Joshua Brown, "Inside the Currency Boiler Rooms," *The Reformed Broker*, April 9, 2011, http://www.thereformedbroker.com/2011/04/09/inside-the-currency-boiler-rooms/.

21 Momtchil Pojarliev and Richard M. Levin, "Do Professional Currency Managers Beat the Benchmark?" *Financial Analysts Journal*, vol. 64, no. 5, September/October 2008, pp. 18–31.

22 Kuntara Pukthuanthong-Le and Lee R. Thomas, III, "Weak-Form Efficiency in Currency Markets," *Financial Analysts Journal*, vol. 64, no. 3, May/June 2008, pp. 31–51.

Chapter 9

1 John C. Bogle, "The Lessons of History—Endowment and Foundation Investing Today," September 12, 2011, http://johncbogle.com/wordpress/wp-content/uploads/2011/09/NMS-9-12-12.pdf.

2 Amy Or, "Investors Show Taste for Hedge Funds," *Wall Street Journal*, July 20, 2011, http://online.wsj.com/article/SB10001424052702303795304576455763504575614.html.

3 Roger G. Ibbotson, Peng Chen, and Kevin X. Zhu, "The ABCs of Hedge Funds: Alphas, Betas and Costs," *Financial Analysts Journal*, vol. 67, no. 1, January/February 2011, pp. 15–25.

4 Mark Gongloff, "Hedge Funds Kiss Their Alpha Goodbye," *MarketBeat*, November 21, 2011, http://blogs.wsj.com/marketbeat/2011/11/21/hedge-funds-kiss-their-alpha-goodbye/.

5 Ilia D. Dichev and Gwen Yu, "Higher Risk, Lower Returns: What Hedge Fund Investors Really Earn," July 1, 2009, *Journal of Financial Economics*, forthcoming, available at SSRN, http://ssrn.com/abstract=1354070.

6 Whitney Tilson, "Notes from the 2004 Berkshire Hathaway Annual Shareholders Meeting," May 1, 2004, http://tilsonfunds.com/brkmtg04notes.doc.

7 Carol J. Loomis, "Buffett's Big Bet," *Fortune*, June 4, 2008, http://money.cnn.com/2008/06/04/news/newsmakers/buffett_bet.fortune/.

8 "Many Unhappy Returns," *The Economist*, August 20, 2011, http://www.economist.com/node/21526326.

9 Doug Friedenberg, "Introducing the New 2 and 20 Index Funds," *All About Alpha*, November 27, 2011, http://allaboutalpha.com/blog/2011/11/27/introducing-the-new-2-and-20-index-funds/.

10 Mebane T. Faber and Eric W. Richardson, *The Ivy Portfolio*, Hoboken, N.J: John Wiley & Sons, 2009.

11 Christopher Faille, "What the Dickens Do Investors Want?" *All About Alpha,* September 1, 2011, http://allaboutalpha.com/blog/2011/09/01/what-the-dickens-do-investors-want/.

12 Robert S. Harris, Tim Jenkinson, and Steven N. Kaplan, "Private Equity Performance: What Do We Know?" September 22, 2011, Fama-Miller Working Paper; Chicago Booth Research Paper No. 11-44; Darden Business School Working Paper No. 1932316, available at SSRN, http://ssrn.com/abstract=1932316.

13 Francesco Franzoni, Eric Nowak, and Ludovic Phalippou, "Private Equity Performance and Liquidity Risk," *Journal of Finance*, 2011, forthcoming.

14 Steven N. Kaplan and Antoinette Schoar, "Private Equity Performance: Returns, Persistence and Capital," NBER Working Paper Series, vol. w9807, June 2003, available at SSRN, http://ssrn.com/abstract=420321.

15 David F. Swensen, *Unconventional Success: A Fundamental Approach to Personal Investment*, New York: Free Press, 2005, p. 147.

16 Options Clearing Corporation, *Annual Volume and Open Interest Statistics*, September 8, 2011, http://www.theocc.com/webapps/historical-volume-query.

17 Jared Woodard, "What Options Are Good For," *Condor Options*, September 8, 2011, http://www.condoroptions.com/index.php/options-education/what-options-are-good-for/.

18 Robert Litterman, "Who Should Hedge Tail Risk?" *Financial Analysts Journal*, vol. 67, no. 3, May/June 2011, pp. 6–11.

19 Jared Woodard, *Options and the Volatility Risk Premium*, Upper Saddle River, NJ: FT Press, 2011, p. 5.

20 Gary B. Gorton, and K. Geert Rouwenhorst, "Facts and Fantasies about Commodity Futures," *Financial Analysts Journal*, vol. 62, no. 2, March/April 2006, pp. 47–68; Claude B. Erb, and Campbell R. Harvey, "The Strategic and Tactical Value of Commodity Futures," *Financial Analysts Journal*, vol. 62, no. 2, March/April 2006, pp. 69–97.

21 "Back to the Futures," *The Economist*, September 17, 2011, http://www.economist.com/node/21529073.

22 Joelle Miffre, "Long-Short Commodity Investing: Implications for Portfolio Risk and Market Regulation," August 31, 2011, available at SSRN, http://ssrn.com/abstract=1920454.

23 Azam Ahmed, "Sluggish Market Stalls Funds That Thrive on Direction," *Dealbook*, July 14, 2011, http://dealbook.nytimes.com/2011/07/14/sluggish-market-stalls-funds-that-thrive-on-direction/.

24 Kathryn M. Kaminski, "In Search of Crisis Alpha: A Short Guide to Investing in Managed Futures," *CME Group*, September 2011, http://www.cmegroup.com/education/featured-reports/in-search-of-crisis-alpha.html.

25 Geetesh Bhardwaj, Gary B. Gorton, and K. Geert Rouwenhorst, "Fooling Some of the People All of the Time: The Inefficient Performance and Persistence of Commodity Trading Advisors," October 6, 2008, Yale ICF Working Paper no. 08-21, available at SSRN, http://ssrn.com/abstract=1279594.

26 Bradford Case, Yawei Yang, and Yildiray Yildirim, "Dynamic Correlations among Asset Classes: REIT and Stock Returns," February 5, 2011, *Journal of Real Estate Finance and Economics*, forthcoming, available at SSRN, http://ssrn.com/abstract=1755592.

27 Mary Pilon, Liam Pleven, and Jason Zweig, "Gold Even Reigns on Stock Market," *Wall Street Journal*, August 23, 2011, http://online.wsj.com/article/SB10001424053111904279004576524890803937206.html.

28 Dennis Jacboe, "Americans Choose Gold as the Best Long-Term Investment," Gallup, August 25, 2011, http://www.gallup.com/poll/149195/Americans-Choose-Gold-Best-Long-Term-Investment.aspx.

29 Chanyaporn Chanjaroen, Nicholas Larkin, and Debarati Roy, "Bullion Vaults Run Out of Space on Gold Rally," *Bloomberg*, September 21, 2011, http://www.bloomberg.com/news/2011-09-21/bullion-vaults-running-out-of-space-as-gold-rally-accelerates-commodities.html.

30 Nicholas Larkin, "Gold Rises as Growth, Debt Concerns Boost Demand, *Bloomberg*, September 5, 2011, http://www.bloomberg.com/news/2011-09-05/gold-climbs-a-3rd-day-as-u-s-europe-economic-concerns-drive-haven-demand.html.

31 Jacob Goldstein and David Kestenbaum, "A Chemist Explains Why Gold Beat Out Lithium, Osmium, Einsteinium..." *Planet Money*, November 19, 2010, http://www.npr.org/blogs/money/2011/02/15/131430755/a-chemist-explains-why-gold-beat-out-lithium-osmium-einsteinium.

32 Eddy Elfenbein, "A Possible Model for Gold," *Crossing Wall Street*, October 6, 2010, http://www.crossingwallstreet.com/archives/2010/10/a-model-to-explain-the-price-of-gold.html.

33 Peter L. Bernstein, *The Power of Gold: The History of an Obsession*, Hoboken, NJ: John Wiley & Sons, 2000, p. 5.

Chapter 10

1 Barry Ritholtz, "Apprenticed Investor: The Folly of Forecasting," *TheStreet.com*, July 7, 2005, http://www.thestreet.com/story/10226887/1.html.

2 Philip Tetlock, *Expert Political Judgment: How Good Is It? How Can We Know?* Princeton, NJ: Princeton University Press, 2005.

3 Transcript, "The Folly of Prediction," *Freakonomics Radio*, June 24, 2011, http://freakonomicsradio.com/hour-long-special-the-folly-of-prediction.html.

4 Jerker Denrell and Christina Fang, "Predicting the Next Big Thing: Success as a Signal of Poor Judgment," *Management Science*, vol. 56, no. 10, June 7, 2010, pp. 1653–1667, available at SSRN, http://ssrn.com/abstract=1621800.

5 James Montier, "Seven Sins of Fund Management," November 18, 2005, available at SSRN, http://ssrn.com/abstract=881760.

6 Ignacio de la Torre, "Astrology and Economic Forecasts," *The Finance Professionals Post*, July 13, 2011, http://post.nyssa.org/nyssa-news/2011/07/astrology-and-economic-forecasts.html.

7 Jason Zweig, *Your Money & Your Brain: How the New Science of Neuroeconomics Can Help Make You Rich*, New York: Simon & Schuster, 2007, pp. 65–67.

8 Steven D. Levitt and Thomas J. Miles, "The Role of Skill vs. Luck in Poker: Evidence from the World Series of Poker," NBER Working Paper no. 17023, May 2011, http://www.nber.org/papers/w17023.

9 Eugene F. Fama and Kenneth R. French, "Luck versus Skill in Mutual Fund Performance," *Fama/French Forum*, November 30, 2009, http://www.dimensional.com/famafrench/2009/11/luck-versus-skill-in-mutual-fund-performance-1.html.

10 Michael Mauboussin, "Untangling Skill and Luck," *Columbia Ideas at Work*, May 25, 2011, http://www4.gsb.columbia.edu/ideasatwork/feature/7317814/Untangling+Skill+and+Luck.

11 Aswath Damodaran, "Luck versus Skill: How Can You Tell?," *Musings on Markets*, March 12, 2011, http://aswathdamodaran.blogspot.com/2011/03/luck-versus-skill-how-can-you-tell.html.

12 Andrew Mauboussin and Samuel Arbesman, "Differentiating Skill and Luck in Financial Markets with Streaks," February 3, 2011, available at SSRN, http://ssrn.com/abstract=1664031.

13 Michael Mauboussin, "Untangling Skill and Luck," *Mauboussin on Strategy*, Legg Mason Capital Management, July 15, 2010, www.lmcm.com/goto.asp?LPObjID=868299.

14 Howard Marks, *The Most Important Thing: Uncommon Sense for the Thoughtful Investor*, New York: Columbia Business School Publishing, 2011, p. 138.

15 "Mental Model: Confirmation Bias," *Farnam Street*, http://www.farnamstreetblog.com/mental-model-confirmation-bias/.

16 Meir Statman, *What Investors Really Want*, New York: McGraw-Hill, 2011, p. 32.

17 Michael J. Mauboussin, *Think Twice: Harnessing the Power of Counterintuition*, Boston: Harvard Business Press, 2009, p. 28.

18 Eli Pariser, *The Filter Bubble: What the Internet Is Hiding from You*, New York: Penguin Press, 2011, p. 88.

19 Hugo Mercier, "The Argumentative Theory," *Edge.org*, May 3, 2011, http://www.edge.org/documents/archive/edge342.html.

20 "Women in Fund Management," The National Council for Research on Women, 2009, http://www.ncrw.org/sites/ncrw.org/files/WIFM%20Report.pdf, p. 7.

21 Stefan Ruenzi and Alexandra Niessen-Ruenzi, "Sex Matters: Gender and Prejudice in the Mutual Fund Industry," October 13, 2011, Paris, December 2011 Finance Meeting EUROFIDAI–AFFI, available at SSRN, http://ssrn.com/abstract=1943576.

22 Alexandra Niessen and Stefan Ruenzi, "Sex Matters: Gender Differences in a Professional Setting," Working paper, February 2007, http://www.cfr-cologne.de/download/workingpaper/cfr-06-01.pdf.

23 Brad M. Barber and Terrance Odean, "Boys Will Be Boys: Gender, Overconfidence and Common Stock Investment," *Quarterly Journal of Economics*, February 2001, pp. 261–292.

24 "Women in Fund Management," p. 11.

25 Ibid., p. 12.

26 Jason Palmer, "Trader's Raging Hormones Cause Stock Market Swings," *New Scientist*, April 14, 2008, http://www.newscientist.com/article/dn13664-traders-raging-hormones-cause-stock-market-swings.html.

27 Ibid.

28 LouAnn Lofton, *Warren Buffett Invests like a Girl, and Why You Should Too: 8 Essential Principles Every Investor Needs to Create a Profitable Portfolio*, New York: HarperBusiness, 2011, http://www.forbes.com/2011/06/21/warren-buffett-invests-like-a-girl-book-excerpt.html.

29 Jason Zweig, "For Mother's Day, Give Her Reins to the Portfolio," *Wall Street Journal*, May 9, 2009, http://online.wsj.com/article/SB124181915279001967.html.

30 Annamaria Lusardi and Olivia S. Mitchell, "The Outlook for Financial Literacy," Pension Research Council WP 2010-25, October 20, 2010, available at SSRN, http://ssrn.com/abstract=1695139.

31 Lauren E. Willis, "Against Financial-Literacy Education," *Iowa Law Review*, vol. 94, November 2008, p. 272.

32 Stephanie Overman, "Do You Actually Know What's In Your Retirement Fund?" *Fortune*, October 18, 2011, http://management.fortune.cnn.com/2011/10/18/do-you-actually-know-whats-in-your-retirement-fund/.

33 Philip Z. Maymin and Gregg S. Fisher, "Preventing Emotional Investing: An Added Value of an Investment Advisor," *Journal of Wealth Management*, Spring 2011, p. 35.

34 Ibid., p. 43.

35 Charles D. Ellis, "The Winner's Game," *Financial Analysts Journal*, vol. 67, no. 4, July/August 2011, p. 6.

36 "Asking the Right and Wrong Questions," Dan Ariely, August 30, 2011, http://danariely.com/2011/08/30/asking-the-right-and-wrong-questions/.

37 Utpal Bhattacharya, Andreas Hackethal, Simon Kaesler, Benjamin Loos, and Steffen Meyer, "Is Unbiased Financial Advice to Retail Investors Sufficient? Answers from a Large Field Study," September 23, 2011, available at SSRN, http://ssrn.com/abstract=1669015.

Chapter 11

1 Annamaria Lusardi, "Americans' Financial Capability," NBER Working Paper Series, vol. w17103, June 2011, available at SSRN, http://ssrn.com/abstract=1857806.

2 Annamaria Lusardi and Olivia S. Mitchell, "Financial Literacy around the World: An Overview," NBER Working Paper Series, vol. w17107, June 2011, available at SSRN, http://ssrn.com/abstract=1857810.

3 Lauren E. Willis, "Against Financial-Literacy Education," *Iowa Law Review*. vol. 94, November 2008, pp. 197–284.

4 Fischer Black, "Noise," *Journal of Finance*, vol. XLI, no. 3, July 1986, p. 534.

5 Carl Richards, "When Television Feeds the Urge to Trade," *Bucks Blog*, June 6, 2011, http://bucks.blogs.nytimes.com/2011/06/06/when-television-feeds-the-urge-to-trade/.

6 "Money in Motion," *CNBC*, http://www.cnbc.com/id/41157529/.

7 Felix Salmon, "Market Reports Are Hurting America," *Reuters*, October 10, 2011, http://blogs.reuters.com/felix-salmon/2011/10/10/market-reports-are-hurting-america/.

8 Nassim Nicholas Taleb, *Fooled by Randomness*, New York: Random House, 2005, p. 60.

9 Mark Gongloff, "Stop Reading the News," *MarketBeat*, May 26, 2011, http://blogs.wsj.com/marketbeat/2011/05/26/stop-reading-the-news-dylan-grice/.

10 Vitaliy Katsenelson, "A Few Simple Rules for Money Managers to Improve Performance," *Institutional Investor*, October 3, 2011, http://www.institutional investor.com/Article/2911282/Search/A-Few-Simple-Rules-For-Money-Managers-to-Improve.html.

11 Rolf Dobelli, "Avoid News: Toward a Healthy News Diet," 2010, p. 6, http://dobelli.com/wp-content/uploads/2010/08/Avoid_News_Part1_TEXT.pdf.

12 Ibid., p. 5.

13 My blog *Abnormal Returns* has been aggregating financial news and opinion since its inception. You can therefore take these views with a big grain of salt.

14 Peter Steiner, "On the Internet, No One Knows You Are a Dog," *New Yorker*, July 5, 1993, http://www.cartoonbank.com/1993/on-the-internet-nobody-knows-youre-a-dog/invt/106197/.

15 Sturgeon's Law, Wikipedia, http://en.wikipedia.org/wiki/Sturgeon's_Law.

16 Milton Friedman, "The Methodology of Positive Economics," *Essays in Positive Economics*, Chicago: University of Chicago Press, 1966, p. 4.

17 Katie Benner, "Hedge Fund Confab Delivers Small Ideas, Not Fireworks," *Fortune*, May 26, 2011, http://finance.fortune.cnn.com/2011/05/26/hedge-fund-confab-delivers-small-ideas-not-fireworks/.

18 Joshua Brown, "Oh No! They're Talking Their Books!" *The Reformed Broker*, June 5, 2011, http://www.thereformedbroker.com/2011/06/05/oh-no-theyre-talking-their-books/.

19 James Altucher, "How to Save the World from Mutually Assured Destruction (MAD)," *The Altucher Confidential*, April 5, 2011, http://www.jamesaltucher.com/2011/04/how-to-save-the-world-from-mutual-assured-destruction-mad/.

20 Wesley R. Gray and Andrew E. Kern, "Talking Your Book: Social Networks and Price Discovery," February 22, 2011, available at SSRN, http://ssrn .com/abstract=1767452.

21 Mebane T. Faber and Eric W. Richardson, *The Ivy Portfolio*, Hoboken, NJ: John Wiley & Sons, 2008, pp. 171–186.

22 Jeff Matthews, "Budding Buffetts: Where to Begin?" *CNNMoney.com*, November 14, 2008, http://money.cnn.com/2008/11/14/news/newsmakers/ buffett_excerpt.fortune/index.htm.

23 There are two great biographies of Buffett: *Snowball* by Alice Schroder, New York: Random House, 2008, and *Buffett: Making of an American Capitalist* by Roger Lowenstein, New York: Random House, 1995.

24 Michael J. Mauboussin, *More Than You Know: Finding Financial Wisdom in Unconventional Places*, New York: Columbia University Press, 2006, p. 209.

25 Andrew Haldane, "Patience and Finance," *Bank of England*, September 2, 2010, http://www.bankofengland.co.uk/publications/speeches/2010/speech445.pdf.

26 Andrew Haldane and Richard Davies, "The Short Long," *Bank of England*, May 2011, p. 4, http://www.bankofengland.co.uk/publications/ speeches/2011/speech495.pdf.

27 Andrew Ang and Knut N. Kjaer, "Investing for the Long Run," November 11, 2011, available at SSRN, http://ssrn.com/abstract=1958258.

28 Merriam-Webster.com, http://www.merriam-webster.com/dictionary/ consilience.

Chapter 12

1 Carl Richards, "Why It Shouldn't Have Been a Lost Decade for Investors," *Bucks Blog*, August 31, 2011, http://bucks.blogs.nytimes.com/2011/08/31/ why-it-shouldnt-have-been-a-lost-decade-for-investors/.

2 James Picerno, "What a Year... What a Decade!" *Capital Spectator*, January 3, 2011, http://www.capitalspectator.com/archives/2011/01/what_a_yearwhat .html.

3 Floyd Norris, "Volatile, but Nearly Running in Place," *New York Times*, November 4, 2011, http://www.nytimes.com/2011/11/05/business/economy/ market-volatility-aplenty-and-a-change-may-be-afoot.html.

4 Jason Zweig, "Too Flustered to Trade: A Portrait of the Angry Investor," *Wall Street Journal*, August 20, 2011, http://online.wsj.com/article/SB10001 4240531119040706045765185842906146 02.html.

5 Andrew Haldane, "Risk Off," *Bank of England*, August 18, 2011, p. 6, http:// www.bankofengland.co.uk/publications/speeches/2011/speech513.pdf.

6 Satyajit Das, *Extreme Money: Masters of the Universe and the Cult of Risk*, Upper Saddle River, NJ: FT Press, 2011.

7 Zheng Liu and Mark M. Spiegel, "Boomer Retirement: Headwinds for U.S. Equity Markets?" *FRBSF Economic Letter*, no. 26, August 22, 2011, http:// www.frbsf.org/publications/economics/letter/2011/el2011-26.html.

8 John Ameriks, "Maybe a Lost Decade for Stocks, but Not for Investors," *Vanguard Blog*, September 28, 2011, http://www.vanguardblog.com/2011.09.28/maybe-a-lost-decade-for-stocks-but-not-for-investors.html.

9 Russel Kinnel, "How Expense Ratios and Star Ratings Predict Success," *Morningstar*, August 10, 2010, http://advisor.morningstar.com/articles/fcarticle.asp?docId=20016.

10 Lisa Gansky, "Do More, Own Less: A Grand Theory of the Sharing Economy," *The Atlantic*, August 25, 2011, http://www.theatlantic.com/business/archive/2011/08/do-more-own-less-a-grand-theory-of-the-sharing-economy/244141/.

11 Derek Thompson, "How Steve Case and His Company Are Driving the Sharing Economy," *The Atlantic*, November 9, 2011, http://www.theatlantic.com/business/archive/2011/11/how-steve-case-and-his-company-are-driving-the-sharing-economy/247997/.

12 Veronica Dagher, "Tax-Wise Funds vs. ETFs," *Wall Street Journal*, December 5, 2011, http://online.wsj.com/article/SB1000142405297020349970457662534 3248337576.html.

13 Wesley R. Gray, "Taxes Are More Important Than Alpha," *Turnkey Analyst*, July 9, 2011, http://turnkeyanalyst.com/2011/07/taxes-are-more-important-than-alpha/.

14 Jason Zweig, "Look before You Leap: Tax-Loss Harvesting Can Backfire," *Wall Street Journal*, December 11, 2010, http://online.wsj.com/article/SB10001424052748703727804576011482935521922.html.

15 Christine Benz, "What Goes Where? The Art of Asset Location," *Morningstar.com*, March 14, 2011, http://news.morningstar.com/articlenet/article.aspx?id=373565.

16 EZLaw Wills and Estate Planning Omnibus Survey, July 19, 2011, http://blog.ezlaw.com/?p=387.

17 John Tierney, "Do You Suffer from Decision Fatigue?" *New York Times*, August 17, 2011, http://www.nytimes.com/2011/08/21/magazine/do-you-suffer-from-decision-fatigue.html.

18 Ibid.

19 Robert Epstein, "Fight the Frazzled Mind," *Scientific American*, August 22, 2011, http://www.scientificamerican.com/article.cfm?id=fight-the-frazzled-mind.

20 Umair Haque, "The Best Investment You Can Make," *Harvard Business Review*, June 24, 2011, http://blogs.hbr.org/haque/2011/06/the_best_investment_you_can_ma.html.

21 Ibid.

22 Tali Sharot, "The Optimism Bias," *Time*, May 28, 2011, http://www.time.com/time/health/article/0,8599,2074067,00.html.

23 Ibid.

Conclusion

1 Mark Hulbert, "Market Undergoing a Huge Change," *Marketwatch.com*, September 30, 2011, http://www.marketwatch.com/story/market-undergoing-huge-change-2011-09-30.

2 Carl Richards, "To Those Who Have Lost Faith in Investing," *Bucks Blog*, August 15, 2011, http://bucks.blogs.nytimes.com/2011/08/15/to-those-who-have-lost-faith-in-investing/.

3 Ben Steverman, "Five Questions: Jack Bogle, Vanguard Index Pioneer," *Bloomberg*, September 27, 2011, http://www.bloomberg.com/news/2011-09-19/five-questions-for-jack-bogle-vanguard-index-fund-pioneer.html.

4 David Merkel, "Advice to a Friend, Again," *The Aleph Blog*, September 22, 2011, http://alephblog.com/2011/09/22/advice-to-a-friend-again/.

Index

About the Author

Tadas Viskanta is the founder and editor of the *Abnormal Returns* blog, which can be found at abnormalreturns.com. In its six years, *Abnormal Returns* has been called a "must-read" and the "best financial blog."

Tadas is a private investor with more than 20 years of professional experience in the financial markets. He is the coauthor of more than a dozen investment-related articles that have appeared in publications, including *Financial Analysts Journal* and *Journal of Portfolio Management.* Three of his articles were awarded Graham & Dodd Scroll Awards from the CFA Institute. Tadas holds an MBA from the University of Chicago and a BA from Indiana University. He lives with his family in the heartland of America.